THE NEW MIDDLE AGES

BONNIE WHEELER, *Series Editor*

The New Middle Ages is a series dedicated to pluridisciplinary studies of medieval cultures, with particular emphasis on recuperating women's history and on feminist and gender analyses. This peer-reviewed series includes both scholarly monographs and essay collections.

PUBLISHED BY PALGRAVE:

Women in the Medieval Islamic World: Power, Patronage, and Piety
edited by Gavin R. G. Hambly

The Ethics of Nature in the Middle Ages: On Boccaccio's Poetaphysics
by Gregory B. Stone

Presence and Presentation: Women in the Chinese Literati Tradition
by Sherry J. Mou

The Lost Love Letters of Heloise and Abelard: Perceptions of Dialogue in Twelfth-Century France
by Constant J. Mews

Understanding Scholastic Thought with Foucault
by Philipp W. Rosemann

For Her Good Estate: The Life of Elizabeth de Burgh
by Frances A. Underhill

Constructions of Widowhood and Virginity in the Middle Ages
edited by Cindy L. Carlson and Angela Jane Weisl

Motherhood and Mothering in Anglo-Saxon England
by Mary Dockray-Miller

Listening to Heloise: The Voice of a Twelfth-Century Woman
edited by Bonnie Wheeler

The Postcolonial Middle Ages
edited by Jeffrey Jerome Cohen

Chaucer's Pardoner and Gender Theory: Bodies of Discourse
by Robert S. Sturges

Crossing the Bridge: Comparative Essays on Medieval European and Heian Japanese Women Writers
edited by Barbara Stevenson and Cynthia Ho

Engaging Words: The Culture of Reading in the Later Middle Ages
by Laurel Amtower

Robes and Honor: The Medieval World of Investiture
edited by Stewart Gordon

Representing Rape in Medieval and Early Modern Literature
edited by Elizabeth Robertson and Christine M. Rose

Same Sex Love and Desire Among Women in the Middle Ages
edited by Francesca Canadé Sautman and Pamela Sheingorn

Sight and Embodiment in the Middle Ages: Ocular Desires
by Suzannah Biernoff

Listen, Daughter: The Speculum Virginum and the Formation of Religious Women in the Middle Ages
edited by Constant J. Mews

Science, the Singular, and the Question of Theology
by Richard A. Lee, Jr.

Gender in Debate from the Early Middle Ages to the Renaissance
edited by Thelma S. Fenster and Clare A. Lees

MEDIEVAL GO-BETWEENS AND CHAUCER'S PANDARUS

Gretchen Mieszkowski

MEDIEVAL GO-BETWEENS AND CHAUCER'S PANDARUS
© Gretchen Mieszkowski, 2006.

First published in 2006 by
PALGRAVE MACMILLAN™
175 Fifth Avenue, New York, N.Y. 10010 and
Houndmills, Basingstoke, Hampshire, England RG21 6XS
Companies and representatives throughout the world.

PALGRAVE MACMILLAN is the global academic imprint of the Palgrave Macmillan division of St. Martin's Press, LLC and of Palgrave Macmillan Ltd. Macmillan® is a registered trademark in the United States, United Kingdom and other countries. Palgrave is a registered trademark in the European Union and other countries.

ISBN-13: 978–1–4039–6341–3
ISBN-10: 1–4039–6341–X

Library of Congress Cataloging-in-Publication Data

Mieszkowski, Gretchen.
    Medieval go-betweens and Chaucer's Pandarus / Gretchen Mieszkowski
        p. cm.—(New Middle Ages)
    Includes bibliographical references and index.
    ISBN 1–4039–6341–X (alk. paper)
        1. Literature, Medieval—History and criticism. 2. Go-betweens in literature. 3. Lust in literature 4. Love in literature. 5. Chaucer, Geoffrey, d. 1400. Troilus and Criseyde. I. Title. II. Series.

PN682.G64M54 2006
820.9'3538—dc22   2006044813

A catalogue record for this book is available from the British Library.

Design by Newgen Imaging Systems (P) Ltd., Chennai, India.

First edition: August 2006

10 9 8 7 6 5 4 3 2 1

Printed in the United States of America.

Transferred to digital printing in 2007.

For
Peter, Katharine, and Jan

CONTENTS

ACKNOWLEDGMENTS

This book has been long in the making and would never have come to be without the support of a large number of colleagues, friends, and relatives. It is with great pleasure and heartfelt gratitude that I thank them here.

First I wish to thank Marie Borroff, who read the manuscript of this book when it was twice as long as it now is, and whose insightful advice helped me reconceive it. Bonnie Wheeler's excellent suggestions for major revisions also made this a far better book than it would have been, and her contagious enthusiasm sustained my own faith in it. Laura Hodges advised me on costume issues, contributed invaluable bibliographical material, and generously read and critiqued my manuscript-in-progress not once but twice, while her interest in my go-betweens kept me believing that other Chaucerians might find them of interest. Verva Densmore also critiqued an early very long version of this book. I especially want to thank her and Angela Howard for their unflagging enthusiasm about this project, confidence in my ability to complete it, and sisterly encouragement. Jan and Katharine Mieszkowski gave me expert detailed editing suggestions, and Agatha Whitney helped me admirably with the many secretarial chores a book entails.

I also owe a major debt to Penny Eley (Old French and Anglo-Norman) and Traugott Lawler (medieval Latin) for their creative assistance with my translations. They contributed far more than simply saving me from grammatical pitfalls. Any remaining errors are, of course, my own.

Finally, I wish to acknowledge the assistance of three institutions: the University of Houston-Clear Lake for two semesters of faculty development leave, the American Council of Learned Societies for funding a crucial year of research, and the Mary Ingraham Bunting Institute of the Radcliffe Institute for Advanced Study for providing both access to Harvard's magnificent Widener library during that year and an office in the most supportive feminist environment I have ever experienced.

My debt to Peter, Jan, and Katharine Mieszkowski for their loving support over the years this book has been a part of their lives is inadequately expressed by its dedication.

INTRODUCTION: GOING BETWEEN

Go-betweens: a queen, a prince, a steward, a merchant, a wizard, a witch, ladies-in-waiting, comrades-in-arms, governesses, nurses, tutors, priests, servants, former prostitutes, peddlers, and beggars. Throughout medieval English and Western European literature, from the top to the bottom of the social scale, go-betweens bring couples together for courtship, marriage, a love affair, or simply for sex. These figures are crucial to a wealth of medieval texts—some famous, some little known—and they are an essential component of Geoffrey Chaucer's *Troilus and Criseyde*. This book uncovers this tradition, the web of cross-fertilizing texts that ultimately yield Chaucer's three main characters: the lover, the lady, and the go-between.

From the eleventh century through the fifteenth century, go-betweens appear and reappear in the literatures of France, England, Italy, and Spain. Most of the secular medieval literary genres include them: romances, fabliaux, allegorical works, exempla, Latin comic tales, novellas, and moralizing poems. Despite the variety of authors who created these stories, the many languages in which they are told, their different countries of origin, and the social, professional, personal, and sexual diversity of their characters, two well-defined and ideologically opposed traditions emerge from them: going between that facilitates idealized love and going between in the service of lust and sexual conquest.

The go-betweens of these two traditions inhabit separate worlds. The facilitators of idealized liaisons are typically aristocratic men and women and their entourages. They are usually the people closest to the lovers, often their best friends or most intimate servants, and occasionally their relatives, and their motives for going between are unimpeachable. They act out of devotion to one member of the couple—often out of devotion to both of them—and without the intervener's help, at least one of the lovers seems to be in imminent danger of death from lovesickness. Since the lovers imagine each other as so unconditionally unattainable that without the go-between's help they could never be united, these go-betweens are often essential for aristocratic couples' wooing. In most cases, they introduce the man and the woman to each other or help them confess they love each other. These courtly go-betweens also arrange trysts, carry messages, out-maneuver meddling relatives, provide an audience for the lovers' eruptions of feeling, and occasionally conceal or disguise the lovers or guard their lovemaking against intrusions. It would be unthinkable, however, for a go-between from this courtly tradition of idealized loving to trick or coerce someone into having sex.

For the go-betweens of the stories of sexual conquest, on the other hand, tricking or forcing one of the couple into a sex act is ordinary behavior. They have no interest in distinguishing between love and lust, and most of them are hired to help men seduce women by any means necessary. The most frequently recurring figure in this group is a lower-class old woman who scrapes together a living by sewing, serving as a duenna, or peddling small items, and who arranges sexual encounters for a price. She first tries to persuade the young woman to accept the man—"Seize the day while you can! Before long, no one will want you!" Though the young woman's compliance is convenient and valuable, once persuasion fails, the go-between intervenes with tricks: an unlocked door, the wrong person in the bed, a concealed rapist, and so forth. The method of entrapping the woman is often the point of the story, many of these stories are salacious as well as comic, and they mock or omit altogether the emotional concerns that provide so much of the interest and energy of the stories of idealized love.

The most important single contrast between the two kinds of go-betweens lies in the conventions governing their methods of bringing men and women together. Idealized go-betweens frequently introduce couples and arrange their meetings, and habitually provide emotional support for them, but they do not mastermind seductions. Winning the other person's love is the aim in the idealized stories. In the stories about lust and sexual conquest, on the contrary, the work at hand is contriving the physical possession of the other person, whether or not she consents. The hired go-betweens in these texts all assume from the start that the woman is to be tricked into compliance by any means, and acquiescence fades into insignificance when the go-between can trap her so that the man can possess her.

The go-betweens of the two traditions bring men and women together by such different methods because opposed conceptions of sexual relation-ships inform their stories. In the idealized works, love takes possession of the lovers—mind, body, and soul. It leaves both men and women in extreme emotional states. They faint or weep uncontrollably, they cannot eat or sleep, and their sufferings drive them to the verge of death. Love inspires the men to perform heroic deeds, most usually battle or tournament feats, and the women match the men's exploits by their heroic suffering. When the lovers' desperate yearning is finally satisfied, their immense joy equals their previous inordinant pain. Instead of trying to thwart the lovers or bring them to their senses, the go-between typically subscribes to and nourishes their extravagant convictions about the worth of love, idealized above all other earthly blessings.

While men or women sometimes suffer from similar outpourings of emotion in the stories of lust and sexual conquest, their feelings are presented as a weakness, a liability, the fortunate piece of madness that will allow the go-between to earn money or rewards, or curry favor with someone important. From the go-between's point of view, love is lust, and as often as not, she or he will be ready with the little dig or turn of phrase that will open up a cruder perspective on the lover's desires. While in the idealized stories love is the entryway into a realm of idyllic experience and finally the passport to ecstasy, in the stories of lust and sexual conquest, love does not ennoble anyone. Ordinarily, it is just sex, and more often than not it turns out to be degrading and expensive sex. The parts these two kinds of go-betweens play are as firmly governed by convention as the roles of the lover and the lady in romances, or the young wife and cuckolded old husband in fabliaux, and the many figures who bring couples together in medieval literature are easily recognized as go-betweens for lust or go-betweens for idealized love.

Uniquely, however, Chaucer's Pandarus fits in neither tradition. He is the offspring of the double tradition itself, an impossible amalgam of the conflicting conventions, as if two photographs had been taken on one frame of film to produce a literary double-exposure. As the lady's relative and the lover's best friend, Pandarus is an ordinary idealized go-between by position and situation, and that is the first role he plays: counseling the lover, comforting him in his yearning, carrying messages back and forth between the lover and the lady, and helping the couple spend time together. On the other hand, essential aspects of his actions violate the fundamental conventions of going between for idealized love. At the same time that he behaves like an idealized go-between, he plays the part of the Old Woman who first tries to persuade the young woman to take a lover and then tricks her into sexual compliance by bringing a man into her bedroom. Although Pandarus has none of the personal traits of the typically lower-class characters who supplement meager incomes by getting women for men, and occasionally men for women, nevertheless, it is their tradition that accounts for the ruses and lies that yield Criseyde's seduction—those crucial elements of Pandarus's role that are altogether foreign to the idealized go-between's supportive befriending.

Pandarus's standard remedies for the difficulties of courting Criseyde derive from the stories of lust and sexual conquest: a lie or a trick or a network of lies and tricks. The most elaborate of these are the two meetings he arranges between Troilus and Criseyde. Their first meeting requires a comically complex script with precisely timed entrances, exits, and cues to support more lies than could possibly have been needed. The effect of all this subterfuge is to deliver Criseyde—without her consent, under blatantly false pretenses—into a room that contains only Troilus, in bed. The later consummation scene is the same kind of production including more lies and a trapdoor that lets Pandarus and Troilus into Criseyde's supposedly heavily guarded bedroom. This is the essential difference between Pandarus's going between and the going between in the stories about idealized love. In idealized love stories, the go-betweens' tricks protect the lovers against powerful figures hostile to their union: relatives or harem guards, for instance. Pandarus, however, does not scheme against lovers' opponents. He schemes against Criseyde, and his schemes are designed to put her in a situation that will make her accept Troilus as her lover. They are the kind of trick the Old Woman plays in the stories about sexual conquest.

Chaucer's Pandarus combines two traditional figures from antithetical types of literature. His methods of going between do not simply violate idealized convention; they introduce an opposed convention that carries with it an opposed conception of the meaning and worth of love. Chaucer creates Pandarus by crossing two literary traditions that had stood in opposition to each other for hundreds of years.

Early in the twentieth century, a generation of Chaucerians discovered with considerable excitement Pandarus's similarity to the go-betweens of the idealized stories, and they seized upon his resemblance to them as an explanation for and vindication of Pandarus's part in *Troilus and Criseyde*.[1] None of these Chaucerians noticed, however, that the courtly intermediaries they were discussing do not play tricks like Pandarus's. They failed to see that the idealized tradition only accounts for the least problematic aspects of Pandarus's role.

Few medievalists have connected Pandarus with the go-betweens for lust and sexual conquest. In 1967, Thomas J. Garbáty discovered the first important link, namely that *Pamphilus*, a Latin comic play in which the major character is a version of the Old Woman figure, was a source for *Troilus and Criseyde*.[2] In 1990, in *Classical Imitation and Interpretation in Chaucer's* Troilus, John V. Fleming pointed out connections between Pandarus and the activities of the classical Old Woman figure while discussing Pandarus as an "interpres," the Latin word for the Old Woman's "specialized office of sexual mediation."[3] Following Fleming, Leyla Rouhi's *Mediation and Love: A Study of the Medieval Go-Between in Key Romance and Near-Eastern Texts* linked Pandarus with the lying bawds of the Latin comic tales and discussed the tension between his role as go-between and his courtly stance, as well as the speeches in which he worries about being a go-between.[4] Yet none of the critics who have considered either the idealized go-betweens or the go-betweens for lust have recognized that there are two traditions, that these two traditions are ideologically opposed, and that Chaucer was using both of them simultaneously, incongruous as they are.[5]

Matchmakers negotiate between families to arrange marriages, and they have no role in these medieval stories. Lovers' helpers, on the other hand, appear in these stories with some frequency, but these figures lie outside the scope of this study. Brangane, Isolde's lady-in-waiting in *Tristan and Isolde*, and Thessala, Fénice's nurse in Chrétien de Troyes' *Cligés*, for instance, are both lovers' helpers, but they do not actually go between. This book concerns the ethical issues raised by the actions of characters who bring people together for sex or love, as Chaucer's Pandarus does, and it is therefore limited to the go-between figure narrowly defined.

Considering characters from several different national literatures, a number of twentieth-century medievalists have traced the history of the go-between for lust and sexual conquest, and most of these scholars emphasize the ubiquitous Old Woman. Joseph de Morawski's early overview (1917) established the parameters of this literary figure and her roots, with emphasis on classical and French texts.[6] William Matthews added a number of other figures in "The Wife of Bath and All Her Sect" (1974), but many of the characters he discussed—the Wife herself, for instance—were not go-betweens.[7] Most recently, Rouhi broadened the focus of the discussion by adding several new classical figures, a number of less well known Spanish go-betweens, and, most importantly, a substantial chapter on Arabic and Persian go-betweens. Rouhi presents many interesting parallels between the near-eastern and western-European traditions, although she does not show that one is the source of the other. Since Rouhi's book studies the "poetics of mediation" and third parties of many sorts in love relationships, she includes confidantes, counselors, parents, and many other helpers who do not in fact go between. Also, because of the particular western-European texts she chooses to consider, she does not single out the tradition of supportive aristocratic friends, servants, and relatives as parallel to the tradition of go-betweens for lust.

Western medieval literary works constitute an intricate intertextual tradition, modifying, manipulating, or adopting one another's conventions, depending on their own form, content, and ideological assumptions. This book does not attempt to chart or survey the vast subject of medieval go-betweens. It concentrates instead on establishing the ideas about go-betweens and their roles that Chaucer would have expected his audience to bring to *Troilus and Criseyde*, and the conceptions of going between within which Chaucer himself worked. I therefore discuss texts that there is either some reason to believe Chaucer may have seen, or seen descendants of, or that belong to textual traditions that were part of his experience. These turn out to be primarily works in medieval Latin and Old French, although some are in Anglo-Norman, Italian, Spanish, and Middle English. The figures that appear in them are sufficiently typical and numerous to establish definitively the parameters of the go-between's part. Since these textual traditions extend into the fifteenth century, I also include some fifteenth-century material to help confirm late fourteenth-century conventions. Cumulatively, the figures considered in this book establish the rich, complex English and European medieval go-between tradition.

The first section of this book discusses going between for lust and sexual conquest. Most of these stories involve extremely misogynistic subject matter: rape as a means of courting virgins, sexual violation, chaste young women tricked into sex acts, the savoring of a young woman's sexual awakening, lewdly imagined erotic scenes, women consumed by flagrant, uncontrollable lust, and presiding over story after story, the predatory Old Woman who sells flesh. Gender is a sociopolitical construct, but it is also an ideological construct; women's place in society yields her treatment in texts, but her treatment in texts in turn helps create her gender and her place in society. One after another, these narratives raise profoundly disconcerting questions about the nature and gravity of medieval misogyny and patriarchal enjoyment of and anxiety about its power over women. As Paul Strohm writes in *Social Chaucer*, "Even in its most apparently aesthetic aspects, narrative cannot help being social, in the way its continuities and discontinuities speak to the purpose and meaning of human action in time."[8] One of the issues this section returns to again and again is how these texts, written by men, relate to "the purpose and meaning of human action in time" for medieval women.

The second section of the book concerns fourteen idealized romance go-betweens. With one exception, these stories all lead to marriages, and none of them fit the notions about the centrality of adultery in medieval loving that C.S. Lewis argued for in *The Allegory of Love* and that dominated thinking about medieval romance in the first half of the twentieth century.[9] The most surprising fact to emerge from these fourteen episodes is how dependent the loving in these romances is on the go-betweens. The lovers' extreme emotions routinely paralyze them, men and women both, and they have to be rescued by their go-betweens en route to their stories' happy endings. Although many go-betweens fit seamlessly into the sequence of action of these romances, others explore the dangers of having a third person so intimately involved in a love relationship. Nevertheless, large as the role the idealized go-between often plays, these stories preserve the couples' consent to love.

Gender issues are an important consideration throughout this book, but they are less important for the romances than for the stories about lust and sexual conquest. The stories about going between for lust are so blatantly misogynistic that they raise gender issues at every turn. The romance episodes, on the other hand, include some powerful, positively presented women and are less obviously misogynistic, although one rarely hears women's voices speaking through these male-authored texts. Going between is typically an episode in a romance, a small piece of a much larger whole, and often the episode yields only the most obvious aspects of the gender relationships the work is examining. The more interesting complications emerge only from analysis of the entire romance. Consequently, gender issues are less extensively discussed in the second section of this book than in the first.

Most Chaucerians will know several of the works discussed in this book. Jean de Meun's *Roman de la rose*, the romances of Chrétien de Troyes, and Boccaccio's *Decameron* and *Filostrato*, for instance, are easily available in English and widely read. Seeing the go-betweens from these familiar works against the whole tradition of going between should encourage medievalists to think about these characters in new ways. Other less well known go-betweens will surprise many medievalists. Galehot, for instance, who goes between for Lancelot and Guinevere in the French Prose *Lancelot*, falls so much in love with Lancelot that he finally dies of love for him, and an old woman in *La Vieille*, the Old French rewriting of a Latin work, protects a young girl's virginity against a would-be seducer by tricking him into having sex with the old woman herself instead of the girl.

Some of the texts considered in this book are well known only to specialists in French, Italian, Latin, or Spanish literature. The very interesting go-between in *Partonopeus de Blois* takes over her sister's relationship so completely that she nearly destroys it. *Partonopeus de Blois* is important in Old French studies, but it has not been translated into modern English and few Chaucerians are acquainted with it. Similarly, medieval Latinists read the Latin comic tales, but only a selection of these is available in English. Some of the texts that are important for understanding the go-between tradition are obscure even for experts. Few Old French specialists, for instance, have read *Claris et Laris*, but its go-betweens push going-between to the extreme limits of romance convention. Since many of the texts that show the growth and development of the double go-between tradition are either not available in modern English or are very slightly known by English readers, I summarize a large number of them. Though readers familiar with them may skip the summaries, many other readers will need them.

The aim of the first two sections of this book, then, is to immerse medievalists in the richness and complexity of the ideologically opposed traditions of going between for lust and sexual conquest and going between for idealized love. The aim of the final section, the Chaucerian section, is to establish and explore *Troilus and Criseyde*'s roots in both of these richly intertextual traditions. There is no comprehensive reading of *Troilus and Criseyde* in this book, and no overview of the poem's characters. This book has nothing to say about the ending of the poem, and little to say about Troilus and Criseyde themselves. I argued previously for a feminist reading of Criseyde in an article, "Chaucer's Much Loved Criseyde,"[10] and I do not repeat that argument here. The Chaucerian section of this book instead focuses quite narrowly on the aspects of the poem directly impacted by the double go-between tradition: Pandarus and his going between.

No matter how sympathetically involved with Troilus and Criseyde Pandarus may seem to be, if the poem is seen through the lens of the stories of lust and conquest, he emerges as invariably pursuing his own agenda. Heterosexually, he is incestuously involved with Criseyde; homoerotically, he desires intimacy with Troilus. He is Troilus's agent who traffics in women for him, Criseyde's predatory sexual adversary, and the go-between who is paid off by his vicarious, or even actual, share in Troilus's sexual pleasures. If, on the other hand, *Troilus and Criseyde* is seen through the lens of the stories of idealized love, Pandarus's compromising behaviors and incriminating aspects dissolve back into the altogether appropriate role of the helpful friend, and Chaucer's poem resumes its place as a stirring tale of doomed romantic love. Some of the most important scenes of *Troilus and Criseyde*—the meeting at Deiphebus's, the consummation night, and the morning-after encounter between Pandarus and Criseyde—depend most precariously on the explosively clashing literary traditions that repeatedly redirect the audience to see the meaning of the actions of the poem in contradictory ways.

The double go-between tradition is of considerable interest in its own right, but its special importance in this book is for Chaucer's *Troilus and Criseyde*. The intent of the final section is to show how to read Pandarus and his going between as medieval audiences would have responded to them, framed as they would have been by the double-faceted medieval go-between tradition.

PART I

CHOREOGRAPHING LUST:
GO-BETWEENS FOR SEXUAL CONQUEST

Lust is the typical subject matter of these stories about going between for sexual conquest, and their plots are full of double-dealing, entrapment, and rape. Often with a veneer of comedy, but sometimes with no veneer at all, their go-betweens coax, inveigle, trick, or force women, and rarely men, into sex acts. Very often these stories concern a man who hires an Old Woman to help him have sex with a young woman who is either indifferent or actively hostile to him. The man is usually desperate for a particular woman and physical possession is almost invariably his goal. Sometimes the man anticipates that the woman will be forced to marry him if he takes her virginity, but such considerations are usually secondary.

The go-betweens of these stories preside over sexual consummation. Most of them trick chaste married women or virgins into sexual relations. The go-betweens ordinarily first try to help seduce the woman by tempting her with accounts of the joys of love. If these preliminary measures fail, they set up a situation in which she can be caught and possessed. The tricks in these stories range from a simple unlocked door to an elaborately staged capture. Sometimes the trick hinges on concealed identity, as when the man dresses up as a woman to gain access to the young woman's bed. In a more usual scenario, the young woman believes she is going to visit another woman for an uncompromising purpose only to discover herself alone in a room with a man intent upon having sex with her. Most of these strategies leave the woman raped.

Of all the current critical approaches to the reading of medieval texts, feminist criticism has yielded the most striking ways of thinking and writing about the encoding of gender. By understanding the body as apprehended virtually exclusively within discursive systems and by analyzing gender as a sociopolitical and ideological construct, captured and even created by texts, feminist critics have opened up new perspectives on a multitude of medieval works.

Because these stories about going between for lust and sexual conquest are such highly gendered works, this is the critical approach that illuminates them best. The sex act, the go-between's goal, raises gender issues at every turn.

The vast majority of these stories are misogynistic as well as aggressively gendered. Some of their female characters are extravagant instances of vices traditionally attributed to medieval women: greed and lust in particular. Other females are so loaded down with vices that they are virtually demonized, and these characters are often the go-betweens. Repeatedly, the ideal woman in these stories is ultrasubmissive and internalizes enthusiastically her abject subordination. Most usually these stories deal with misogynistic subject matter: the violation of young, innocent and fatally naive women. Sometimes the young woman's violation is camouflaged by diverting attention to another woman, typically the go-between; at other times, however, nothing diverts attention from the violation. Frequently women are passed from man to man as property, and often the violation the story highlights is violation of the property rights of the woman's father or husband. Similarly, in some of these texts, what at first seems to be a story about women and men develops instead into a homosocial story about what one man owes another. And not only are most of these stories about women, most of the go-betweens are women.

It is hardly surprising to find such a high level of misogyny in medieval stories. The official culture of the Middle Ages was fundamentally misogynistic. Medically, theologically, and morally, woman was considered weak, inadequate, unstable, an occasion for sin, and the cause of man's corruption. Medically she was conceptualized as an incomplete male. Aristotle, a dominant source of medieval medical theories beginning in the twelfth century, explained the sex of the child as determined by generative heat at the time of conception. Sufficient generative heat produced a male; insufficient produced a female. Moreover, the female's sex organs matched the male's except that they were internal instead of external—undescended because of insufficient generative heat. Consequently, by nature females were cold and wet compared with males, and they menstruated to rid themselves of excess moisture and the toxic substances that built up because they lacked the male's greater heat to burn them off. Women were sexually insatiable because their innate coldness left them constantly desiring the hotter male. Physiologically, then, woman was inadequate, incomplete, a partial being, desperate for a male to bring her the heat she lacked.[1]

According to the thinkers whose works grounded medieval Christianity, women were also profoundly inadequate theologically and spiritually. St. Augustine believed that woman's very nature separated her from God. Although as humans women were created in the image of God, he argued, as females they were not. Augustine also speculated about why God had created such an inadequate being as woman. His answer: so that she would give birth and man would not need to be concerned with progeny.[2] In the thirteenth century, eight centuries later, St. Thomas Aquinas raised the same issues and arrived at the same conclusions. Why, he wondered, should God have created woman since she is an incomplete male, and nothing incomplete should have been created in the first creation? When he answered himself with the argument that woman is needed to help man by giving birth to children, he spelled out that for any other kind of help, another man would have sufficed.[3]

The ascetic tradition inherited from the writings of the church fathers identified man with the aspects of life medieval moralists most valued: spirit, reason, form, and God; and woman with the aspects of life they most feared: the body, the senses, the temporal, and the worldly. Woman was decorative, cosmetic, associated with "life's little idle shows," as St. Jerome described her. Man alone had "claim to full Being."[4] Sexually, women were insatiable temptresses who reenacted the Fall, and woman's love "enervates a man's mind."[5] Because woman was innately wet physiologically, she was soft and inconstant. Albertus Magnus, writing in the thirteenth century, explained these connections: " 'A woman's *complexio* is more humid than a man's, but the nature of the humid is to receive easily and retain badly. Whatever is humid is easily changed, and so women are inconstant and always seeking new things. . .there is no faith in woman.' "[6] Light, fickle, and unstable, woman was dismissed as incapable of any serious thought because her soft wetness retained so poorly.

These learned explanations of woman's defective nature are gentle compared with the many virulent texts that denounced her straightforwardly. Since the church condemned sexual pleasure even in marriage, woman was portrayed repeatedly as a wicked seductress, Eve's true descendant and heir. Richard de Bury, writing in the fourteenth century, described woman as a " 'biped beast' " who should be avoided " 'more than the asp and the basilisk.' "[7] In one of the most repeatedly quoted medieval diatribes against women, Walter Map, a twelfth-century archdeacon of Oxford, argued that they are all to be feared, the good as well as the bad, and he warned a friend that they are chimeras, with the beautiful face of a noble lion but a viper's tail and a goat's belly—an allusion to woman's constantly denounced lechery. Map even contended that a series of affairs is better than a marriage since being sick repeatedly is less wretched than living with a single incurable illness. Map also narrates the story of a man who, weeping, recounted to his friend the recent death of his third wife. All three of his wives had hanged themselves, one after the other, on a tree in his garden. The friend's first response was to marvel that the man should be crying when he had had such good luck, and the friend next asked the man for some branches of his tree to plant in his own garden.[8]

A second, classical tradition also depicted women as greedy, fickle, conniving, and heartless, ready to trick and deceive men at every turn, and it joined with the church's hostility to sexual pleasure to fuel medieval misogyny. Ovid is its most important source, in particular his *Amores, Remedia Amoris, Ars Amatoria*, and *Metamorphoses*. In the twelfth century, Ovid's popularity surpassed Virgil's and his works and references to them appear in France, England, and Germany, in handbooks, commentaries, imitations, songs, and denunciations.[9] Most important of all, he was taught in cathedral schools.[10] As Peter Allen writes, "Whether copied, imitated, or opposed, Ovid was an essential part of twelfth-century literary conscious-ness."[11] Ovid wrote his love poems about relationships with courtesans and their management of their love affairs. Hair styles, perfumes, jewelry, and the artful winning of expensive gifts while juggling several wealthy lovers at a time are all professional requirements for a courtesan, but when details of this sort reappear in medieval writings they become evidence of the essential triviality and viciousness of women. Similarly the *Metamorphoses*, filled with the gods' transformations to seduce and rape mortals, illustrate the dangers of desire. While the asceticism of the church fathers and Ovid's arch, cynical accounts of the excitement and sensual delights of love affairs should have made uneasy bedfellows, the two traditions shared their con-tempt of women and together fed the misogyny that generated so many of these medieval stories of going between.

The most frequent intermediary in these stories about going between for lust and sexual conquest reads as if she had been birthed in a misogynist's nightmare. Her invariable traits are her age and her gender: she is a very, very old woman, an ancient, sexually repulsive crone. She is usually exceedingly poor, or pretends to be poor, ostentatiously pious, an expert on sexual matters, and proud of her lost youth when she was desirable and a prostitute. Often a peddler, occasionally a witch, she is consistently cleverer than the rest of the characters and notably unscrupulous. She ordinarily contrives what-ever tricks are played in these tricky stories, and she is usually paid for going between, sometimes with money and sometimes with goods and services.[12] She is not limited to a specific genre, and appears in exempla, allegories, twelfth-century Latin comedies and their later adaptations, thirteenth-century fabliaux, fourteenth-century *Decameron* stories, and even a romance.

Most often, these Old Women are predatory figures who use their sexual expertise and experience to hunt down women for men. Typically they convince virgins or chaste wives to take lovers, or trick them into being seduced, or set them up for rape. Because these go-betweens are old and female, the reader expects them to protect young women. Instead, they collect fees for corrupting them, for exposing them to harm, or for betraying them into sex.

These ancient hags suffer their age. They are not simply women of the young people's parents' generation. They are much, much older, and they croak, creak, and totter about, lamenting their aches and pains. In an early fourteenth-century Anglo-Norman poem, *Pamphile et Galatée*, for instance, a young man remembers his go-between as on the verge of death: "Fronchie estoit et esdentee, / Si vielle que flairoit le biere" (908–09).[13] [She was wrinkled and toothless, so old that she smelled of the grave.] And the Old Woman laments her ancientness to the young man:

"Vielleche, li suer a la Mort,
Par vis, par dens, par tout me mort,
S'ai maintes goutes en l'eskine.

. . . .

Vielle sui, si n'ai dent en geule." (995–97, 1001)

["Old age, Death's sister, is gnawing at me all over—at my face, at my teeth, all parts of me—and my spine is full of rheumatism. . . . I am old and I haven't a tooth in my jaw."]

At least tell your servants to help me a little, she concludes, begging for a bit of wood for her fire or a little milk to help her headache.

Typically these old go-betweens gain access to women by complaining about their poverty and begging. Here is Dame Sirith, for instance, in a thirteenth-century English fabliau,[14] as she arrives at the home of Dame Margery, the woman whose seduction she is arranging. She hobbles up to Margery's door, sighing and groaning pitifully. "Woe to old wives who live their lives in poverty," she laments. "No man knows as much about pain as a poor wife who falls into hardship." Hunger, thirst, and cold have already so nearly killed her, she claims, that she can hardly control her old limbs, and she bewails her life and wishes she would die: " 'Warto liueþ selke a wrecche? / Wi nul Goed mi soule fecche?' " (313–14) ["Why does such a wretch live? / Why won't God take my soul?"] Dame Sirith's approach is eminently successful. Dame Margery greets her with loving pity and open-handed charity. She commiserates with her over her poor shoes and clothes, invites her into her house, offers her meat, bread, and something to drink, and tries to cheer her up.

These Old Women also often camouflage their profession with links to the church. They say rosaries repeatedly and showily, perform a church function, wear a nun's habit, or talk about spending their time in convents. When Dame Margery welcomes Dame Sirith with such kindness, for instance, the Old Woman thanks her with lengthy references to God and Christ (322–26). Similarly, in *Le Prestre teint*[15] [The Dyed Priest], another fabliau, Dame Hersent is the sacristan of her church despite the fact that she

boasts: " 'Il n'a bourjoise en tot Orliens / Qui par moi son ami ne face!' "
(162–63) ["There is no townswoman in all Orléans who does not find her
lover through me!"].

Houdée, the Old Woman who goes between in *Pamphile et Galatée*, also
hides behind the appearance of piety:

> Si con de l'ordre des apostres,
> En sa main unes patrenostres
> De noiaus traués de cherises
> Dont elle fait ses sacrefices. (1261–64)

[Just like a member of the order of the apostles, in her hand she has a
rosary made from carved cherry pits, with which she says her prayers.]

And in an early thirteenth-century Old French version of the Dame Sirith
story, "De la male vielle qui a conchié la preude fame" [Concerning the
evil old woman who played a dirty trick on the good wife],[16] the go-
between disguises herself as a nun:

> Dras aveit de religion
> Et s'apuiout o un baston;
> Bien semblout chose esperitable,
> Et ce esteit membre a deable,
> Quer por maus engienz porpenser
> N'aveit en tot le mont sa per. (1771–76)

[She wore a religious habit and leaned on a staff; she seemed to be a
spiritual being, but she was the devil's henchwoman, for in the whole
world she did not have her equal for thinking up evil tricks.]

Piety is the last attribute one would expect from as robustly secular a
character as the Old Woman in Boccaccio's *Decameron* who lectures a
homosexual's wife on making the most of her youth by having many
affairs.[17] Nevertheless, from start to finish, the Old Woman is portrayed as
obtrusively pious. When she is first introduced, there is a slight suggestion
that her piety is a cover-up for her real occupation. She is described as
seeming to be more saintly than "santa Verdiana che dà beccare alle serpi"
(318) ["Saint Verdiana feeding the serpents"] (370). She always carries a
rosary when she walks around town, attends every public pardoning, talks
repeatedly about St. Francis's stigmata and the lives of the church fathers,
and most people believe she is a saint (318). The Old Woman sustains this
image of herself even while she goes between. When the wife tells her that
she wants lovers, the go-between assures her that God supports satisfying
the flesh: " 'Figliuola mia, sallo Idio, che sa tutte le cose, che tu molto ben

fai; e quando per niuna altra cosa il facessi, sí il dovresti far tu e ciascuna giovane per non perdere il tempo della vostra giovanezza." (319) [" 'My child, God knows, for He knows everything, that you are acting for the best; and if you did it for no other reason, you and every other young woman should do it in order not to waste the opportunities your youth affords you.' "] (371). Finally, after the Old Woman has boasted about her effectiveness as a go-between and cannot have any motive for trying to hide her occupation, as she leaves she promises that if the wife is generous with her, she will include her in all her Our Fathers and indulgences, and then God will look after the souls of her dead (372). The conventional association of this stock figure with religious trappings and sentiments is so strong that they characterize her even when they seem altogether out of place. What first appears to be a way of hiding the go-between's role becomes a sign of it.

This mark of the old go-between's role becomes her name itself in the early fourteenth-century Spanish *Libro de buen amor*[18] in which she is called Trotaconventos, "convent-trotter." As Sir Love tells the Archpriest of Hita how to find an ideal go-between, he captures the dangerous aura around the Spanish old woman figure, associated with magic, witchcraft, and the church:

> "[unas] viejas
> que andan las iglesias e saben las callejas:
> grandes cuentas al cuel[l]o, saben muchas consejas,
> con lágrimas de Moisén escantan las orejas.
>
> . . . .
>
> Andan por todo el mundo, por plaças e [por] cotas:
> a Dios alçan las cuentas querellando sus coitas:
> ¡ay!, quanto [de] mal saben estas viejas arlotas." (438–39)

["one of those old crones that frequent the churches and know all the back alleys—the ones with the huge rosaries dangling from their necks. They are in on many secrets and possess magic arts with which to enchant maidens' ears. . . .They go everywhere, in the marketplace and on the hillsides, lifting their rosaries to God and bewailing their miseries, but ah! how much wickedness these old witches know!"]

Like piety and begging, peddling camouflages the Old Woman's erotic activities. The Archpriest describes Trotaconventos as she makes her way through town hawking tablecloths, rings, and pins, and jingling bells to announce her coming (723). When the Archpriest wants Urraca, another old go-between, to arrange an affair for him, she knocks on the woman's door pretending to have a jewel to sell, "ca de uso lo an" (1324) ["as they all do"]. Once in the house, Urraca continues her sales pitch—" 'Señora,. . .conprad

traveseros e aviesos' " (1325) [" 'Lady, buy my bolsters and my borders' "]—
before arguing successfully the advantages of a good lover over a bad husband. The Archpriest locates these old go-betweens as dangerous,
frightening, but commonplace figures in the village scene:

> éstas echan el laço; éstas cavan las foyas;
> non ay tales maestras como estas viejas troyas.
>
> Como lo an de uso estas tales buhonas
> andar de casa en casa vendiendo muchas donas,
> non se reguardan d'ellas, están con las personas,
> fazen con el mucho viento andar las atahonas. (699–700)
>
> [These are the ones who lay snares and dig traps. . . .There are none more mas-
> terful than these old harlots. . . .These old women regularly go from house to
> house, peddling little gifts. Nobody takes note of them; they mingle freely
> among the people and turn windmills with their hot air.]

Peddling gives them access to women, and their rosaries and ostentatious
piety conceal their corruption and their real trade.

The obvious choice for a go-between in a story would be a servant,
since servants already have access to the women of their households.
Nevertheless, from the late eleventh through the fifteenth century, in
England, Italy, France, and Spain, this poor, physically repulsive, unscrupulous Old Woman who peddles, begs, associates herself with the church,
and claims expertise in all things sexual is the most frequent go-between in
stories of lust and sexual conquest.

Medievalists have offered a number of explanations for this strange
choice. In "The Wife of Bath and All Her Sect," the first overview of this
figure in English, William Matthews argues that these Old Women derive
from Dipsas, the ancient hag who counsels the courtesan in methods of
fleecing a whole stable of lovers in Ovid's *Amores* 1.8.[19] John V. Fleming,
in *Classical Imitation and Interpretation in Chaucer's* Troilus, likewise identifies
Dipsas as "the Great Mother of all medieval literary bawds."[20] However, there
is a major difficulty with this derivation for Western European literature's
Old Woman. As Philippe Ménard points out, Dipsas is not a go-between.[21]
She is a chronic drunk and a witch, and her function in the *Amores* is to
scold a courtesan for wasting her time with a poet when she should be
spending her youth and beauty charming the largest possible number of
gifts out of admirers with something better to give than verses. The
techniques Dipsas advises include displaying presents other men have sent,
pretending it is the courtesan's birthday, making a rich lover jealous by
indications that she has been having sex with another man, telling a handsome but poor man to find rich male lovers to get money to buy gifts for
her, having her mother, sister, and nurse ask men for more gifts on her

account, and so forth. Although most of these techniques reappear in the *Roman de la rose* whose Old Woman is indeed modeled directly on Dipsas, there is no connection between Dipsas's advice and the activities of the typical Old Woman who goes between in medieval texts. Her job is to capture young women, not to teach them how to sell themselves more profitably. Important as Ovid was for literature of this period, Dipsas does not account either for the ordinary role of the Old Woman go-between or for her customary attributes.

Near Eastern texts yield figures much more like the Old Woman of medieval Western literature, but which tradition originated the figure and which one adopted it remains undecided. One work that contains Arabic stories, the *Disciplina Clericalis* of Petrus Alfonsi, written in Latin by a converted Spanish Jew early in the twelfth century, includes an anecdote about an old woman who dresses as a nun and tricks a chaste wife into an affair.[22] The anecdote is the core of the Dame Sirith story, and the *Disciplina Clericalis* was ultimately very widely read in Western Europe. Seventy-six medieval manuscripts of it have survived, the whole work was translated into French three times, and parts of it were translated or reworked in French, English, Italian, Hebrew, and perhaps Icelandic.[23] Other Near Eastern texts offer similar figures. Leyla Rouhi, describing Arabic and Persian go-betweens in *Mediation and Love*, finds old women in fourteenth-century erotological treatises who go between by playing tricks, setting traps, and posing as seamstresses, hairdressers, and religious women. Similar old women who stress their piety and play tricks to trap young women appear in the Indian, Persian, and Arabic stories that make up *The Thousand and One Nights*.[24] All these Near Eastern texts, however,—including the Arabic stories of the *Disciplina Clericalis*—are either later than or contemporaneous with Western European texts that use the tricky Old Woman as a go-between. Since so many similar figures appear in Near-Eastern and Western medieval literature, the two traditions must be linked. Probably the Persian and Arabic stories traveled west, as so much of that rich culture did in the twelfth century, but it is also possible that the Western European stories traveled east.

The loathsome portrait of the Old Woman who goes between in Western literature, however, has another more obvious and powerful source. Every aspect of this figure has its counterpart in medieval beliefs about old women. Young and middle-aged women were dismissed as inadequate males in the Middle Ages, but old women were not merely inadequate; they were physiologically pathological, malignant, and intensely toxic.[25] Menstruation was thought to purify the female body, which was too cold to burn off its own poisons as male bodies did. Shulamith Shahar writes about the "obsessive preoccupation with the contaminating and injurious effect of menstrual blood" in the Middle Ages.[26] Old women were believed to be toxic because the old woman's unmenstruating body retained all that perilous contamination. Moreover, according to the thirteenth-century *De Secretis mulierum*, attributed to Albertus Magnus, poor old women were most poisonous of all because they lived on "nothing but coarse meat" and had "no natural heat left to consume and control this matter."[27]

Jole Agrimi and Chiara Crisciani, in "Savoir médical et anthropologie religieuse: Les représentations et les fonctions de la *vetula* (XIIIᵉ-XVᵉ siècle)," offer an overview of appalling ideas about old women, culled predominantly from ecclesiastics. Thomas Aquinas, for instance, like Albertus Magnus, explained poor old women's evil powers by their inadequate diet. He also pinpointed as a source of their wickedness the vapors that accumulated because they no longer menstruated. Repeatedly preachers claimed that old women worked for the devil or the devil worked through them. Twelfth-century moralists cited by Agrimi and Crisciani maintained that the devil uses old women as his mask to seduce men or kill sleeping babies by sucking their blood. Old women are the devil's mouth just as preachers are God's mouth.[28] Aquinas believed the devil gave old women their dreaded evil eye as payment for pacts they made with him, presumably promising him their souls. By their evil eye, old women could poison babies in cradles, and the spells they cast were so powerful that even priests and theologians suffered from them.[29] Although old women's dreams, visions, and melancholia led to witchcraft and evil spells and made them easy prey for devils and magicians,[30] the root of their evil was in the Garden of Eden itself according to Alexander of Hales, a thirteenth-century English scholastic philosopher. At the time of the Fall, the devil taught Eve sorcery, and woman has passed her secrets down to her daughters ever since.[31] By the later Middle Ages, convictions such as these, voiced by some of the most respected and influential thinkers of the period, were sending old women to execution as witches.

Fear of the power of old women appears repeatedly in Agrimi and Crisciani's citations from twelfth- and thirteenth-century exempla, sermons, and moral treatises. Preachers proclaimed the old woman who goes between as a new bestiary creature: "la bête 'chronocrate', mi-louve, mi-chienne, qui, conjuguant la voracité du chien et la cruauté du loup, corrompt et prostitue vierges, épouses et veuves."[32] [the beast called "chronocrate" (she who rules time), half she-wolf, half bitch, who, combining the voraciousness of the dog and the cruelty of the wolf, corrupts and prostitutes virgins, wives, and widows]. Her wrinkles reveal the death she carries within her and her single tooth witnesses to her deadly poison. Although the old woman is guilty of multiple sins such as greed, gluttony, backbiting, envy, and laziness, these writers assert repeatedly that the root of her wickedness is unsatisfied lust. She turns to lechery and alcohol to retrieve the heat her body lacks and she involves herself in the affairs of young people to satisfy vicariously her old body's futile lasciviousness. She makes love potions from consecrated host, causes abortions, and curses couples with sterility and impotence,[33] but her primary endeavor is to lure women into sexual relationships and corrupt them to do the work of the devil.

Bernard of Sienna (1380–1444), cited by Agrimi and Crisciani, attributes to St. Jerome his account of the old go-between's method for beginning her seductions. Weighed down by decorated baskets of goods, she arrives at homes, offering her services—to scour, peel fruit, pluck a chicken—and she tells fables and tales.[34] St. Bernard's stereotype completes the picture. The preachers, moralists, and stories all agree about the image, nature, and activities of the Old Woman who goes between.

Medieval laws and court practices add to this picture. Going between was punished in the Middle Ages in both civil and church courts, and a mid-thirteenth-century English poem gives a glimpse of such a punishment. When a young man asks an old woman to go between for him, she spells out her fears of being caught by the local authorities:

> "For al þe world ne wold I nout
> Þat Ich were to chapitre ibrout
>   For none selke werkes.
> Mi iugement were sone igiuen
> To ben wiþ shome somer-driuen
>   Wiþ prestes and wiþ clarkes."[35]

["Not for all the world would I be brought before the ecclesiastical court for doing such a thing. My judgment would be quickly given: to be driven in shame on a packhorse by priests and clerks."]

Public shame remained the English punishment when London's customary law was compiled in the *Liber Albus* in the fifteenth century. Women convicted of "bawdry" were to be led to the pillory " 'with minstrelsy' " and have their hair cut or shaved off. Convicted a second time, they would be sentenced in addition to ten days in prison, and a third time, they would be banished from London.[36] As Ruth Mazo Karras suggests, writing about *Common Women: Prostitution and Sexuality in Medieval England*, laws such as these that stress public shame may have been directed particularly at "the casual go-between."[37] Most of the women in the stories about going between have other professional commitments and go between "casually." Karras reports illuminating statistics from London church courts. Accusations against procurers: 324 men, 1,593 women, 810 couples; accusations of corrupting young girls: 14 women, 11 couples, no men. As Karras points out, "Persuading women into sin seems to have been blamed particularly on women."[38] Discussing "the powerful literary motif" of the corrupting old bawd, Karras sees its correspondence with the court record sterotypes; when a woman is presented as a passive victim of sexual activity, blame falls on another woman, not on a man. "Literary representations and court prosecutions worked together to construct an image of the bawd that reflected a deep distrust of the sexual nature of older women,"[39] Karras writes. Church, court, and story assigned the same place and nature to the Old Woman.

Latin Comedies

The earliest of the Western European genres to include go-betweens for lust and sexual conquest is a strange hybrid made up of brief narratives told so predominantly through monologue and dialogue that some scholars believe they were intended for performance.[40] Called Latin comedies, they are written in Latin elegiac distichs unmistakably inspired by Ovid. Their plots, however, concern the tricky servants, raped women, and unscrupulous go-betweens that would later populate the fabliaux. The typical language of these poems is self-consciously clever and full of elaborate word play and rhetorical devices, and they were used to teach Latin and rhetoric in the cathedral schools that began late in the eleventh century and became very important in the twelfth century.[41]

Go-betweens operate in five of these stories: *De nuntio sagaci, Pamphilus, Baucis et Traso, Lidia*, and *Alda*. They date from 1080 to 1170 and were written, for the most part, in northern France in the Loire valley. The last three, from approximately 1150 to 1170, are contemporaneous with the fabliaux, but the first two, 1080 and 1100, precede them.[42] Why the subject matter and characters of the Latin comedies and fabliaux are so similar is as yet unexplained since the Latin and cathedral context of the one and the vernacular and lay context of the other would seem to separate them.

These five works are patently misogynistic. They feature sexual violation, crude jokes about a young girl's first sexual experiences, women as the exchangeable property of males, a homosocial power struggle, lewdly portrayed female lust and erotic scenes, an Old Woman used to divert attention from sexual violence, and portraits of a wildly lustful woman and an old witch. As would be expected, the pleasures of these poems are frequently voyeuristic.

Three of these five Latin comedies, *De nuntio sagaci, Pamphilus*, and *Alda*, deal with young men who have intercourse with young women who either do not agree to the act or have no idea what is being done to them.

A number of recent critics have debated what a historical reading of these poems would be. This issue arises most compellingly because these poems quote, echo, and refer to Ovid repeatedly, in an insistent intertextuality that forces the reader to consider them from an Ovidian perspective. In cathedral schools, boys learned Latin from these comedies, but they also learned Latin from Ovid's *Ars amatoria*,[43] and the *Ars amatoria* famously advises the would-be seducer that some force is permissible. Women often like to be taken by force, Ovid contends, and though they pretend to be glad to be spared, they are actually disappointed if the man does not force them.[44] If the idea behind these rapes is that "no" really means "yes," then no actual violence occurs, and medievalists need to consider whether medieval readers, especially boys taught by clerics, would have understood the events of these stories this way. If so, then accepting that these are "Ovidian" non-rapes would constitute a historical reading of them.

One way to explore this issue is to consider the satisfactions these poems offer. The least problematic of these attractions appear in *Alda*,[45] written in approximately 1170. It tells the story of Pyrrhus, a young man who becomes ruinously depressed and is wasting away to skin and bones because of his passion for Alda whom he has never seen. His twin sister is Alda's companion, and Alda is so beautiful that Pyrrhus has fallen in love with her from her reputation alone. Although Alda is an adolescent, she has never seen a young man. Her mother died giving birth to her, at which point her father locked her away from all contact with men. Her chaperon and nurse, named only "anus" (old woman) or "nutrix" (nurse), is so knowing about love that she recognizes Pyrrhus's symptoms at once and weeps and pleads until she coaxes him into telling her his secret. She then dresses him in his twin sister's clothes, teaches him to speak, act, and walk like a girl, and has him take his sister's place as Alda's companion. Pyrrhus returns beaming with joy after a week of sex, the old woman is triumphant, Alda discovers herself pregnant without ever suspecting that her companion for a week was not his twin sister, and her father lets Pyrrhus marry Alda to save the family's honor since his daughter is pregnant although she has never seen a man.

This piece has more to offer than its tricky plot. Since Alda is altogether ignorant of sexuality, every act she engages in with Pyrrhus is excitingly new to her. He begins by claiming that her nurse has just taught him how to win immortality, and he instructs Alda to mimic his actions as he kisses and caresses her, yielding a lusciously described sequence. Once he has sex with her—"Sumpta satis Pyrrus post oscula cetera sumit. / Defloratus abit uirginitatis honor" (465–66) (After Pyrrhus took enough kisses, he takes the rest. He deflowers her virginal honor.)—as described in nearly fifty verses, Alda marvels at the amazing lesson Pyrrhus has been teaching her about winning immortality. She would be happy to repeat that lesson, she says. Indeed, she would be happy to repeat it ten times over. She begs him to tell her where to get something capable of such wonderful work. Pyrrhus laughs and explains that he bought his instrument when a salesman arrived in town selling them, but he only had enough money for a small one, and right now it is dripping with sweat and worn out by the labor of the battle it fought with her; what was formerly swollen is resting, what was formerly proud and rigid hangs limp. And Alda wishes her friend had had more money to spend when the salesman came.

There are no class issues between this couple. Pyrrhus and Alda are of equal birth and their fathers are equally wealthy. On the other hand, part of the pleasure of this story comes from Pyrrhus's outfoxing Alda's father who locked her away—the old man denying the young man sex. Young male readers in particular would identify with Pyrrhus's victory. Alda's father is Pyrrhus's single adversary, and when he agrees to let Pyrrhus marry Alda because she is pregnant, Alda, who as yet knows only Pyrrhus's sister, not Pyrrhus (other than carnally), becomes a homosocial exchange between the two men.

The chief satisfactions of this story, however, are more evident. The most obvious is voyeuristic savoring of its intimate sexual scenes. The second and far more pervasive satisfaction derives from seeing a woman tricked into sex. This is a story about male conquest, and its pleasures arise from identifying with the conquering male. Enthusiastic and full of desire as Alda becomes in response to her sexual experiences, she loses her virginity to a trick. She does not know Pyrrhus, and has no idea what a sexual relationship or virginity is. She does not understand the societal meaning of any of these acts, how her loss of "honor" changes her value as a woman, or even how pregnancy occurs. She cannot be said to want this relationship, and without an understanding of the meaning of having sex, she cannot be said to consent to it. She is simply tricked into sex. Effectively, *Alda* narrates a rape, and the pleasure of the story derives predominantly from that aspect of it.

Standing behind all this erotic action is the "anus," the Old Woman, and a final satisfying aspect of the poem is surely the audacity of her trick. As Alda's nurse and chaperon, she has shared her life intimately since she was born and is responsible for guarding and protecting her, not dressing up young men in women's clothes to take her virginity. Although the Old Woman is never described and has no dialogue, she remains an ominous figure of betrayal and treachery, the Old Woman who goes between.

The earliest of these Latin comedies, *De nuntio sagaci* [Concerning the Clever Messenger] *c.* 1080, also narrates a rape. When Ovid advised force with women who say "no" when they really mean "yes," he was writing about a seduction tactic: the woman is wooed to the brink of accepting the man and then pushed over it. *Facetus*, a mid-twelfth-century Latin art of love,[46] contains an Ovid-inspired medieval version of this ploy. *Facetus*'s step-by-step account tells the would-be lover to touch the woman's clothes, then her hip and side, then kiss her, then, after long, passionate embraces, caress her breasts, her thighs, and her stomach. At this point, they should both have their clothes off, and if she resists consummation, he should force her, because only prostitutes seek out intercourse.[47] This is not at all what happens in *De nuntio sagaci*. The young man rapes the young woman, but rape is virtually his only interaction with her. Nothing between them prepares for this moment. Strange as this sounds, the young woman relates nearly exclusively to the go-between. Most of *De nuntio sagaci* is dialogue, and the young woman and the go-between speak all of it; the young man is limited to occasional summaries of action. The go-between, not the man, courts the woman.

In *De nuntio sagaci*, Davus, the go-between, is the young man's servant and the sole character who is given a name. He takes gifts to the young woman, interests her in sex, persuades her that she should meet with the young man, leads her to the meeting, consoles her over her lost virginity, and even convinces her to continue an affair with the man, despite the rape. Davus leaves only the sex act to his master, and even during that, the young woman is calling to Davus to protect her. This is not a poem about a relationship between a man and a woman. It is a poem about a go-between who delivers a young woman to a man for sex.

The young woman is ambivalent about her situation. On the one hand, she is very naive, afraid of sex and love, and half aware of how much she is risking. On the other hand, she is attracted by the idea of the young man and wants to be in love with him. Davus tantalizes the woman with glimpses of forbidden experience, luring her on with language that half conceals its sexual meanings. When he tells her she would praise "the act" if it were to occur, for instance, she becomes very upset. " 'Laudarem factum? Quod factum? Nescio factum. / Dic quid sit factum. Puto quod non sit bene dictum' " (123–24)[48] ("I would praise 'the act'? What act? I don't know anything about any act. Tell me what this act can be. I think it's not a good thing to talk about").

Davus's veiled sex talk laced with allusions to future delights arouses the young woman's interest, but he also promises to protect her honor and stay with her when she meets the young man (104–05, 139–40). The young man is as virginal as she is, he assures her: " 'Si bene cognosses, velut agnum tangere posses. / Quid sit amor nescit: pudor est ubi femina tangit.' " (146–47) ["If you knew him well, you would be able to pet him like a lamb. He does not know what love is; he blushes when a woman touches him."] Nevertheless, despite Davus's soothing speeches, when the young woman is about to go to the man's house, she remains clear about what she fears: " 'Quam cito dimittis si forte fores michi claudis; / Et mox sum victa, postquam sum sola relicta' " (153–54) ["How quickly you will abandon me if you shut the door on me—and the second I'm left alone, I'm done for!"].

This story focuses so improbably on going between that even during the rape nearly everything the young woman says is directed at the absent go-between. At a sign from Davus, the young man maneuvers her into a room with a bed and shuts the door. She laments, protests, and denounces Davus. She sounds so grief-stricken and amazed at her situation that she seems to have trusted the go-between. "Where are you, where are you?," she cries. "The young man wants love!"

> "Audis clamare? Debes hic tu prope stare.
> Quo tu venisti? Numquid fantasma fuisti?
> Facta fides fuerat, sed eam quis nunc michi servat?
> O maledicta Fides, aliis te taliter offers?" (192–95)

> ["Don't you hear me calling you? You ought to stay here by me. Where did you go? Were you some sort of apparition? You gave me your word of honor, but who now keeps it for me? Oh cursed Honor, do you treat others this way?"]

And she laments the thousand promises Davus made to her, and how duped she has been. If Davus were there, she says, she would have him put to death.

The rape is announced noncommittally: "Talia cum loquitur, lecto prope stante locatur. / Cetera que restant, Venus associata ministrat." (202–03) [As she is saying these things, she finds herself placed on a nearby bed. As for the rest, Venus joins in and takes care of it.]

Even after the rape, the young man has nothing to say; it is Davus who talks to the young woman. He begins with lies, swearing he cannot imagine why she is weeping and that he was right beside the door and never heard a word, but ultimately he switches tactics, arguing that her initiation into sexuality was all for the best. She is the right age for love; sex is a fact of life, why should she grieve so about it? Many other women have been trapped just as she was. The young woman is very clear about how meanly she has been treated: " 'Fas est plorare: sum perdita, nescio quare' " (241) ["It is right for me to weep; I am lost without knowing why"], but she then agrees to accept her situation. When Davus urges her to kiss her lover, she talks openly about how long she has wondered what having sex was really like. Now at last "factum" no longer frightens her. And she hugs the young man and covers him with kisses.

Unlike *Alda*, most of the interactions in *De nuntio sagaci* are basically realistic. No clever tricks divert the reader's attention from the rape, and its technique is so ordinary that Davus's role, this time played by a woman, appears in *Facetus*, the thirteenth-century art of love: "sapienter nuncia curet / Artibus ut trahat hanc ad loca tuta jocis" ["let his messenger take charge of ingeniously luring the girl to a place safe for sport"].[49] Anne Schotter, in "Rape in the Medieval Latin Comedies," groups *De nuntio sagaci* with comedies that justify rape "implicitly with assumption that it is women's true desire,"[50] presumably because the young woman accepts the man as her lover after the act. Similarly, Leyla Rouhi in *Mediation and Love* claims that there are no victims in these Latin comedies and that the apparent victims in fact "end up enjoying the sexual trap set for them or at least put up little resistance at the crucial stages."[51] Surely this is too benign a representation of the rape in *De nuntio sagaci*. The young woman ultimately accepts what has happened to her, but she resists loudly and frantically while she is being raped and she is miserable and accusing afterwards. Moreover, with the go-between doing all the wooing, her rape does not fit the erotic Ovidian model. The titillation of the narrative comes from anticipation of her capture and betrayal and the taboo pleasures of imagining a scene in which a young woman loses her virginity to violence. Rape understood as rape is essential to such a story.

De nuntio sagaci was not an obscure text. Two hundred years after it was written, it was still widely read, a dozen verses from it became proverbs, it was quoted in florilegia; in 1280, Hugh of Trimberg, schoolmaster of Bamberg and author of the *Registrum Multorum Auctorum* [List of Many Authors], identified it as a text used in all the schools; and it was still being copied at the end of the fifteenth century.[52] Since *De nuntio sagaci* is incomplete in all surviving manuscripts, and what remains of the end of the text is chaotic, it must have been the go-between's role and the rape that engaged medieval interest.

De nuntio sagaci was popular, but *Pamphilus*, a Latin comedy modeled on *De nuntio sagaci*[53] and written approximately twenty years later, was ten times as popular. *Pamphilus* was one of the very widely read texts of the Middle Ages. It has survived in 170 manuscripts[54] from throughout the continent; it was frequently translated; it is widely cited in florilegia; the word "pamphlet" derives from it; and a large number of authors quote it or allude to it, among them both Chaucer and Gower.[55] It also influenced a number of important works that include go-betweens. One of the most important of these is Chaucer's *Troilus and Criseyde*, as will be discussed later.[56] *Pamphilus* was also a major source for the *Roman de la rose*. Not only did the characterization of the go-between lead directly to the Old Woman, Ernest Langlois argues that both Guillaume de Lorris and Jean de Meun used *Pamphilus* as their source for the subject, method, and several of the allegorical figures in the *Roman*.[57] *Pamphilus* may have begun as a text to teach rhetoric, but it was soon read far outside the cathedral school confines.

Pamphilus contains the first fully developed characterization in medieval Western literature of the feared and reviled Old Woman who dominates the medical treatises, sermons, and religious writings of the Western Middle Ages. By substituting the Old Woman for Davus, *Pamphilus* combines the voyeuristic and sadistic pleasures of observing rape with a satisfying, socially acceptable target for misogyny, an easy female figure to loathe. Could it be that the Old Woman accounts for *Pamphilus*'s enormous popularity?

Pamphilus is a darker, harsher piece of work than *De nuntio sagaci*, and Anus, the Old Woman, is a much more formidable go-between than Davus was. At the close of the rape sequence in *De nuntio sagaci*, the young woman is kissing and embracing the young man, but at the matching point in *Pamphilus*, she is weeping, lamenting her wretchedness, cursing her betrayer, and swearing that all her love for the young man has been destroyed. Furthermore, the *Pamphilus* rape is no simple act of passion; it is an heiress rape. No class differences separated the *De nuntio sagaci* couple, but Pamphilus lacks both the money and high birth to make him eligible to be the husband of Galatea, the young woman. Once he rapes her, however, she must marry him to save her honor. The Old Woman is a hired professional, and she traps Galatea into this rape.

The Old Woman is the central character of *Pamphilus* and appears and speaks more often than either of the young people. She is a traditional Old Woman figure, "anus subtilis et ingeniosa / Artibus et Veneris apta ministra satis" (281–82) (a subtle and clever old woman, a very suitable helper in the arts of Venus).[58] She bewails her age, poverty, and physical weakness, and laments how rich she was when she was young, suggesting that she had been a prostitute (323). She alerts Pamphilus immediately to the importance of paying her well. In fact, if she succeeds in winning Galatea for him, she says she expects to be supported as part of his household. Even in her last line, which is the last line of the poem, she returns to the subject of what she is owed: " 'Per me felices, este mei memores!' " (780) ["Made happy by my efforts, remember me!"]

The Old Woman lies so often that the events of the story are hard to follow. In the course of a 780-verse poem, she tells or acts out ten substantial lies. For instance, she warns Pamphilus about another man who is trying to hire her to intercede with Galatea. Even though this young man is honest and would make a good husband, she says, she will not help him because he is only offering her a fur piece and some old gowns. This competing suitor is never mentioned again and is apparently one of the Old Woman's many prodding fictions. Another of her lies concerns her relationship with Galatea. As soon as Pamphilus mentions Galatea to her, she assures him that she is Galatea's confidante, that Galatea proceeds only on her advice, and that no one will win Galatea without her support (307–10). As soon as she and Galatea converse, however, it is obvious that even young, naive Galatea is wary of the Old Woman, and there is no special relationship between the two of them.

The Old Woman's most serious lie concerns Pamphilus's social position and financial status. She assures Galatea that she has investigated his family tree and chosen him for her because he equals her in birth and wealth. He is handsome, noble, charming, and generous, a paragon among young men, she insists, and he is wise, honest, rich, and the son of a distinguished family. With Galatea, of course, the Old Woman pretends to have thought of the Pamphilus marriage entirely on her own. When Galatea questions her motivation, she defends herself sanctimoniously. She may be poor, she insists, but she manages with what she has and would never commit such a crime as to take money to further a relationship (387–88).

The Old Woman manipulates Pamphilus skillfully, keeping him anxious and dependent on her, twisting him back and forth between joy and despair. At one point she tells him she has seen a magnificent wedding dress at Galatea's house, ready for her marriage with another man. At the next moment, she claims instead that Galatea will do anything Pamphilus wants. This is as much a lie as the story about the marriage. Galatea has only very timidly admitted to sharing " 'vera. . .amicitia' " ["a true friendship"] with Pamphilus (434).

The rape in *De nuntio sagaci* was an end in itself; the young man desired the young woman. But Pamphilus's rape of Galatea is his means to an end, to force her family to let him marry her. The Old Woman spells out his role:

"Si vos nostra simul solertia collocat ambos
     Et locus affuerit, te precor esse virum.
Mens animusque manet inconstans semper amantis:
     Parvaque forte tibi quod petis hora dabit." (545–48)

["If my clever plan arranges a meeting between you two, and the opportunity is there, I entreat you to be a man. The mind and spirit of a girl in love are always wavering, and a small moment will perhaps give you what you desire."]

Since Galatea and Pamphilus meet only once, briefly, before the rape, she knows and desires him nearly exclusively through the Old Woman's praise of him and of the joys of love. Torn between desire, modesty, and fear, Galatea cannot understand why Pamphilus does not ask her parents to let him marry her. As the Old Woman awaits the arrival of Pamphilus who is coming to rape Galatea, she lectures Galatea on the inextinguishable fires of Venus in a standard seize-the-day speech. If Galatea resists Venus,

" 'Insipiens temere, male perdis gaudia vite.' " (637) ["Rashly foolish, you wickedly throw away the joys of life"]. " 'Parce iuuentuti, complectere gaudia vite.' " (645) ["Take pity on your youth; embrace life's joys!"]. Galatea is still conflicted. She is both frightened and drawn to Pamphilus, but she is never given a chance to decide whether to risk being alone with him. The Old Woman coaxes her into eating fruit and nuts at her house, Pamphilus pretends to burst the door bolts, and the Old Woman exits on the pretext that a neighbor is calling her. As she shuts her door behind her, she announces for the benefit of the neighborhood that now no one is at her home; the house is empty.

The Old Woman is playing the standard rape trick: trap the young woman alone with the man in such a compromising situation that she cannot extricate herself from it without losing her reputation. *Pamphilus* dramatizes the harsh reality of sexual assault. Galatea is realistically wretched, and the scene is pathetic. Pamphilus initially begs Galatea for love and tries to seduce her with promises of the pleasures that lie ahead for them, but the seduction very quickly becomes a rape, and all sensuality is lost in violence. Pamphilus forces Galatea while, graphically and repeatedly, she pleads with him to stop. Detail after detail charts the progress of the rape: Galatea bewails her subdued hands, her bruised breasts, and her lack of strength—a woman's weakness pitted against a man's force. She cries out against Pamphilus for hurting and betraying her, threatens to scream, and finally, sadly and anticlimactically, she vows never again to come to the Old Woman's house or let the Old Woman deceive her. At last she denounces Pamphilus: " 'Huius victor eris facti, licet ipsa relucter, / Sed tamen inter nos rumpitur omnis amor!' " (695–96) ["You'll win this time, no matter how much I resist, but it will destroy our love forever!"]

In a desperate maneuver, Pamphilus tries to blame Galatea for her own rape because her beauty tempted his passion. " 'Culpe communis fer patienter onus' " (720) ["We're both to blame; you should bear your share patiently"], he counsels her, but she is still weeping inconsolably when the go-between returns. The Old Woman pretends to know nothing at all about what has happened, but this time Galatea has been too blatantly betrayed to be fooled. She compares herself to a fleeing hare that has died in the trap, and she denounces the Old Woman's treachery: " 'Sic piscis curvum iam captus percipit hamum, / Sic avis humanos capta videt laqueos!' " (763–64) ["Just so, the caught fish feels the hook, and the caught bird sees the trapper's snare!"]. The Old Woman's response is cold, practical, and prudent. Since it is too late to change what has happened, Galatea and Pamphilus must marry, and since she has matched them up so well, they must take care of her.

Pamphilus is a sad little story of betrayal in which the means to the marriage may well have destroyed the love, just as Galatea claims, and the go-between's callousness and insensitivity to the people involved in the relationship she was hired to create may actually have made the relationship impossible. Galatea is the most obvious casualty of the Old Woman's going between. As the poem opens, Galatea is a beautiful, innocent, cheerful young woman who is full of eagerness to love and much attracted to Pamphilus. By the end of the poem, her innocence, her consent, and her body have all been violated. Pamphilus is the agent of her violation, but the Old Woman is its instigator. And while Galatea is the Old Woman's primary victim, the go-between corrupts Pamphilus as well when he allows her to redefine desire as rape for him.

Two major adaptations, both from the early fourteenth century, retell the entire *Pamphilus* story: a French version, *Pamphile et Galatée*, and the Spanish *Libro de buen amor*. Both reproduce the ending in ways that show how their authors read it. The French version stresses how exclusively rape is a tool for Pamphilus. When the old woman go-between warns him to "be a man" as soon as she manages to create the situation he needs, she then adds, " 'Pensers d'amours plus tost se mue / Qu'ome pouilleus ne se remue' "[59] ("Thoughts of love change faster than a timid man runs away"), making explicit how passionless this act is. The Spanish Galatea first denounces go-betweens:

> "¡Ay, viejas tan perdidas!
> a las mugeres trahedes engañadas, vendidas:
> ayer mill cobros me davas, mill artes, mill salidas,
> oy que só escarnida, todas me son fallidas." (882)[60]

["Ah, damned old women! You betray us and you barter for us! Yesterday you promised me a thousand ways, a thousand tricks, and a thousand escapes. Today, I am scorned: they all failed."]

She then elaborates movingly and pathetically the metaphors the Latin version used to describe the grief of the raped Galatea.

> "Si las aves lo podiesen bien saber e entender
> quantos laços les paran, non las podrían prender:
> quando el laço veen, ya las lievan a vender;
> mueren por el poco çevo, non se pueden defender.
>
> Sí los peçes de las aguas, quando vëen al anzuelo,
> ya el pescador los tiene e los trahe por el suelo." (883–84)

["If the birds could know and understand how many traps are prepared for them, they would never be caught. But by the time they see the trap, they are already being hauled to market. They die for a scrap of bait and have no defense. And the fish in the water—by the time they see the hook, the fisherman has caught them and thrown them on the ground."]

The raped young woman then draws the grim analogy with herself:

"La muger vëe su daño quando ya finca con duelo,
non la quieren los parientes, padre, madre nin avuelo.
El que la á desonrada, déxala, non la mantiene;
vase perder por el mundo." (884–85)

["A woman sees her ruin only when she is already in grief, and is thrown out by her father, mother, and grandparents. The man who dishonored her leaves her without support and she wanders about the world to her ruin."]

Scholars concerned about ahistorical readings of rape scenes from these Latin comedies discuss *Pamphilus* far more than any of the others. Alastair Minnis, for instance, describes *Pamphilus* as a comic text for the "all-male elementary schoolroom" of clerics and quotes Galatea's entire speech while she is being raped, only to conclude that she illustrates Ovid's precepts that women enjoy rape and want to be forced.[61] Jill Mann takes a similar Ovidian position. Concerning this scene between Pamphilus and Galatea, she writes:

It is not, of course, a scene of outright rape, as Galatea's protestation that she *will* scream makes clear (why not simply scream?). Pamphilus's forcefulness is based on the familiar assumption that decorum obliges a woman to say no even when she means yes, and that it is therefore a man's duty to save her face by taking on himself the responsibility and guilt of copulation—as Pamphilus does.[62]

If this scene is to be understood as a seduction rather than a rape, no indication of that is given in the text. Nothing Galatea says during the sexual act or after it indicates she is being seduced. Even Pamphilus seems to be acting more out of duty than desire. Alison Elliott, in the introduction to her translation of *Pamphilus*, notes that *labor*, meaning "hard work," "drudgery," appears twenty-seven times in this 780-line poem, "an essentially unromantic, rather cynical view of love."[63] This rape seems to be "*labor*" for Pamphilus. And Galatea has an excellent reason for not screaming; she must protect her reputation. As Anne Schotter points out in "Rhetoric versus Rape in the Medieval Latin *Pamphilus*," Galatea is very concerned about *fama* [reputation] and talks about her fear of scandal throughout the poem.[64]

Elliott, Schotter, and Marjorie Woods all agree that Galatea's characterization and response to Pamphilus make it clear that she is raped rather than seduced.[65] Schotter, building on Elliott's reading, describes *Pamphilus* as "giving voice to a female rape victim" and exploring the real-world problem of rape.[66] Woods, on the other hand, argues that the "apparent 'realness' of *Pamphilus* as a text and the seeming 'strength' " of Galatea are the effects of classroom rhetorical techniques rather than medieval exploration of female psychology, and she sees the poem as concerned with "issues of power and powerlessness" rather than sex.[67]

Given the wide audience *Pamphilus* attracted for centuries, it unques-
tionably appealed greatly to medieval readers, and medieval readers were
predominantly male. Surely sympathy with the voice of a female rape victim,
present though it may be in *Pamphilus*, would not have sustained that level
of interest. The Ovidian readings deny that there is a rape and the feminist
readings emphasize sympathy for Galatea. Could it be that the debate over
ahistorical readings of *Pamphilus* grows out of ahistorical reluctance to
acknowledge the attractions of rape for medieval male readers? *Pamphilus*
was so popular in the Middle Ages because it fed readers' appetite for
reading about rape. Galatea's rape offers a variety of attractions: a male
dominates a female; a less powerful male—less rich, less noble—rises in
stature by conquest of a higher-class female. And then there are the more
evident taboo pleasures of viewing a titillating scene and imagining the
female body forced and penetrated. Of course, *De nuntio sagaci* also offers
much of this. Why then was *Pamphilus* so very much more popular than *De
nuntio sagaci*? Surely the answer is the Old Woman. *Pamphilus* had hit on a
winning combination. With the Old Woman distracting attention from
the sexual violence, the vicarious pleasure of the rape becomes less illegitimate. Since the Old Woman told Pamphilus to rape Galatea, the rape is less
his fault or responsibility, leaving the reader free to identify with him,
enjoying the prurient sexual pleasures of reading about rape while the
loathsome Old Woman carries the blame. The audience of *Pamphilus*
would have been responding to being offered, as Kathryn Gravdal puts it,
"the unacceptable fantasy of rape in an acceptable way,"[68] protected from
recognizing that the taboo source of pleasure of the work is rape.

The women in the last of these Latin comedies are unambiguous
instances of the evils of women as they were preached and philosophized
about throughout the Middle Ages. Baucis, the central figure of *Baucis et
Traso*, which dates from the third quarter of the twelfth century, is a traditional Old Woman who goes between. She sells women for a living in a
town underworld of pimps, bawds, thugs, and bullies where men urinate
on other men and punch, maul, and tear out the hair of women. Poor and
very old—"Annos quingentos vixisti, nec nisi nugis; / Os tibi dente caret,
falsa remiscet adhuc. / Tu senii fex es." (141–43)[69] ["You have lived five
hundred years, totally frivolously; your mouth has no teeth in it and still
mixes together lies. You are the dregs of old age.]—Baucis is also a former
prostitute. During the course of the poem, various people call her "meretrix"
or "meretrix annosa" (151) [old whore], and while they might simply be
insulting her, her aggressive tactics suggest that she is an old hand at selling
sex. Her initial clientele in this narrative is a group of men, and she hawks
a young woman to them, taking bids for her outright, until she chooses the
man most likely to buy.

One of the standard accusations against old women by preachers and the legal system was that they practiced black magic. According to studies of inquisition trial records in Spain, for instance, go-betweens were routinely thought to be witches.[70] Baucis is a witch. When she quarrels with another go-between, he accuses her of being able to control the fertility of both human beings and the earth:

> "Non herbis, ut tu, segetes subvertere novi,
>> Uberiora tibi carmine rura dare,
> Non pueris orbare patres, matri dare partum.
>> Nuper enim vidi lecta venena tibi." (153–56)

> ["I do not know, like you, how to ruin crops with herbs or make your own grow with a charm, or deprive fathers of children, or bestow childbirth on a mother. Recently I saw potent herbs gathered at your house."]

Baucis never denies any of these charges, and the woman she sells in this narrative is a prostitute that Baucis has turned into a virgin by witchcraft.

The narrator describes Baucis's witchcraft without commenting on it. After giving the prostitute a new, poetic name, Glyceria, Baucis teaches her to speak and act elegantly and modestly and then lengthens her face, enlarges her forehead, narrows her shoulders, thins her mouth, elongates her fingers, contracts her hands, and makes her hair more luxuriant and her neck more enticing (3–7). Next, with a soldier, Traso, promising to pay a high price to possess a virginal Glyceria, "Baucis, virgineum temptans revocare pudorem, / Provida proposite colligit apta rei." (307–08) [Prudent Baucis, attempting to call back a girl's virginity, gathers together the things she needs for her purpose]. Her list begins with herbs, unguents, potions, and drugs, but before long it names impossibilities: the whiteness of a crow, some smoke, three puffs of wind, the sight of a blind man, hair from the forehead of a bald man, a eunuch's sexual member, and so forth. The narrator then announces that once Baucis has these things prepared, she turns the prostitute into a virgin. Baucis's list may be a joke about the impossibility of regaining lost virginity. On the other hand, she may be as adept at black magic as she is at fraud. The end of the poem reports Traso's enjoyment of Glyceria's high-priced first favors, and he never complains that he has been cheated.

As a procurer, Baucis is tough, clever, aggressive, and manipulative. She sells Glyceria to man after man:

> Hanc probat, hanc cuivis spondet, dat dantibus huius
>> Primos concubitus virgineumque decus—
> Huic primos, illi primos. . .Quid plura referrem?
>> Tot spondet primos quot sibi dona ferunt. (15–18)

[To whoever pays, she gives the girl's "first time ever, her cherry—really"; to this guy "the first time ever," to that guy "the first time ever." What's more to say? She promises as many "first times" as there are men to give her gifts.]

To sustain her trick as long as possible, she promises the young woman to different men under different names and they compete with each other by comparing the attractions of the women they expect to possess. When Traso, her best prospect, arrives on the scene, she ingratiates herself with him, " 'O miles, Amoris alumpne, / Miles, honoris honos' " (33–34) ["Oh Sir Knight, love's disciple, Sir Knight, honor's pride"], and hawks her wares: " 'Virgo, sed virga, sed flos, sed fructus amoris, / Lumen virgineum, forma decore nitens' " (37–38) ["She's a virgin, a tender sprout, a blossom, a peach ripe for love, a fresh flame; her beauty just glows"]. As soon as Traso is ready to rush to Baucis's house, "Anxius ut fiat, ut crescat flamma calentis" (41) [to tease him, to make him even hotter], Baucis pretends to be about to leave. This maneuver reduces Traso to pleas to be able to see the young woman, but Baucis holds him off with accounts of Glyceria's extreme delicacy. Glyceria is sleeping, Baucis explains, and she becomes ill if she is awakened. If she is kept waiting when she is ready to eat, she sends away the meal when it is brought. If she is kept waiting for a drink, she refuses it. And Traso finds all these details of the woman's finickiness exceedingly enticing. To extract as much money from Traso as possible, Baucis leads him through the marketplace while she shops and he pays. Sometimes she borrows the money from him; sometimes she persuades him to purchase what she needs as gifts for Glyceria. Then suddenly Baucis disappears, leaving Traso so beside himself with rage and frustrated passion that he is reduced to beating his slaves.

Conventionally, going between is an individual matter of trickery and persuasion, but in this violent context it becomes a fight over who will have the privilege of duping Traso. Davus, Traso's slave, sees through Baucis's tricks and wants to go between for Traso himself. When Traso tells his story about Baucis's sudden disappearance in the marketplace after tantalizing him with the beautiful virgin, Davus rushes to Baucis's house to rail at her for fleecing his master—" 'Tu dolus es et origo doli, scelus aut sceleris fons, / Summa mali nobis omnibus, immo malum' " (129–30) ["You are deceit incarnate, and you spawn deceit; you are wickedness, and you make others wicked; for all of us, you are the height of evil, or rather you are evil itself"]. The two get into a slapping, hair-pulling, mauling fight, and then agree to split whatever amount can be made from Traso.

Baucis's going between concludes with a standard speech that a number of old go-betweens give, and it is especially comic because Glyceria is an ex-prostitute. When Glyceria shrinks from Traso, protesting that her virginity is her only dowry, love frightens her, and Traso must leave her alone, Baucis intervenes, lecturing Glyceria on seizing the day and the importance for a woman to learn about love while she is still young. Traso is so grateful that he once again pays Baucis a large sum and promises her more (273–98).

Baucis is a demonized portrait of an Old Woman. Poor, ancient, physically repulsive, greedy, mercenary, a witch, a procurer, corrupt herself and living off the corruption of others, Baucis operates at the bottom of society, below even the rest of these Old Women who go between. The magical powers she boasts of or men suspect of her—her capacity to control fertility and to turn a prostitute into a virgin—tap men's fear and resentment of woman's sexual power, and from time to time the generic disgust with woman that supplies the energy of this poem breaks through to the surface: " 'Femina, flamma nocens, dolor intimus, hostis amico. / Femina, summa mali, femina digna mori, / Femina fetoris dat semina, femina mortem.' " (89–91) ["Woman, destructive flame, pain in the gut, enemy to the man who loves you. A woman is the greatest evil of all; a woman is better off dead; woman gives the seeds of decay; woman kills."]

Women were believed to be sexually insatiable in the Middle Ages, and the sin most insistently attributed to them was lust. *Lidia*,[71] written in approximately 1155, is the last of these Latin comedies that include go-betweens, and it is a poem about woman's lust. Its major character is so wild with lust that to convince the young man she lusts after that her desire is real, she kills her husband's favorite falcon, pulls five hairs out of his beard, and extracts a good tooth from his jaw. Even more so than *Baucis et Traso*, *Lidia* is an act of aggression against women, and this generalized aggression yields much of the satisfaction of the work. One woman was demonized in *Baucis et Traso*, but in *Lidia*, all women are demonized. Lusca, the nightmare figure who goes between for Lydia, loathes her mistress and holds her up as a pattern of all women, detailing and denouncing the magnitude of their lust. The voice speaking via Lusca is of course a male voice—a male voice denouncing females via a female voice—and his audience is also male, the cathedral school audience of these Latin poems. As Sheila Fisher and Janet E. Halley write, citing Anne Cruz, "the female speaker invented by a male author is the mark of female absence, because the male author is speaking not through, but across the female in order to address other men."[72] In this case, since the male author is vilifying females, the female voice functions to validate the accusations. This is not one sex reviling the other; the speaker is reveling in the torrid secrets of her own sisters.

Lydia is a duchess, and Lusca is her maid. Although she is characterized as "Vna ministrarum fidissima" (57) [one of the most faithful of servants], she is a parasite who preys on the depravity of a mistress she despises. Moreover, she adopts this role in full self-awareness. All of these go-betweens exploit other people's vices; Lusca flaunts how effective she is at exploiting the duchess's.

Lydia is consumed by lust for Pyrrhus, a young knight in her husband's retinue. Instead of trying to distract her mistress from Pyrrhus, Lusca cultivates Lydia's lust and glories in it. Boasting that she knows every trick Lydia knows, Lusca spells out how she wins her own profit from her mistress's lewdness:

> "Non tam cara forem si sibi casta foret.
> Si grauis esset hera, mihi quid grauitate lucrarer?
>   Est leuis, illius sum leuitate potens.
> Parca quidem grauis est, quia nil frons nuda ueretur;
>   At lasciua uiri prodiga spargit opes." (142–46)

["I would not be so dear to her if she were chaste. If the mistress of the house were serious, what would I get out of it? She is frivolous, and her frivolity makes me powerful. A serious woman is stingy; she presents an open face to the world, and fears nothing; but a loose, wasteful woman scatters her husband's wealth."]

Lusca then denounces women in general as cesspools of lust. Even Hercules in the shirt of Nessus never burned the way women burn, Lusca claims. Passion drives a woman mad. In the grip of passion, " 'Audet et aggreditur, temptat agitque nefas. / Hec furit, hec gannit, hec gestit uersa lepore' " (98–99) ["she is daring and aggressive; she tries anything; she does the unspeakable. And using her charm, she rages, she yelps, she wriggles."]. Women are insatiable, Lusca announces. They want parades of men, not a single lover. Ten men would not satisfy Lydia, and all women are equally lustful:

> "Nulla timet, nulla denegat, immo petit.
> Non habet una modum, nec in omnibus una modesta;
>   Illud quando mouet est modus absque modo.
> Turpis, formosa, trux, mitis, diues, egena,
>   Sulcat, arat, uellit, quassat, aduncat, hiat." (104–08)

["None of them is timid, none says no, but begs for it. Not one is restrained; there's not a modest one in the whole lot; once aroused, they behave without restraint. Ugly, beautiful, fierce, mild, rich, poor, she ploughs, tills, tears out, shakes, hooks—and spreads her legs wide."]

Women yearn after whatever kind of man they do not already have. Sexual novelty lures them on so senselessly that a woman with a well-endowed lover wants a small lover, one with a small lover wants a large one; or a thin one a fat one, or a short one a long one. Their passions obscure even their self-interest, and they all make poor bargains selling themselves.

Lydia, Lusca reports, is so promiscuous that the duke's house is bountiful, the gatekeeper is inviting, and there is no charge for entrance. The duchess welcomes everyone shamelessly, one after the other, whoever comes: " 'Malleus incude terque quaterque sonat; / Sustinet hos et adhuc aperit fabrilia quassans.' " (124–25) ["The hammer rings out on the anvil three or four times; she sustains these and still is open, shattering the tools."] Lusca then imagines Lydia asking Pyrrhus to press his thigh against hers; he refuses; she begs him more feverishly, and the chase is on, never mind her husband. Lusca turns back again to women in general. What good are marriage bonds and a shared bed? The Penelopes and Lucreces of the past have all vanished, leaving only generations of Thaïses. Women may seem to be faithful, but poison lies just beneath the surface (126–38).

This ominous, parasitical female voice reviles women with no intention of moderating their lasciviousness. Lusca's only interest is in profiting from their vices. In some unclear but sinister way, she identifies herself with darkness. Lusca means "one-eyed" in Latin, and she is blind in one eye, but she claims to have been named after the horned moon. When she thinks about herself as outshining all Lydia's other servants, she compares herself to the moon surpassing all the stars and giving her light to them. Night is her time, and light is jealous of her, she says (157–58, 162–67).

As a go-between, Lusca carries Lydia's messages to Pyrrhus and attempts to convince him to have an affair with her mistress, but without success. Initially Lusca terrifies Pyrrhus with her descriptions of Lydia's passion. Doubting both the duchess's sincerity and her power in her marriage, he refuses to consider her propositions. Pyrrhus's rejection sends Lydia into convulsions of despair and fantasies of Pyrrhus in the arms of a prostitute or a woman from the country. She sends Lusca back to Pyrrhus to plead her case again, and buy him if necessary. Instead, Lusca, "uerbis et rebus subdola" (231) [crafty in word and deed], appeals to Pyrrhus as one underling to another, with an underling's special understanding of vulnerability. She compares Pyrrhus and Lydia to Hippolytus and Phaedra. Phaedra, Theseus's wife and Hippolytus's stepmother, lusted after Hippolytus. When he refused to become her lover, she accused him of making advances to her, and her enraged husband, Theseus, his father, had Hippolytus killed by a sea monster. Diana, goddess of chastity, Lusca points out, rarely avenges herself when her votaries break their vows, but thwarted lustful women are capable of horrendous acts. Lusca's analogy balances Pyrrhus's fears of the duke with new fears of the duchess. Caught between the two, Pyrrhus speculates that either the duke is spineless or his wife is mad, and he agrees to become Lydia's lover if she kills her husband's favorite falcon, pulls five hairs from his beard, and extracts a good tooth from his jaw.

Capturing the person lusted after is not the object of the tricks in *Lidia*. They are designed to pain and shame the powerful duke who is about to be cuckolded by one of his young, dependent knights. The plot justifies the dead falcon and pulled hairs and tooth on the grounds that they are needed to convince Pyrrhus of Lydia's power and determination, but no reason is given for the poem's conclusion, a final outrageous illustration of Lusca's claims about woman's lust. Pyrrhus means "pear tree" in Latin, and after Lydia fulfills Pyrrhus's impossible demands, she celebrates Pyrrhus's name in a grand finale flourish of contempt for the cuckolded duke. While the duke watches, perched in the top of a pear tree, convinced that what he sees so clearly is an illusion, Lydia copulates with Pyrrhus at the pear tree's base.[73]

Lidia announces itself as a didactic narrative that will teach men what to expect from women, and its principal source of pleasure is most obviously and least ambiguously its outright denunciation of women as sexual beings. Other sources of satisfaction familiar from the rest of these Latin comedies include seeing a young man best an older, more powerful father or husband and imagining the copulating couple in the final pear tree scene. These more ordinary sources of interest, however, leave important aspects of this piece unaccounted for. Lust can be presented comically, as any fabliau reader appreciates, and some of the *Lidia* imagery for the sexually aroused female body is subtly suggestive: open doors, the duke's bountiful house, the welcoming gatekeeper. For the most part, however, this imagery is aggressive and borders on the gross. The physical descriptions conjured up by saying that women plough, till, shake, hook, and gape, for instance, are crude, with too much literal potential, and without any of the clever seductiveness of good fabliau imagery. There is nothing lighthearted about any of these descriptions.

Beneath the surface of this narrative lies a reservoir of fear of women, and it fuels the harshness of *Lidia*. Conjuring up women as insatiable and devouring, the male voice that speaks through Lusca's female voice is haunted by anxiety about male sexual inadequacy. This powerful under-current of the poem surfaces most explicitly in its frightening image of Lydia welcoming man after man, whoever comes: " 'Malleus incude terque quaterque sonat; / Sustinet hos et adhuc aperit fabrilia quassans.' " (124–25) ["The hammer rings out on the anvil three or four times; she sustains these and still is open, shattering the tools."] The crucial detail here is the shattered tools.

The generic expectations of narratives that picture rape as part of the courtship of virgins, or feature women driven by flagrant, uncontrollable lust, or include an old witch hawking a prostitute pressure the reader to join in their misogyny. To laugh at the joke or enjoy the action, the reader must assent to the conception. Reading these Latin comedies with attention to the desires they arouse and seek to satisfy and the means by which they do so yields a new experience of the misogynous Middle Ages.

Alda, De nuntio sagaci, Pamphilus, Baucis et Traso, and *Lidia*: two Old Women and a young man tricking young virgins into being raped, an Old Woman practicing witchcraft to prepare other women for sale, and a middle-aged woman exploiting as she itemizes her female employer's lust. How profound the misogyny of a society must have been for it to have raised its young sons on material of this sort! And yet initially these Latin comedies were texts for cathedral schools. Their Latin was simpler than Ovid's, and students probably studied them right before they studied Ovid.[74] Gender yields texts, but texts also yield gender. What "man" or "woman" is comes into being in part from a society's texts. These Latin comedies are the product of a deeply misogynous culture, but they also increase that misogyny. Surely choosing these texts for young boys is cultural indoctrination in woman-loathing and violence against women. As Marjorie Woods writes, commenting on *Pamphilus* as a school text, "The continuity of this tradition of using rape for pedagogical purposes is disturbingly powerful—and disturbingly overlooked."[75]

These Latin comedies, written over the course of nearly a century, did not remain simply school texts. Some of them were studied, translated, and read for centuries after they were written, and one, *Pamphilus*, became immensely popular. The Old Woman who goes between, first developed at length in these comedies, grew to be a formidable intertext for Western medieval literature. These are seminal texts in the long history of medieval misogyny, important expressions of patriarchy's enjoyment of and anxiety concerning its power over women.

Fabliaux

The fabliau has more in common with the Latin comedies than with any other medieval genre. Fabliaux are brief rhymed comic tales in the vernacular, typically written in French between the early thirteenth and the mid-fourteenth centuries.[76] Of the five fabliaux that include go-betweens, four are in French and one is in English. The social class of the fabliau audience has been debated since the late nineteenth century when Joseph Bédier maintained that they were written for the bourgeoisie. By mid-twentieth century, Per Nykrog insisted that, on the contrary, the fabliau is a courtly

genre. Charles Muscatine, in *The Old French Fabliaux*, disagrees with both
Bédier and Nykrog. The fabliau, he writes, is not "somehow more natural
and congenial to one social group than to another." Fabliaux had a
"socially heterogeneous and mobile audience,"[77] they were "shared by and
within all classes,"[78] and their attitudes reflect town and commercial life as
well as life in small rural communities. As for their authors, Muscatine proposes that while jongleurs would have recited them, many were probably
written by clerks, the only social group positively presented in the fabliaux
on a regular basis.[79]

R. Howard Bloch, who argues that the fabliaux are about writing
poetry, attacks sardonically the "virtual academic cottage industry" of
dissertation writers who imagined that the fabliaux mirrored the daily life
of the Middle Ages. "The assumed transparency of the fabliaux has been
summoned to prove just about anything and everything concerning the
social reality of the High Middle Ages,"[80] Bloch points out. Although
Muscatine never assumes transparency, unlike Bloch he hears "a colloquial,
everyday voice" in these poems and believes they see the world realistically.
"Fabliau imagery overwhelmingly records ordinary experience," he writes.
"Its circumstantial realism is far from incidental: it is central to its style and
to its ethos."[81]

If the details of *Le Prestre teint*[82] [The Dyed Priest], an anonymous, early
thirteenth-century fabliau, indeed record attitudes from daily experience, it
offers a glimpse of a community's ambivalent feelings about an Old
Woman who goes between. Dame Hersent, the Old Woman, is a former
prostitute, "la pautonniere" (121) [the whore], and the other characters all
recognize her as a professional go-between. The narrator stresses her expertise and experience. She knows so much about going between that

> Il n'a el mont prestre ne moigne,
> Ne bon reclus ne bon chanoine,
> Se tant feïst qu'a li parlast,
> Que de s'angoise nel getast. (90–93)

> [there is no priest or monk or good hermit or good canon in the whole
> world whom she could not rescue from his anguish if he would only
> consult with her.]

And yet, despite being a recognized go-between, Dame Hersent is an
accepted neighbor and the church sacristan. When she arrives at the home
of the beautiful wife a priest wants to seduce, the wife receives her very
kindly. So long as the wife does not realize why Dame Hersent is paying
this visit, she welcomes her like any other respected fellow villager and
honors her by inviting her to sit on the bed rather than on the floor.

The priest's initial response to Dame Hersent exposes the other side of her community's attitude toward her. When he first sees her, he is sitting on his doorsill beside himself with lust. The beautiful wife has driven him out of her house and beaten him with a stick for propositioning her, and he is furious because he cannot think of any way, "Ou par avoir ou par proiere" (59) [either by money or by pleading], to seduce the wife. At this moment his solution walks down the road in the form of Dame Hersent. Nevertheless, despite the great self-control it costs him, the priest does not call out to her. When she is close enough to see him, he motions discreetly to her to come to him and explains that he would like a few words with her. "Lors si la prist a acoler, / Mes il garde aval la voie: / Grant paour a que l'en nel voie" (105–07). [Then he embraces her, but he keeps one eye on the road: he is very much afraid that someone will see them.]

Thinking about Dame Hersent as a go-between rather than a parishioner, the priest is ashamed to be seen greeting her familiarly. And when Dame Hersent proposes the priest to the wife as a lover, the wife slaps her in the face, curses her, and drives her away from her house with " 'Dame Hersent, de vostre escole / Ne veu ge mie encore estre!' " (153–54) ["Dame Hersent, I never want to be at your school again!"] Dame Hersent's disreputableness is specifically the product of her going between. When she is not thought of as a go-between, she is a person of some stature in her town. Going between, however, is shameful and reprehensible, and as a go-between, she is dismissed with contempt.

Although Muscatine acknowledges that the same cast of characters appears in the Latin comedies as in the fabliaux, he describes the comedies as "purely clerical" and points out that the "fabliau authors do not refer to them, and fail to imitate them in fundamental traits."[83] The clerks who wrote most of the fabliaux, however, were church-educated,[84] and since the comedies were taught in cathedral schools, some of those clerks probably studied the comedies. Moreover, by the late twelfth or early thirteenth century, Pamphilus was in the jongleur repertoire in southern France,[85] and one of the fabliaux, the English Dame Sirith,[86] echoes the Latin comedies in form. So much of it is long speeches that a current commentator argues it was actually a play,[87] the same argument that is often made about the Latin comedies. At issue here is the Old Woman who goes between. Dame Hersent is an unelaborated instance of the Old Woman, but the fabliaux also embed this figure in much richer contexts, and when they do, she is remarkably like the parasitic, manipulative, sinister character who controls the action in Pamphilus. It is of course possible that her fabliau characterization did not derive directly from Pamphilus itself. The powerful support that preachers, medical ideas, and legal attitudes would have lent to the idea of the Old Woman portrayed in Pamphilus may have made this characterization an intertext as early as the late twelfth century.

However the Old Woman who goes between finds her way from the Latin comedies to the fabliaux, she is strikingly developed in two of them, playing similar roles and generating similar issues and a similar ethos. One of these fabliaux is in French and the other is in English. *Auberee*, in French, dates from the late twelfth or early thirteenth century.[88] It appears eight times in manuscript collections, which makes it one of the most often copied of any of the fabliaux.[89]

Auberee is named for the Old Woman who goes between in the poem. It is her fabliau, and none of the rest of the characters have names. She is a poor old beggar, the poisonous Old Woman of the preachers and medical writers, and she is dangerous: shrewd, sly, subtle, and cleverer and far more devious than any of the men in the poem. At the bottom of the social scale herself, she reaps profits from attacks on the bourgeois marriage contract. Auberee alone generates every aspect of the unraveling of the story's tricky plot, calculating each action and response and leaving nothing to chance. Everything remains entirely in her power. She directs the action so secretly that not even the young man who hires her knows what is going on at any point.

The young man lusts after a proper young woman from a poor family. When he courts her, she tells him flatly that unless he wants to marry her, he is wasting his time, but that she would be happy to be his wife. His rich father, however, threatens his son with death if he ever speaks of such a low match again, and the young woman becomes the bride of a rich man who marries her one month after the death of his first wife.

The young man hires Dame Auberee, but unlike most of these Old Women, she does not piece together her price from assorted cloaks, dresses, and shoes. She will not even begin working on his behalf until he steals forty pounds from his father to pay her, a sign of the new money economy of the late twelfth century. In addition to going between when the occasion offers itself, Auberee has an ordinary public occupation. She is a seamstress, which accounts for an important prop for her machinations. The wealthy young man wears an elaborate, very fashionable surcoat trimmed with squirrel skins. Auberee attaches her needle and thimble to this surcoat, rolls it up very tightly, and hides it under her cloak.

Every aspect of Dame Auberee's going between displays her experience and cunning. She is introduced as one "Qui de meint barat mout savoit" (108) [who knew a great deal about all sorts of trickery], and the most extravagant claim made for her going between rates her as invincible: "Ja si ne fust fame enserree / Qu'a sa corde ne la treïst!" (113–14) [Never was a wife kept so tightly under lock and key that she [Auberee] could not reel her in on her line!] She arrives at the new bride's doorsill as a beggar, grieving over the death of the first wife and stressing her special status as a regular recipient of charity from this household. The first wife never refused her

anything, she laments, and then begs just a small loaf of bread and a little of
the wife's white wine for the pain in her daughter's side. Auberee's strategic
begging wins her admission into the young bride's house on a special footing.
She is not a threatening figure; she is simply an old woman in need. And
when she leaves, she carries off gifts of wine, peas, bacon, and bread.

Auberee's tricks depend on her sexual professionalism and able reading
of character. She maneuvers herself into the wife's bedroom by playing on
the insecurities of the very young bride of a previously married man:

> "Ha! Com il avoit l'autre chiere!
> El avoit mout de son delit!
> Bien vodroie voer ton lit:
> Lors savroie certainement
> Se tu gis ausi richement
> Com fesoit la premiere fame." (187–92)

> ["Ah, how dearly he loved the other one!
> She had a great deal of pleasure with him! I would
> like to see your bed: then I would know indeed
> whether you lie as richly as the first wife did."]

The sexual issues exert their special pressure—the cherished first wife, the
richness of the marriage bed—and the young bride trustingly ushers the old
woman into her bedroom. Dame Auberee is very reassuring:

> "Puis la Pentecouste
> Ne vi ge mes si riche lit!
> Plus as asez de ton delit
> C'onques n'ot l'autre, ce me semble!" (215–18)

> ["I haven't seen such a rich bed since
> Pentecost. It seems to me that you must have much more
> pleasure with him than the other ever had!"]

While the wife is busy exhibiting her furs and dresses, Auberee slips the
tightly rolled surcoat with her needle and thimble in it under the quilt that
covers the white straw of the bed.

The hidden surcoat drives the new bride straight into Dame Auberee's
power. When the husband returns tired from market and lies down for a
nap, he discovers a man's coat in his bed and is so mad with jealousy that
he stands speechless for hours. After nightfall, without a single word of
explanation, he throws his wife out of the house. She has done nothing
wrong and has no idea what is happening to her, or why, and she begs
Dame Auberee to take her to her father. Instead, Auberee offers her comfort, shelter, and a more experienced woman's understanding of the men in

her life. She must not run to her father's house, Auberee warns. Her father will believe the worst of her, just like her husband, and her husband is probably drunk. Her best course of action will be to spend the night at Dame Auberee's and wait for her husband to sober up. Auberee then installs the wife between her white sheets and locks the bedroom door.

Auberee thinks of herself as a trapper of women, and she uses a hunting image when she reports her success to the young man: " 'je tieng t'amie en mes laz: / Avoir en puez touz tes solaz / Jusqu'a demein aprés ceste eure!' " (339–41) ["I have your love in my snares: you can have all your pleasure of her until at least this time tomorrow!"]. What should he do, he asks, if the wife turns away from him in shame and screams? With the imperturbable aplomb of the old professional who has been through scenes of this sort many times before, Auberee replies:

"Va, si te couche,
Et se point vers toi se corouche
Et ele crie, et tu deus tans!
Lieve la robe, si entre ens!
Si tost com el te sentira,
Autrement la besoigne ira:
Meintenant la verras tesir,
S'en porras fere ton plesir!" (355–62)

["Go and get into bed, and if she is at all angry with you and screams, you scream twice as loud! Lift up the gown and go right in! As soon as she feels you, things will take a different turn: then you'll see her quieter, and you will be able to do as you please with her."]

The situation Auberee has created virtually guarantees success for the rapist. By all appearances, this bride seems to be waiting for an assignation. She is in bed at the house of a known go-between, both the young man and the wife are undressed when he awakens her, and when she threatens to rouse the whole street with her screams, he tells her she will only shame herself if people of all ranks and importance see her completely naked beside him in the middle of the night. As he says: " 'N'i avra un seul qui ne cuit / Que j'aie fet a grant plenté / De vostre cors ma volenté' " (386–88) ["Not a single person will believe that I have not had my way with you over and over again"]. At first the young woman does not know what to do, but when she thinks about how publicly she will be shamed, she lets him quiet her and kiss her, and they have sex.

Each trick in *Auberee* outdoes the previous one. Auberee not only provides the wife as a sexual partner for the young man, she then reunites the wife successfully with her husband. Once again the participants have no understanding of their actions. In the middle of the night, Auberee takes the young woman to church and surrounds her with crosses and lighted candles as she lies in front of the statue of the Virgin Mary. Auberee then hits and kicks on the husband's door, denouncing his wicked treatment of his beautiful young wife. He is mad, she says, to send his wife to matins in the middle of the night when she should be at home behind the bed curtains. The husband cannot imagine what to think, but when he finds his wife praying in the church, just as Dame Auberee had described her, he takes her back home to bed and tells her he had been drunk the night before.

Dame Auberee's final trick knits up the last loose strand of the story to restore the husband's faith in his wife. The old go-between groans and shrieks in the village street that the provost is about to confiscate all her earthly possessions because she owes thirty sous for losing a surcoat a young man hired her to mend. When the husband finds Dame Auberee's needle and thimble in the surcoat, he is convinced his life is back in order again. At the close of the couple's day and two nights of sex, Auberee promises to reunite them, and so her tricks win an ongoing affair for the young man.

Fabliaux tend to value good sex over marital chastity, and the sexually successful conclusion of *Auberee* encourages the audience to enjoy it as a cheerful comic story about the beginning of a much desired affair for a rich, virile young man. Auberee herself contributes to this comic mood. Unlike the Old Woman in *Pamphilus*, Auberee has an engaging side. Fabliaux value cleverness and ingenuity, in particular trickery played out effectively against conventional power structures. As Muscatine writes, "The fabliaux do not honor vice for its own sake, but they do celebrate the getting of money, goods, or pleasure through wit—whether legally or illegally."[90] The Old Woman in *Pamphilus* traps Galatea, but there's nothing clever about her method of trapping her. Auberee's tricks, on the other hand, are exceedingly clever, and so are her techniques for getting into the bride's house and bedroom. Auberee, the poor old beggar, outwits the middle-class types in her story and undermines the village social structure that guarantees a rich burgher possession of his proper young wife. Moreover, Auberee undermines conventional morality in the service of lust, another fabliau value.

Rouhi, in *Mediation and Love*, contends that works like fabliaux show "the bawd's essential weakness and lack of impact, which stand in such strong contrast to the image of power and evil projected when she enters the scene."[91] Rouhi minimizes the importance of Auberee's going between with the argument that she only provides the trick, the "preamble" to the affair, and it is the young man who actually argues the young woman into accepting him. Auberee, Rouhi says, has "little or no interest in the intellectual dimension of seduction, that is, the power of speech and reasoning. She stands on the margins of the seductive space, showing once again that her reputation exceeds her ability."[92] Dame Auberee's work, however, is far more sinister than speech and reasoning. It is entrapment, and she is a master of it.

María del Pilar Mendoza Ramos, in "Auberée la alcahueta: Similitudes y diferencias con sus homólogas literarias hispanas," succumbs to the temptation of reading *Auberee* benignly, in the process revealing the elements that refuse to be integrated into such a reading. She characterizes Auberee as engaged in reuniting lovers separated by a money-driven marriage. The fabliau, however, neither states nor implies that the young woman loves the young man before her father arranges her marriage. She would be happy to marry him if he would marry her properly, but that is the extent of the description of her feelings. Similarly, Mendoza Ramos writes repeatedly about the young bride's old husband, "un viejo burgués" [an old burgher], but her husband is never said to be old, only rich and a widower.[93] Reading *Auberee* as a poem about reuniting lovers casts the Old Woman herself in a fairy godmother role, conniving on behalf of a wrongly separated couple, a far more admirable motive than her forty pounds.

Avoiding sexual violence in *Auberee* would have been a simple matter. A few lines about the young woman's initial love for the young man, her grief over her marriage, and her yearning for her lost lover would have changed the story at its core. *Auberee* would have been the poem Mendoza Ramos wanted to read. But instead of the young woman's love for the young man, we hear about her concern for making a proper marriage. No detail suggests that she married her wealthy husband unwillingly or is unhappy with him. Instead there is the rich marriage bed that Auberee is so enthusiastic about (217–18). And nothing indicates that the bride wants an affair with the young man. Quite the contrary, when he is kissing and caressing her in the bedroom at Dame Auberee's, she thinks only of her fear of shame, not of her love for him. *Auberee* is not a story about lovers; it is a story about rape. And vicarious participation in male violence against a woman is one of its sources of satisfaction. Dame Auberee delivers the bride to the young man as a passive, powerless victim, taken by surprise and trapped for violation. Once the young wife's point of view is acknowledged, *Auberee*'s cheerful comic surface cracks. Another layer operates beneath it to satisfy less conventional interests.

Nevertheless, comedy prevails in *Auberee*. The fact that twenty-four hours of pleasurable sex follow the rape moderates its impact, and, as in *Pamphilus*, the fabliau protects its taboo pleasures of sexual violence by displacing the violence onto the Old Woman rather than the young man. Although Auberee is the source of every comic moment, she remains a sinister character who knows too much, manages too well, and holds her cards too close to her chest to be part of the comedy herself. As an Old Woman, she is by nature dangerous and frightening. It is women who corrupt women, the fabliau contends, and the ending of one version of *Auberee* makes this contention the poem's moral:

> Par cest fabliel vous wel prouer
> Comme puet en feme trouer
> Qui de son cors fache meffait
> Se par autre feme nel fait
> Tele va hors de droite voie
> Se feme n'iert ki le desuoie
> Qui seroit bone *et* pure *et* fine. (530–36 Text J)

[Through this fabliau I want to prove to you that rarely can one find a woman who misbehaves sexually unless she does so because of another woman. A woman may leave the straight and narrow path, a woman who would be virtuous and chaste and pure were it not for another woman who leads her astray.]

The thirteenth-century English fabliau *Dame Sirith*[94] features the Old Woman figure in a role quite similar to Auberee's. The story of the trick she plays circulated in the very popular early twelfth-century Latin *Disciplina Clericalis* as well as in the *Exempla* of Jacques de Vitry, but neither is the direct source of the English poem.[95] Dame Sirith herself is a typical Old-Woman go-between. Ancient and frail, she bemoans her aching body, and like Auberee, she uses her status as a beggar to gain access to the home of the chaste wife she has been hired to trap. She arrives groaning over her aches and pains and hunger, and Margery greets her generously with bread, meat, something to drink, and pity.

In *Dame Sirith*, far more than in *Auberee*, the Old Woman's trick is stressed as an act of violence against the young woman. Margery, the wife, innocent, appealing, generous, and charitable, is outspoken about her love for her husband. When Wilekin, a clerk, learns that her husband is out of town and declares his love for her, she refuses him angrily. Her husband has gone to the fair, she says, but even if he were a hundred miles beyond Rome, she would never love another man. "My husband, my spouse, brought me with great honor to his house as a maiden," she protests. "He loves me and I love him; our love is as true as steel" (91–95). And when the clerk continues his pleas for love, she scoffs at him: " 'We, we! oldest þou me a fol? /. . .Ich am wif boþe god and trewe. / Trewer womon ne mai no mon cnowe / Þen Ich am.' " (115, 121–23). ["Good heavens! What do you take me for, a fool?. . .I am a true, good wife. No man can find a truer woman than I am"].[96] Dame Sirith's going between, however, is so effective that by the close of a brief visit, Margery is begging her to bring Wilekin to her to become her lover.

Going between is illegal and disreputable, and when Wilekin first tries to hire Dame Sirith, she maintains she is no go-between; she is an old, sick, lame " 'holi wimon' " ["holy woman"] who lives on charity and spends her days praying for the souls of the people who give her alms. Wilekin has to give her twenty shillings to buy sheep and pigs and promise her " 'Moni a pound and moni a mark, / Warme pilche and warme shon' " (224–25) ["many a pound and many a mark, a warm fur coat and warm shoes"] before she will agree to help him. Even then she is worried about being taken to ecclesiastical court and publicly shamed. Like Auberee, Dame Sirith works all alone and keeps her plot entirely to herself. Wilekin decides she has gone mad when he sees her feeding pepper and mustard to her dog, but she dismisses him out of hand as a " 'boinard' " [buzzard, lazy fellow] and tells him to keep quiet. " 'I shal mit þis ilke gin / Gar hire loue to ben al þin' " (289–90) ["By this trick I will win all her love for you,"] she gloats. Going between is her business, not his.

As Dame Sirith eats at Margery's house, she weeps and wails over her tragic loss of her beautiful blond daughter, " 'Feiror ne miȝtte no mon se' " (340), ["No one could ever see a fairer woman"], who was happily married to a very generous husband whom she loved all too well. One day when her daughter's husband was out of town on an errand, Dame Sirith explains, a clerk declared his love for her, and when her daughter persisted in refusing him, by witchcraft, the clerk turned her into a dog. At this point Dame Sirith exhibits her weeping dog:

> "Þis is mi douter þat Ich of speke:
> For del of hire min herte brekeþ.
> Loke hou hire heien greten;
> On hire cheken þe teres meten." (355–58)
>
> ["This is my daughter that I have been telling you about; my heart breaks with sorrow for her. Look how she weeps; the tears meet on her cheeks."]

It is no wonder her own heart is bursting, Dame Sirith grieves, and she offers advice to anyone involved in a similar situation:

> "A, wose euer is ȝong houssewif,
> Ha loueþ ful luitel hire lif,
> And eni clerc of loue hire bede,
> Bote hoe grante and lete him spede!" (361–64)
>
> ["Ah, whoever is a young housewife, if any clerk asks her for love, she loves her life very little unless she grants him love and lets him succeed with her!"]

Innocent, naive, credulous Margery is terror-stricken. She blurts out at once the story of Wilekin's proposals and wishes repeatedly that she had had sex with him. Dame Sirith never mentions Wilekin to Margery, and

Margery never shows any sign of suspecting that Dame Sirith is going between for Wilekin. The weeping dog trick works so neatly that it is Margery herself who pleads with Dame Sirith to bring Wilekin to her, and she is just as earnest and eager as Wilekin was when he begged the old woman to go between for him: " 'Euermore, nelde, Ich wille be þin, / Wiþ þat þou feche me Willekin, / Þe clarc of wam I telle' " (385–87) ["I will be yours forever, old woman, if you will bring Wilekin to me, the clerk I'm telling you about"]. And she promises her gifts. Dame Sirith agrees, so long as she will be " 'wiþhoute blame,' " and the young wife's anxiety reaches a new pitch: " 'Bote þat þou me Wilekin bringe, / Ne mai I neuer lawe ne singe / Ne be glad.' " (400–02) ["Unless you bring Wilekin to me, I'll never laugh or sing or be glad again."] Not only has Dame Sirith won the woman's consent for the man, she has tricked the woman into hiring her to bring the man to her, and the couple has sex.

Class and competition between men are issues in *Dame Sirith*, unlike *Auberee*. Margery lives in a beautiful house and has lovely clothes, which suggests that her husband is richer and more powerful than a clerk like Wilekin. Wilekin complains that no man can have a private conversation with Margery while her husband is in town (70–72), which suggests that the husband is jealous and possessive, a suitable sexual adversary. When Wilekin has sex with Margery, then, he triumphs over his social superior who guards his wife against other men. The more general issue of woman as man's possession, however, applies to both *Dame Sirith* and *Auberee*. Here, as in *Auberee*, unauthorized sexual access to a woman's body threatens the social order. But surely the amount of comedy and interest generated by these matters does not account for much of the pleasure of *Dame Sirith*. If these were crucial elements, more would have been made of them. As in *Auberee*, there is some erotic pleasure to be had from seeing a woman made available to a man who lusts after her, and Dame Margery is surely an objectified erotic body by the end of this poem. But again, these interests are not elaborated.

More important than either of these sources of pleasure is the sexual violence exercised against Margery. This is not literal violence; once Dame Sirith has played her trick, Margery is desperate to have sex with Wilekin. Nevertheless, Margery's chastity, her sense of herself as an honorable, loving woman, and her self-definition are all violated. Moreover, Margery, reduced from a chaste wife to an unchaste wife, is radically devalued from the point of view of her society. As E. Jane Burns writes, "Sexual violation symbolizes and actualizes women's subordinate social status to men."[97] Part of the patriarchal pleasure of this story, then, is to watch male power enacted and appreciate woman's subduing. The Margery we hear in her first conversation with Wilekin is a proud, self-confident young person, secure in her valuing of herself: "I am a true, good wife. No man can find a truer woman than I am" (121–23). By the end of the story, this voice has been silenced.

Margery is the victim of a cruel trick. If she were actually willing to have sex with Wilekin, the story would lose all interest. Her unwillingness creates its conflict, but the more unwilling she is, the more nearly the story ends in rape. Whatever pleasure listeners derive from the trick played on Margery arises from the listener's misogyny, but even in the thirteenth century, blatantly misogynistic pleasures are half-guilty pleasures. To preserve the sex act ending as comic, the listener's attention must be diverted from the cruelty of the trick. Like Dame Auberee's, this is the role Dame Sirith plays: she diverts the listener's attention from the serious human costs of the trick and redirects it to herself. Like Auberee, Dame Sirith is a frightening and hateful figure, frightening because she is so cunning and hateful because she takes vicious advantage of Margery's generosity, charity, and naiveté. A beggar in a story about prosperous villagers, Dame Sirith is at once the least powerful figure in the story and the most powerful because her deviousness corrupts the story's prize. She is easy to hate, a satisfying target for free-floating misogyny, and instead of concentrating the listener's attention on the sexual violation of Margery, the story trains it on the Old Woman and her weeping dog. Finally, just as in *Auberee*, Dame Sirith diverts attention from the actual violator, the man. It is as if the Old Woman were violating the young woman.

At the poem's close, the Old Woman drops her role as a diversionary tactic and laughs outright at the violation. Once Margery welcomes Wilekin to her home, the clerk sends Dame Sirith away, " 'Wile Ich and hoe shulen plaie' " (438) ["While she and I play"], and Dame Sirith indulges in sexually explicit parting advice. Gloating, she anticipates with relish the sex act her client is about to perform:

> "And loke þat þou hire tille
> And strek out hire þes.
> God ȝeue þe muchel kare
> ȝeif þat þou hire spare,
> Þe wile þou mid hire bes." (440–44)

["And see to it that you plow her and stretch out her thighs. If you spare her while you're with her, may God curse you with suffering!"]

Perhaps there is some voyeuristic erotic pleasure in this moment, but for the most part it focuses on the female body used for sex. Dame Sirith's final stanza follows these lines, but it is not addressed to either Wilekin or Margery, and it suggests that this piece is either a minstrel's poem or a play.[98] Dame Sirith turns to an audience of listeners, assures them of her excellence at her work, and offers to sell them her services (445–50).

With the sinister Old-Woman figure orchestrating the violation of young wives, the misogyny of *Auberee* and *Dame Sirith* is unmistakable and emerges as their controlling point of view. The amount and significance of misogyny in fabliaux, however, is a matter of some debate. Philippe Ménard, for instance, dismisses it as "un motif mineur" [a minor motif] and offers as counterevidence five fabliaux about faithful wives who resist the advances of priests.[99] Lesley Johnson similarly contends that the usual argument that fabliaux are antifeminist grows out of a "generic portrait of Woman through enumerating her so-called vices," and that when women play large parts in these poems, they are rarely condemned.[100] Charles Muscatine says the "so-called 'antifeminism' in the fabliaux is so various in its quality and tone as more often to support the claim of admiration for women than fear and hatred."[101] Two final fabliaux that use go-betweens are involved in this debate.

Both Ménard and Johnson include *Constant du Hamel*[102] [*Constant of Hamel*], from the early thirteenth century, among their fabliaux that portray women positively. Johnson admires in particular Isabel, the beautiful wife in this story, who rescues herself and her plowman husband from the power of a priest, a provost, and a forester who all want to have sex with her. When she refuses them, they gang up on the couple with the idea of forcing her to yield by ruining them financially. Unless the plowman pays enormous bribes, the priest will drive him out of the church, the forester will have him beaten for poaching, and the provost will have him hanged for theft. Isabel's solution is to make each man believe she has agreed to have sex with him. Galestrot, her maid, then goes between with them for her.

Galestrot, like Isabel, is clever and conniving, and Isabel works through her. As Galestrot goes between, she sees to it that she is doubly hired. Isabel promises her a fur-lined cloak for luring the men into her trap, but when Galestrot arrives at each house, she presents herself as working for the man. With the priest she claims to have fought so hard she convinced her lady to reverse herself: " 'Vos n'i avenissiez des mois / Se ge ne m'en fusse entremise.' " (439–42) ["You would not have gotten so far in months if I had not gone between for you."] The priest must bring Isabel everything he originally promised to bring to her, Galestrot warns. As for herself, she is only asking for a thick wimple, despite all her work. The priest fills up a fat purse with money for Isabel, collects the jewels he had promised, and then adds an extra present of twenty sous for a fur-lined cloak for Galestrot. Before Galestrot and the priest leave his house, the poet describes the beautiful cloak of richly dyed fine fabric that the priest puts on, and this too will be part of the two women's spoils. At the provost's, Galestrot raises her price to one hundred sous. Night and day she has been laboring in his service, she complains, and then asks for a large loan for the plowman's wife, which she assures him the wife will repay. Twenty sous seems to be the going wage for Galestrot, however. Despite her new tactics, the provost responds with twenty sous for a new coat for her and a well-stuffed money bag for Isabel.

At the forester's, Galestrot modifies her approach somewhat. At first she sounds as if she is about to try to interest him in herself:

> "Ge sui, dit el, musarde et fole!
> Qu'ai ge de ce vassal afaire?
> Se il ne fust si debonnaire,
> Ge n'alasse por lui plain pas." (587–90)
>
> [She says, "I am a silly fool; what does this man have to do with me? If he were not so agreeable, I wouldn't stir an inch for him."]

Then she whispers to him to come to her lady, describes how hard she has worked for him, and even seems to be claiming to have aroused Isabel sexually on his account: " 'Mais ge l'ai pointe jusqu'au cuer / Sovent, et tenue et tastee, / Tant qu'el est por vos eschaufee.' " (595–97) ["But I have often stung her to the heart, and held and touched her until she is on fire for you."] The forester is poorer than the priest and provost, and, despite Galestrot's come-on, he only adds ten sous for her to the gold ring he promised Isabel. Galestrot's going between, however, is considerably more lucrative than her individual payments from the priest, the provost, and the forester suggest. She and Isabel together persuade each of the three men in turn to strip for a bath to prepare for sex, and the women then hide away the men's money, clothing, and even shoes, as well as the gifts they have brought.

Norris J. Lacy asks in "Fabliau Women," "If a woman is praised for her scheming and craft, is it legitimate to conclude *ipso facto* either that we are witnessing an approbative view of woman (since she *is* praised) or that the text is antifeminist (because it praises her for less than admirable qualities)?"[103] Galestrot is certainly a smart, strong, effective woman. She is not, however, portrayed as admirable. She is more nearly a type figure than a character; her name means "trotter for joy," "go-between." She goes between six times in this story, and the language of the poem stresses her going between. Each time she is sent to get a man for the plowman's wife, the poet emphasizes through metaphor and exclamation how fast Galestrot "trots." Here, for instance, she hurries to the priest's:

> Et cele escorce ses trumeaus,
> Qui gros furent par les talons:
> Une vasche qui sent tahons
> Ne vi plus galoper par chaut

Que Galestrot s'en vait le saut!
Mout se pena de tost aler. (429–34)

[And she runs her legs off, even though they were fat around the ankles: I never saw a cow, bitten by a horsefly, gallop faster in the heat than Galestrot shoots off! She strove to go as fast as she could.]

The copyists of the manuscripts of this fabliau pick up on Galestrot's special name. Four times they use the verb "troter" to describe her as she hurries to go between.[104] Going between is disreputable even when the go-between is not a semiprofessional like the Old Woman figure. Furthermore, although nothing in the plot indicates that Galestrot is a prostitute, she is introduced as "une goulue pautoniere" (405) [a greedy whore], and the plowman's wife calls her "pute asnesse" (662) [stupid slut] in the midst of a conversation, with no motive for deliberately insulting her since the two of them are very successfully gulling six people. Is going between such a low trick that a "trotter for joy" is automatically a "pute asnesse"?

Once Galestrot arranges with the three would-be seducers to come to the plowman's house, the women's timing and setup operate with fabliau neatness. As they usher the first prospective lover into a tub of hot water to wash himself in preparation for sex with Isabel, the next one knocks on the door, and Isabel convinces the bather to hide in a barrel of feathers by assuring him that the person knocking must be Constant, her husband. When the third would-be lover is bathing, the knocker is indeed Constant, and once the priest, provost, and forester find themselves naked in the same barrel of feathers and see Constant storming around the room brandishing an enormous axe, they realize they have been hoodwinked and trapped.

The story devolves into brutal revenge. Isabel, who planned the trapping of the three men, proposes the next counterblow as well. Since the three tried to have intercourse with her, she argues, Constant should rape their wives while the husbands watch from the barrel. This fabliau is approximately 950 verses long. One hundred twenty-seven of them are used to describe these rapes. Galestrot goes between three more times, this time inviting each of the three wives to share a bath with Isabel. These are Isabel's women friends of long standing. When the provost's wife is undressed and about to get into the bath and Constant challenges her angrily, she protests that she has been there many times before, and when Constant tells the forester's wife that he is going to rape her, she says he must be joking. The rapes are brutal and described with attention to position, the women's attempts at self-defense, what the action looked like from the hole in the barrel as the three men peeped out, and how each husband reacted. For instance, the priest's wife is first, and as Constant is raping her, the provost asks the priest whether he can recognize her from the buttocks and surrounding regions visible through the barrel hole. As Constant completes each rape, the wife is pushed out the door leaving behind most of her clothes. After raping the three wives, Constant sets fire to the barrel of feathers and the three men run naked through the village trailing smoldering feathers while their own dogs hunt them down.

These vengeance rapes are a homosocial exchange; Constant rapes the wives in repayment for their husbands' attempts to have sex with his wife. But considered from the point of view of the three wives, their cheating husbands were violating their marriages as well as the plowman's marriage, and the wealth offered to Isabel in exchange for sex was their wealth as well as their husbands' wealth. Instead, the wives are viewed entirely as the men's property to be abused in satisfaction for the men's wrongdoing.

As a chaste wife who defends her beleaguered husband, Isabel is one of the positively portrayed characters Ménard and Johnson point to in defense of fabliau women. However, as attractively as Isabel is characterized—beautiful, chaste, and cunning—her positive portrayal is overwhelmed by the general misogyny of this story. Galestrot's subtlety is undercut by her low role of go-between, and she supplies most of the women's action in this poem. But far more important are these vengeance rapes that operate altogether from the assumption that a wife is exclusively her husband's property, not a suffering person in her own right.

Of the five fabliaux featuring go-betweens, only one is not misogynistic, *Le Prestre et Alison*[105] [The Priest and Alison], from the early thirteenth-century, and there anticlericalism takes the place of misogyny. The go-between helps defeat a lustful priest and expose his hypocrisy. If he had carried out his plans, he would have taken the virginity of a twelve-year-old, but instead three women—Dame Mahaut, the girl's mother; Hercelot, the go-between; and Alison, the village prostitute—trick and publicly shame the priest. The priest wants to buy Dame Mahaut's daughter, Marion, and at every opportunity, Hercelot plays cunningly on his vanity and lasciviousness to increase her profits. When she goes to his house to invite him to dinner at Dame Mahaut's, Hercelot greets the priest with love language, wishing him good day on behalf of " 'vostre amie et vo drue: /. . .Marion au cors gent' " (218–19) ["your love and your darling,. . .Marion, with the lovely body"]. This is just what the priest wants to hear, and he rewards Hercelot with a leather belt-purse full of silver and promises of more if she keeps his secret. Hercelot then claims to be responsible for the success of the whole plan for his night with Marion: " 'Par moi est toz li plaiz bastiz!' " (227) ["The whole plan has been devised by me!"] This time the priest calls to his clerk to give Hercelot two pieces of new, fresh linen.

Hercelot brings about the intricate maneuvers that protect Marion at the same time that they fleece and publicly humiliate the priest. At dinner, in the priest's hearing, Dame Mahaut instructs Hercelot to prepare a bed rich enough for a king. As the price of pretending to be virgin, Alison has been promised the coat and skirt the priest is paying for Marion's virginity, and Hercelot smuggles Alison, bathed, through a secret door into the bedroom. Next, with the priest watching, Hercelot leads Marion into the bedroom and conceals her in an attic. As Hercelot finally conducts the priest to the bedroom in which she claims to have just put Marion to bed, Hercelot appeals to his sadism. The girl is " 'Molt dolente et molt esploree' " (325) ["full of grief and very tearful"], she warns him. It was very hard for her to comfort her, and she convinced her to go through with the bargain only by reminding her about the dresses and jewels the priest had promised her. Although he has paid fifteen pounds of sterling silver for this twelve-year-old and never courted her in any way, he enjoys imagining himself as an elegant, successful lover wooing a lady. Hercelot sustains his illusion by decorating her advice about proper behavior with expressions from romantic stories where the lover is " 'saiges et cortois' " ["wise and courteous"], the lady " 'plus blanche que flor d'espine' " ["whiter than the hawthorn flower"], and lying together " 'desoz la cortine' " ["beneath the bed-hangings"] is a euphemism for intercourse (338–43). The priest gives Hercelot another purse of twenty silver pieces, underscoring the success of her techniques.

Alison, the prostitute, "Qui bien en sot le maiestire" (364) [who was a past mistress of the art], pretends to suffer martyrdom while the priest joyfully possesses her, hour after hour, for a total of nine times. Finally Hercelot, who is spending the night in that same bedroom, sets fire to a mattress and yells "Help! Fire!" until the whole village comes running. The villagers knock a hole in the wall, break down the door, and reveal the priest, naked, holding Alison, the town prostitute, by the hand. The villagers beat the priest, and the poet reminds the reader once more that the priest could have hired Alison for a penny at her brothel any day.

The discrepancy between what the priest actually does, what he intends to do, and what he enjoys imagining himself doing produces the comedy of *Le Prestre et Alison*. The priest is actually having sex with the town prostitute; he intends to be taking the virginity of a bought twelve-year-old; and he enjoys imagining himself consummating a refined relationship with a young lady whom he has been courting. Hercelot unmasks all these dimensions of the priest's hypocrisy, pretentiousness, and lust, and her mattress fire quite literally exposes the duped priest to the whole village. Hercelot, Dame Mahaut, and even Alison play easily admired roles in this fabliau, rescuing a young virgin from a sexual predator and fleecing him in the bargain.

Lacy, in "Fabliau Women," weighing in on the debate about the degree of misogyny in the fabliaux, offers an overview of them based on their explicit commentary and morals. In the fabliaux, he writes, "when men are criticized, it is because they are less than admirable individuals; when women are criticized for the same failings, they are most often presented as representatives of their sex." Apropos of the poets' attitudes toward women, he notes the "nearly invariable axiom" that when a writer has a choice between two morals, he'll choose "the one most critical of women."[106] The attitudes toward women found in the fabliaux that include go-betweens support Lacy's conclusions. Predominantly, these are tricky stories about convincing chaste wives to have sex with seducers or about punishing men for their lusts. The tricks typically produce the comedy of the stories and provide their central interest. Misogyny animates most of these works and is expressed through disagreeable or sinister portraits of the go-betweens and through pleasure in the raping of chaste women.

The Birth of Heroes

A third small group of stories, told and retold between the twelfth and the fifteenth centuries, breaks with the traditions of both the Latin comic tales and the fabliaux. Magic takes the place of the go-between's usual intrigue and traps, and although these go-betweens are powerful and dangerous, and the central concern of each episode is their sexual victims, their texts never seem to be criticizing the go-betweens for what they do, either implicitly or explicitly. These stories are all Arthurian, and the sexual relations engineered by the go-betweens result in the conception of heroes: King Arthur, Galahad, and Helain le Blanc. As Otto Rank describes in *The Myth of the Birth of the Hero*, for thousands of years sexual transgressions of one sort or another have been motifs in heroes' birth stories.[107] Going between yields the sexually transgressive elements of these three Arthurian conceptions, and their mythic dimensions absolve the go-betweens from the very significant amount of blame that humanly should be theirs.

Unlike in the fabliaux and Latin comic tales, males as well as females are victims of this group of go-betweens. A virginal young woman is used as an instrument of destiny in one of these stories, the tale of Galahad's conception, and a chaste wife is raped in another, the story of King Arthur's conception; but males are also egregiously tricked into undesired sex: Lancelot and Bohort, another knight. All the go-betweens in these stories are mysterious figures: Merlin, the great Arthurian enchanter and adviser to kings, and two women from aristocratic or royal households whose going between is nearly as magical as Merlin's. In all three stories, operating by enchantment, the go-betweens ride roughshod over the desires and commitments of the tricked people, bewitching them into feelings they have never had before and will never have again or duping them by shape-changing and potions. Through the go-betweens' magic, the characters have intercourse when they do not intend to or with the wrong people. Once the charms pass, so does their attraction or mistaken perception, but some of the charmed people remain emotionally devastated by what they have done.

Igraine, King Arthur's future mother, is a chaste wife as meanly tricked into adultery as any fabliau victim. The go-between is Merlin, and her story was told from the twelfth through the sixteenth century, beginning with Geoffrey of Monmouth. In Thomas Malory's English version (1469), the text used here, when King Uther falls sick from desire for Igraine, the wife of one of his dukes, Merlin promises her to the king if he will give Merlin the child she conceives. Igraine's response when she first realizes King Uther desires her is to flee through the night to the protection of her husband's castle, so, to make Igraine willing, Merlin transforms Uther to look exactly like her husband. Igraine welcomes Uther to her bed in that guise and conceives the future King Arthur. A few hours before Uther has sex with Igraine, her husband is killed battling Uther's troops, and when Igraine learns the time of her husband's death, "she merveilled who that myghte be that laye with her in lykenes of her lord" [she marveled who that might be who lay with her and looked just like her lord], but she mourns secretly and says nothing.[108] Given the nature of the trick played on her, she has nowhere to turn and no one to object to about what has been done to her.[109]

Similarly, a young man is forced into an unwanted sexual relationship in the thirteenth-century Prose *Lancelot*. The go-between is a princess's nurse, an old woman who "savoit de charaies et d'enchantemens a grant plenté" (193)[110] [knew a great deal about charms and enchantments]. Helain le Blanc, future Emperor of Constantinople and Grail knight, is to be born of this union, but Bohort, the young destined father, is committed to virginity. Although he wins the princess as his wife in a tournament, and she desires him, he has no interest in her. The nurse gives Bohort a ring " 'qui a si grant force qu'il vos amera, vueille il ou non' " (195) ["which has such great power that he will love you whether he wants to or not"]. As soon as he puts it on, he desires the princess, and they spend the night together in her bedroom and have sex. When the nurse comes to lead Bohort back to his room, he is "molt joians" [very joyful], but once the ring falls off his finger, he realizes that he has been deceived "si fu molt dolens et soffri jusqu'al jor" (199) [and he was full of grief and suffered until dawn]. He then leaves the king's court, continuing his original quest, and the princess gives birth to Helain le Blanc. Bohort's response to the princess is entirely externally instigated. Without the magic ring, he feels nothing for her and regrets his lost virginity and broken vow.

The famous Lancelot story about Galahad's conception is also driven by destiny. Both the thirteenth-century Prose *Lancelot* and Malory (1469) tell this story,[111] and its go-between, Dame Brusen, is "one of the grettyst enchaunters that was that tyme in the worlde" (584) [at that time one of the world's greatest enchanters]. She tricks Lancelot with a less dramatic version of the trick that Merlin played on Igraine, and the story stresses the overwhelming cost to Lancelot of his infidelity to Guinevere. Dame Brusen's trick brings about the conception of Galahad, who is destined to see the Holy Grail, rescue the land of King Pelles from an ancient curse, and be the best knight in the world. Although Dame Brusen brings Lancelot to the bed of Elaine, daughter of King Pelles, she is not Elaine's go-between. Elaine neither desires Lancelot nor has any say in her role in the episode. She is a dutiful, passive daughter following her father's orders. Elaine is destined to conceive Galahad, and Dame Brusen is effectively King Pelles's go-between, tricking Lancelot into fathering Galahad at the request of Elaine's father.

Dame Brusen plays a bed trick. She knows by magic that Lancelot cannot love anyone except Guinevere, and she therefore deceives Lancelot into thinking Guinevere is expecting him to spend the night with her in a castle near King Pelles's castle. Servants transformed by enchantments to look like Guinevere's servants carry messages to Lancelot, and Elaine lies in the bed where Dame Brusen tells Lancelot he will find Guinevere. Dame Brusen ensures the results of their encounter by giving Lancelot a cup of enchanted wine to drink: "and anone as he had drunken that wyne he was so asoted and madde that he myght make no delay, but wythoute ony let he wente to bedde" (585) [and as soon as he had drunk that wine he was so madly infatuated and out of his mind that without the slightest delay, he went to bed immediately]. The next morning, when Lancelot opens a window and the enchantment breaks, he threatens to kill both Elaine and Dame Brusen, " 'for there was never knyght disceyved as I am this nyght' " (586) ["for no knight was ever as deceived as I am this night"]. Elaine makes her peace with him by telling him that she was obeying the prophecy her father commanded her to fulfill; that " 'I have in my wombe bygetyn of the that shall be the moste nobelyste knyght of the worlde' " ["I have in my womb, begotten by you, the noblest knight in the world"]; and finally, that she has given him her virginity, " 'the fayryst floure that ever I had' " ["the fairest flower that I ever had"] (586).

Elaine is a virgin sacrificed to destiny in this episode rather than a seducing woman. She does not desire Lancelot, and the only pleasure she is said to have in their night together is her satisfaction at conceiving Sir Galahad.

Once the child is born, knights have visions of the Holy Grail in his presence and hear prophecies that he will sit in the Siege Perilous and be a much better knight than his father.

All three of these episodes depict men and women tricked into and entrapped by relationships they do not want. The enchanted ring in Bohort's episode is a relatively tame trick but it produces the same effect as Dame Brusen's bed trick and Merlin's shape-changing. An external magical force alters Bohort's feelings and directs his actions so that he compromises his values and his concept of himself, committed to virginity. Similarly, Merlin's shape-changing robs Igraine of her chastity, and the bed trick Dame Brusen plays on Lancelot tricks him into violating his commitment to Guinevere, the bedrock of his existence. In Lancelot's case, the result is so crushing that it drives him mad for two years.

Despite their Arthurian trappings of enchanted rings, mysterious potions, and destined children, and their cast of famous characters from romance, these three episodes operate from the same assumptions about the meaning of sexual acts as the rest of these stories in which sex is not idealized. Prophecy and destiny make their atmosphere seem solemn, as if the importance of the outcome somehow justified the tricks, but sex is entirely a means to an end in them. Lancelot and Bohort are tricked into paternity and Igraine is tricked into maternity as thoroughly as fabliau characters are tricked into sex. Desire, here, is a falsely generated tool for conception.

Four Thirteenth-Century Go-Betweens

The stories of the conceptions of heroes are outliers from the main body of this branch of the go-between tradition. Although Dame Brusen and the princess's nurse are probably old, they are not type figures like the Old Women of the Latin comic tales and fabliaux. Four additional thirteenth-century stories return to the tradition's central issues, offering new twists on the Old Woman and her role. In one of these stories, *Le Roi Flore et la belle Jehanne*, she is barely characterized. In another, Jean de Meun's Myrrha story, she is reduced from a highly sympathetic classical prototype to an appalling instance of indefensible wickedness. The third story contains one of the best known of all the Old Women who go between, La Vieille from the *Roman de la rose*, and the fourth old woman, from *De Vetula*, translated in French as *La Vieille*, never actually goes between at all.

Dame Hiersent: Women as Property

Through their portraits of the Old Woman go-between and their accounts of her clever tricks, *Auberee* and *Dame Sirith* maintain the comedy of their stories by diverting attention discreetly away from the pleasures of vicariously enjoyed violence against women. *Le Roi Flore et la belle Jehanne*,[112] a thirteenth-century French prose narrative, operates in the opposite fashion. Dame Hiersent,[113] its go-between, is not substantially described or characterized and the trick she sets up is of no special complexity. Nothing about her distracts the audience's attention from the viciousness of the attempted rape she arranges. Instead, the rapist's violence is kept in full view. Moreover, lust, with its comic potentials, plays no part in this rape; sexual violence here is exclusively a homosocial matter. Unknown to the bride, of course, the rapist and the bride's husband, both knights, have bet 400 pounds of land on her chastity. The wager reifies the wife as property, leaving the rapist attacking the husband's property doubly: both the wife and through her the land.

Dame Hiersent is a familiar misogynistic figure of evil greed. Bought outright and easily, she first tries to interest Jehanne, the bride, in Raoul, the rapist, and then when tales of the pleasures of extramarital sex have no impact on Jehanne, and her husband is about to return home, the Old Woman offers to stage a rape. Her total price is sixty pounds of silver. With the castle empty of other servants, she promises to persuade Jehanne to bathe in her own room in preparation for her husband's arrival. With Jehanne in the bathtub, Dame Hiersent sends for Raoul. Raoul drags Jehanne out of the tub, and she is able to prevent her rape only because he catches his spur in her bedclothes and crashes to the floor with her naked in his arms. Although she strikes him in the face with a stick, he sees a wart and a black mark on her groin and convinces her husband that he has possessed her.

Jehanne triumphs over all aspects of her victimization. Once she is believed to be unchaste, she disguises herself as a male and ultimately makes her husband rich, defeating her double equation with property.[114] Since the point of her story is her eventual success, the attack on her is presented virtually realistically, and the easily bought Old Woman who betrays her is developed without flourishes.

Myrrha's Wicked Nurse

Most of the Latin comic tales and fabliaux that portrayed go-betweens were circulating in the twelfth and early thirteenth centuries. By the second half of the thirteenth century, probably from a combination of written texts, sermons, and oral storytelling, the Old Woman who goes between was well established as a type figure. One striking instance of the rewriting of a famous text attests to the virulence of the Old Woman's fame. The contrast between this writer's source and his portrayal of the go-between is so extreme that it amounts to clear-cut rejection of the meaning of the original, and the original is a far richer and more interesting account both of the episode the two poets are relating and of the Old Woman who goes between.

In approximately 1275, Jean de Meun retold the Greek myth of the act of incest by which Myrrha conceived Adonis.[115] An Old Woman maneuvers Myrrha, daughter of King Cinyras, into her father's bed where she has sex with him. She then turns into a myrrh tree as she gives birth to Adonis, their child. Jean does not suggest any motivation at all for the extraordinary trick ["trop estrange semille"] the Old Woman plays to get Myrrha into her father's bed. The situation does not offer any reason for her action, and even the narrator marvels at it. It is as if calling the go-between an Old Woman, "la vielle," were explanation enough for her wickedness. King Cinyras, Jean writes, was a good man until he was deceived by Myrrha, his blond daughter, "que la vielle, que Dex confonde, / qui de pechié doutance n'a, / par nuit en son lit li mena" [whom the old woman—may God confound her—who has no fear of sin, brought to his bed by night].[116] The king has sex with his daughter without realizing who she is.

Jean's source for this episode is Ovid's *Metamorphoses*, but when Ovid tells this story, the old woman is a richly intelligible character, and there is even an admirable dimension to her actions.[117] She has loved Myrrha since she was born, and now that Myrrha has grown into a self-destructive adolescent torn apart by desire and shame, the old woman tries to protect her against herself, literally snatching Myrrha back from death when she discovers her trying to commit suicide by hanging herself from a rafter. The old woman had been Myrrha's wet nurse when she was a baby, and she pleads by her shriveled breasts, gray hair, and years of cherishing that Myrrha must let her help her. Once Myrrha blurts out a half-veiled lament about envying her mother's marriage, however, the nurse recoils in horror. At no point does the nurse minimize the seriousness of incest. Incest is an affront to nature and the gods; suicide, however, is an even greater affront. The nurse's primary identification throughout Ovid's story is with birth, milk, and the sustaining of life. When the only possibilities for Myrrha are suicide or incest, it is quite in character for her old nurse to help her commit incest.

Jean de Meun's version of this story omits altogether the conflict Ovid developed so carefully between the old woman's horror at incest and her love for Myrrha, and Jean omits as well Ovid's persuasive depiction of Myrrha's deadly passion. All that remains is a grossly wicked old go-between who, quite unaccountably, positions a daughter in her father's bed. Myrrha's loving old nurse who stands gallantly between her and her death has turned into a sadly impoverished figure of inexplicable evil: the Old Woman who goes between.

La Vieille: Sex Commodified

Jean de Meun's version of the myth of the birth of Adonis is an episode in his portion of the *Roman de la rose*, his immense, encyclopedic allegorical poem that recounts a seduction or a rape, depending on how it is interpreted. The *Roman* was enormously popular and survives in approximately 300 manuscripts, more manuscripts than any other French vernacular text.[118] One of the most famous allegorical figures in the *Roman* is the most complexly developed and literarily influential of all the Old Women who go between, La Vieille.[119] Although Ovid's Dipsas from *Amores* 1.8 is one of the sources of the Old Woman in the *Roman*, the go-between tradition itself is her principal source. Details stress her great age: she hobbles about leaning on a stick or a crutch; when she tries to climb stairs quickly, her legs tremble; and one of her repeated laments is that her beauty and desirability have decayed into wrinkles and gray hair. Jean includes other traditional elements: she is connected with the church (12471–72); she was formerly a prostitute; and she refuses to go between before she is well paid. When the Old Woman completes her going between, Jean uses the go-betweens' verb for her, "troter" (14661), the same word that appears in Galestrot's name and will be used for Trotaconventos, the Spanish go-between in the *Libro de buen amor*.

La Vieille's going between is remarkably straightforward: no weeping dogs or men dressed up as their twin sisters, just a chaperon betraying her charge for a price. The Old Woman is supposed to be keeping under lock and key a character named Fair Welcoming, Bel Acueil, a personification of the young woman's capacity to respond to a lover. Instead, bribed by gifts and 100 marks, the Old Woman convinces Bel Acueil to meet with the Lover and leaves a secret backdoor unlocked to give the Lover access to him. That is all her going between amounts to. The Old Woman's fame derives from her account of her life and convictions.

Fair Welcoming, Bel Acueil, introduces repeated rich gender confusions into the narrative of the *Roman*. The personification of the desired young woman, the Rose, is feminine, but Bel Acueil, the Rose's capacity to respond, is a young man. When the Old Woman entices Fair Welcoming into meeting with the Lover, for instance, she is speaking to a male, and her entire lecture on fleecing rich lovers is also delivered to a male. Acueil is a masculine noun, which is the most obvious explanation for Fair Welcoming's gender, but the majority of recent commentators believe the text here exploits homoerotic meanings almost as much as heterosexual meanings. As Marta Powell Harley gently proposes, "To expect an audience to suppress a consciousness of the gender of a character (or *personi*fication) in an allegory of sexual seduction is perhaps to expect too much."[120] Karl D. Uitti describes the homoerotic imagery of the Lover's initial attraction to the rose: "One cannot conceive of a more phallic, masculine sort of rose, in my judgment, than the rose described here as it reposes, closed in its budlike shape, on its long and stiffly upright stem," and he stresses the protagonist's initial desire to hold this rose in his hand.[121] Simon Gaunt, who argues for a homoerotic reading of Bel Acueil and the *Roman* allegory as a whole, describes the plot as motivated "not by a man's attraction for a woman, but rather by the mutual attraction of two masculine figures." The *Roman*'s literal narrative, he writes, "inclines towards the homoerotic while the allegorical (or 'improper'?) narrative inclines towards the heterosexual."[122] Much of the Old Woman's lecture can apply to either a male or a female.

The Old Woman boasts and swaggers as she proclaims her mastery of sexual relations and their uses. A former prostitute, she preaches the commodification of sexual relationships: the business of arousing and gratifying lust. She is not talking about going between. She is describing prostituting herself. She is both the seller and the thing sold, the merchant and the merchant's wares, and the relationships she describes are altogether exploitative. The villain in her lecture is desire. So long as young women protect themselves against love, they can maintain their sexual power over men and live off them. Once they fall in love, however, they become victims instead of subjugators. Relationships are a seesaw of exploitation; the woman exploits the man's desire for her, but as soon as she starts to feel passion, the man exploits her desire for him. This is the game of love as the Old Woman describes it, and the formula for winning at it is never to love.

The Old Woman's going between is designed to satisfy the Lover in the short run and defeat him in the long run because she is using her lecture to try to convert Bel Acueil to her own way of life. Since Bel Acueil will be a smarter, abler, more sophisticated version of herself when she was young, she (or he) will be able to wreak vengeance on the men who now turn up their noses at the Old Woman. The Old Woman wants to arm Fair Welcoming's youth and beauty with her own hard-won understanding of the game of love. With the wisdom of age and the beauty of youth, together they will be able to take control of men and amass the fortune the Old Woman kept letting slip through her fingers until it was too late. Fair Welcoming will be her disciple.

This is the Seize-the-day! theme with a new twist. Where most of these go-betweens warn women not to miss out on the joys of sexuality, this Old Woman warns Fair Welcoming not to miss out on its power. She is teaching him to exploit sex; to use men and keep from being used by them; to make sex his life's work and means of support. The Old Woman, then, is attempting to corrupt this young person's understanding of desire and its possibilities by substituting exploitation of the other person for any notion of love.

As Sarah Kay comments, "Whilst misogyny may be endemic, it none the less manifests itself particularly strongly in specific historical outbreaks," which, some argue, "correspond with anxieties created by political and economic conditions."[123] Although Kay was discussing late thirteenth-century intellectual and academic debates, her points apply equally to Jean de Meun's exposé of the Old Woman's commodification of sex. In the late thirteenth century in Western Europe, the feudal agrarian peasant economy by which workers were tied to the land was slowly losing its once near absolute control. Market towns were increasing in importance as were their bourgeoisie of independent merchants selling goods. The Old Woman, whose goods are sex, satirizes this disconcerting new independent-agent activity. Old Women who go between are nearly always selling someone's sex. What makes La Vieille a threat of a new sort is that she is lecturing on selling herself. Perennial misogynistic concerns expressed through her calculations about how to best market herself tap deep anxieties about the new economic climate and its impact on everyday life and values.

The Old Woman's sex partners are customers, not lovers. She describes crowds of men competing for her with her door swinging open all day and men fighting over her at night. Sometimes she would have to hide one man while she entertained another, and, like crowds of active bidders at a hot auction, the quantity of competitors intensified each other's interest in the product.

At issue is the woman's body as an item for sale, and La Vieille instructs Fair Welcoming in showing off her wares. Here, for instance, she explains displaying a pretty foot:

> "Et se sa robe li trahine
> ou pres du pavement s'encline,
> si la lieve ancoste ou devant
> si con por prendre un po de vant,
> ou por ce que fere le sueille
> ausinc con secourcier se vueille
> por avoir le pas plus delivre.
> Lors gart que si le pié delivre
> que chascun qui passe la voie
> la bele forme du pié voie." (13515–24)

["And if her dress drags or hangs down near the ground, she should lift it up a little on the sides or at the front, as if to let in a little air or because she is accustomed to tucking up her dress to have a freer stride. Then, she should take care to reveal her foot so that anyone who passes by should see its lovely shape."]

The Old Woman continues with pointers for a woman who wants to wear a coat. Since the woman will also want to draw attention to her fine figure, as well as to the cloth of her dress, decorated in silver and small pearls, and the expensive fur lining she has added, and her purse, which should be prominently displayed, she should hold out the sides of her coat in both hands, " 'soit par bele voie ou par boe' " (13537) ["whether she is walking on fine paths or on mud"], and make a wheel of it, the way the peacock makes a wheel with its tail. E. Jane Burns sees the Old Woman as preserving "women's access to pleasure in the face of male exploitation." Women "put *themselves* on display," she writes, and "their acts of beauti- fication are designed to take the lady out of an enclosed and controlled space." Apropos of this passage about wearing a coat, Burns continues: "Here clothing is not principally looked upon by the aspiring suitor but more specifically manipulated by the woman who looks out at the specta- tor from a body she has arranged, assembled, and displayed, a body she has fashioned from cloth."[124] Burns stresses the woman's agency, that this adorning is her own act; however, the purpose of the act is not to give herself pleasure but to market herself. "Arranged, assembled, and dis- played" are the presentational activities of a shopkeeper with wares to sell. The Old Woman is describing her own prostitution here, her commodi- fication of herself. It is difficult to see how she escapes male exploitation by prostituting herself.

Not all wares are as attractive as they might be, however, and the Old Woman details methods of increasing marketability. If a woman's breasts are too heavy, for instance, she should tie them up with a towel wrapped around her ribs. If she has ugly legs, she should wear beautiful stockings. If her breath smells, she should keep away from people's noses. Wares must also be kept up to date, and damaged goods must be repaired. If the woman's hands are scabbed from insect bites or pimples, she should wear gloves. If her hair is thinning, or a drunk has pulled it out, she should patch it with pads of material or a dead woman's hair. And she should be sure to keep her private parts clean.

Instead of hiring out for a fee, the Old Woman advises "plucking" men: " 'Fole est qui son ami ne plume / jusqu'a la darreniere plume' " (13667–68) ["Whoever does not pluck her lover down to the last feather is a fool."]. It is here that Jean borrows most directly from Ovid's Dipsas, the drunken old witch in *Amores* 1.8 who instructs a courtesan on how to trick more gifts out of her lovers. La Vieille echoes Dipsas's counsel concerning teaching servants and relatives how to nudge admirers into buying more. The goal is to separate the men from their money, jewels, coats, gloves, and shoes (13679–710). Most especially, the Old Woman lectures, a woman should sell her "rose" as an exclusive item. Even with a thousand men promising her gifts and payment for love, she should swear to each one that he alone will ever have her "rose."

Scarcity and difficulty of attainment increase the value of goods to the buyer, and the successful merchant sees to it that the customer believes he is getting his money's worth. Sometimes, to intensify sexual interest with fear, the Old Woman made her sex partner arrive by climbing in her window, or she would hide him suddenly, or pretend that both she and he were in desperate imminent peril from her jealous husband. Sometimes logistics yield the difficulties that enhance desire. If the young woman's husband will not let her out of the house, La Vieille counsels, then she should get him drunk, or drug him with herbs, and entertain her lover at home. Or, even if she has a tub at home, she should convince her husband that she must go to the public baths to steam herself, and meet her lover there.

And always—except when the Old Woman let her own foolish passion deflect her—she saw to it that she got paid, even if it was only a few pennies pledged at the wine seller's. The point of her genial lecturing never changes. The imperative at its heart is that men must pay for love as long as possible and at as high a rate as possible. A smart, good-looking woman can feather her nest very nicely, but only if she makes the most of what she has to sell.

Goods, however, grow old, decay in worth, become obsolete, or sometimes simply lose their desirability for buyers, and when the goods are a woman's sexual attractiveness, they are certain to lose their marketability. Virtually elegiacally and with full awareness of her sexual symbolism, the Old Woman laments her door that had once been opened again and again and now stands on the doorsill day after day and night after night. " 'Nus n'i vient hui ne n'i vint hier, / pensaie je, lasse chetive! / En tristeur esteut que je vive' " (12806–08) ["No one comes today, and no one came yesterday," I thought. "Miserable wretch! I must live in sadness"]. Her glory years are gone. The same men that desired her so much they could never be satisfied by her and fought in the streets to be able to possess her now call her wrinkled and old, and look the other way as they pass her by.

Passion is the villain in the Old Woman's description of her career, " 'l'estuve / ou Venus les dames estuve' " (12721–22) ["the hot bath where Venus makes ladies sweat"]. Instead of getting rich and marrying a lord, she herself fell prey to the same kind of passion she is teaching Fair Welcoming to exploit. In its grip, she squandered her wealth on an abusive, gambling, drinking husband who cared nothing for her, and by the time he had wasted everything she earned, she was too old to attract anyone else. She presents her advice to Bel Aceuil as if her only purpose were to increase the woman's wealth, but sex is her way of injuring men as well as exploiting them. Both the woman and the man are engaged in acts of predatory violence in her imagery for intercourse: " 'Et s'ele pluseurs en acroche / qui metre la vueillent en broche.' " (13571–72) ["And if she hooks several of them who want to put her on the spit."]. Her appetite for making men suffer surfaces as she warns the woman against double booking. She must not schedule two men for the same hour since if several arrived at once they might be angry and leave, and she would lose what they would have paid her.

> "El ne leur doit ja riens lessier
> don il se puissent engressier,
> mes metre an si grant povreté
> qu'il muirent las et endeté,
> et cele an soit riche mananz,
> car perduz est li remananz." (13581–86)

["She should never leave them anything that they can fatten themselves up on; instead, she should impoverish them so completely that they die in misery and in debt and she becomes rich and wealthy, for anything they keep is lost to her."]

Medieval texts rarely offer a voice that can be claimed with confidence as a woman's voice, but feminist scholars struggle to hear whatever traces of such a perspective might be lodged in male writings. Burns, Kay, Krueger, and Solterer write about the need for women to search for "a female subjectivity that comes to us through a literary tradition that neither reifies nor ventriloquizes it," and they propose that "if there can be no totalizing or coherent woman's voice in medieval French literature (or elsewhere), neither can the dominant male voice—whether of literature or culture—dominate totally or unproblematically."[125] Given the Old Woman's independence, self-reliance, and vitality, and the strength of her voice, it is a great temptation for women to want to claim some part of this speaker for their own. Sarah Kay deconstructs the Old Woman's lecture arguing that her advice "contains some clear reversals of misogynistic *topoi*. You seduce men by appealing to *their* sensual desires. And you need many lovers because men are basically unreliable and untrustworthy." (The *topoi* that Kay sees reversed here are that women are libidinous and fickle.) Kay sums up her position with "The Vielle's teaching overall is that women share the same material nature as men (and like them have a right to sexual pleasure) whilst their moral character stems from the need for self-defence against male exploitation."[126]

True, the husband the Old Woman doted on exploited her and she denounces men for betraying women, but her lecture stresses neither these points nor woman's right to sexual pleasure. Her subject is her own cleverly calculated, richly remunerative, emotionally rewarding exploitation of men, and her lecture teaches that selling sex is woman's route to wealth, status, and power. The voice of the Old Woman, then, loud and clear, proclaims the male message of misogyny. She incarnates the idea of woman attached for two centuries to the Old Woman who goes between and now revamped and reinvigorated by anxiety generated by the new economy of independent merchants and shopkeepers. The Old Woman is a nightmare summary of why women should be feared. Women are greedy, lustful, power-hungry liars and cheats, and they are good at their work. This strident, virulent voice is bizarrely intolerant of any human impulse related to sexual relations; it is dedicated to reducing to hire and salary all attraction from one sex to the other. Despite Kay's valiant efforts to claim this voice for women, it drowns out any hint at a woman's perspective.

The Old Woman Who Does Not Go Between

By the mid-thirteenth century, one writer, probably in France, reversed the traditional portrait of the Old Woman. His old woman refuses to go between. She appears in the one substantial narrative section of an encyclopedic Latin poem called *De Vetula* [Concerning the Old Woman]. *De Vetula* was read and copied in England and Italy as well as in France, where it first circulated,[127] and it includes sections on such diverse subjects as mathematics, astrology, the Jews, God, life after death, and castration. It was rewritten in the mid-fourteenth century in French as *La Vieille*,[128] and the French version, which will be discussed here, doubles the length of the old woman's story.

The old woman in this poem is very old and very poor, two of the type figure's primary traits, but no matter how much she is begged, bribed, or threatened, she refuses to go between, and there is no indication that she has ever gone between in the past. Poor as she is, instead of conniving to get more money out of the seducer, she resists his requests, keeps him at bay, and protects the young girl. And when the seducer finally thinks she has agreed to arrange what he wants, she betrays him.

The seducer, Ovid, lusts after a fourteen- or sixteen-year-old girl (her age is given variously at different points in the poem). Berthe, the go-between, is a beggar who works in Ovid's sister's kitchen, but she was the girl's nurse when she was tiny, which gives her entrée into her household. When Ovid asks her to go between for him, she recoils in horror. The girl's father would kill any go-between, she tells him, and she begs him to leave her alone in her poverty and wretchedness. The more the old woman protests, the more certain Ovid is that she can be won over. After many counterarguments to her arguments, he gives her gifts: a nanny-goat, wheat, beans, peas, lentils, a wimple and kerchief, a tunic, a mantle, a fur-lined cloak, boots, and three pieces of cloth for a chemise, with different grades for the collar, sleeves, and back. At last Berthe agrees to go between for him.

For weeks, Berthe keeps Ovid dangling with tales of the courtship she is allegedly carrying on for him. Finally, when he loses patience, she says she believes the girl loves him but is too shy to admit it, and she proposes that he take her by surprise. Normally the girl sleeps in her mother's bedroom, Berthe explains. Berthe washes the girl's hair, however, and the next time she is asked to do so, she promises to leave the house door unlocked and arrange to have the girl spend the night in a little room just off the entryway. Ovid is to undress in silence and darkness, and enter the bed where Berthe assures him he will find the young girl naked. He should possess her at once, she counsels, because as soon as he takes her virginity, she will love him.

Ovid's progress to the young girl's room is described in detail, as is his great joy and, literally, rising desire. The woman in the bed, however, is Berthe. Before he realizes who she is, he embraces and possesses her, the firebrand of his lust extinguished in her old flesh, as he describes his experience graphically: "Et tele rose fut viellie / Qui encor n'avoit esté cueillie" (3173–74) [And that rose, which had never been plucked before, was already old].

This is a sexual nightmare, the unplucked, withered rose and "la belle" transmogrified at the moment of sexual possession into a "vielle chauve ridée" [an old, bald, wrinkled woman]. But the author's concentration on young flesh contrasted with old flesh takes more dramatic forms. When Ovid first falls in love, he describes the girl in an extravagantly long catalogue: 120 verses in the original Latin poem and 200 in the French. Much of this material is a conventional list of desirable attributes: her hair, arms, hands, eyebrows, eyes, nose, nostrils, and so forth, all discussed in detail. As the description concludes, however, it becomes virtually titillating. For instance, he dwells on the girl's tiny breasts, which seem to say to the idlers who study them "Que bien veulent estre pressées, / Et que point ne soient lassées / D'amant par amours acoler" (2759–61) [that they really want to be squeezed, and that they never weary of holding a lover in love's embrace]. Matching this, in some macabre fashion, is the much briefer, unconventional, but more memorable catalogue account Ovid gives of the old go-between's body. As he recoils in disgust from her, he lists the attributes that led him to realize that this was not the young girl: her wiry neck, bald head, and pointed shoulders; her dirty skin, wrinkled up like a wet purse; her breastless, nippleless, sluggish, hard chest and earth-hard stomach, furrowed as if from a plowshare; and her dried-up loins, thighs hollowed out by want, and swollen knees as hard as stones for making walls (3184–98).

Finally, lying in his own bed at home, Ovid conjures up a punishment for Berthe by magnifying her two primary attributes into a double curse— unmitigated poverty and the torments of old age: may she beg without finding anyone to give her a scrap to eat; may her meat and bread always be spoiled and her fish stinking; may she only drink bitter wine; cough constantly, wracked with fever and chills; weep incessantly; vomit when she tries to spit, and on and on in a summary of the miseries of being poor, sick, and old (3239–96).

There is some voyeuristic pleasure in the attempted rape of the young girl, and considerable prurient misogynistic pleasure from imagining the Old Woman's body and her withered "rose." Ovid's gross sexual defeat is also perversely satisfying since someone so far beneath him in social position and wealth accomplishes it. From a feminist perspective, however, Berthe herself is the most interesting character in *La Vieille*. Since Ovid narrates his own bed trick story, it describes only the aspects of the old woman that engage his interest or attention: whether she will go between for him and the hideousness of her old body. The implications of his story, however, yield other elements for a characterization of this old woman who triumphs over Ovid as she protects the young girl against rape by being raped herself. Berthe is said to be wise, which her actions surely support, and Ovid calls her an old sorceress, "la vielle sorciere" (3250), but there is no evidence of sorcery in her portrait—only cleverness, and considerably more decency than the alleged lover shows.

There is a twentieth-century coda to *La Vieille*. A distinguished Chaucerian and New Historicist has misread this episode so egregiously that his misreading begs for interpretation. First in *Speculum* in " 'For the Wyves love of Bathe': Feminine Rhetoric and Poetic Resolution in the *Roman de la Rose* and the *Canterbury Tales*,"[129] then in *Chaucer and the Subject of History*,[130] and finally in a collection of articles as "Feminine Rhetoric and the Politics of Subjectivity: La Vieille and the Wife of Bath,"[131] Lee Patterson argues that this poem provides "an important example of the eroticism of feminine discourse" and "suggestive precedents for the *Wife of Bath's Prologue and Tale*."[132] Writing about "the rhetoric of the Wife's discourse" and Chaucer's "verbal sporting" to create her, for instance, Patterson says that

> the most relevant of *La vieille*'s strategies is its exploitation of the erotic possibilities of the old woman's garrulity. The ambivalent sexuality that invests the old woman is here expressed in *La vieille*'s interlacing of delectable accounts of the young girl's body with self-pitying laments for her own age and poverty. Titillation and tedium alternate in her discourse, successfully arousing Ovid to a state of all too blind lust.[133]

Here Patterson links Berthe's rhetoric and the Wife of Bath's, which is essential for his point about the "eroticism of feminine discourse."

However, he has mistaken Berthe for a go-between. Earlier he describes Ovid as "Teased by her [the old woman's] long-winded descriptions of the lady's beauty into a frenzy of anticipation"[134] but while Berthe does indeed lament her old age and poverty, she never once mentions the girl's body. Berthe has no titillating rhetoric because she is not going between. Quite the reverse, the ancient beggar-woman is defending the young girl against this wealthy, powerful, upper-class lecher. It is Ovid who muses on how desirable the young girl is and the poem's many lengthy "delectable" accounts of her body are all his.

Similarly, Patterson pictures Berthe as lascivious, despite her great age. Describing Ovid's experience during the bed trick, Patterson writes, "the lustful poet makes furious love to the woman awaiting him in the assigned bed," and later, "The human being he confronted when the sun rose on his bed of shame those many years ago was an image of his own future: an aged but unabated sexuality veiled by garrulity and nostalgia."[135] In the poem, however, there is no discovery at sunrise, and Ovid never confronts anyone in his bed. Nor did he make "furious love" to anyone. He knew who his partner was as soon as he penetrated the old woman and he left at once in the night, the firebrand of his lust extinguished in her old flesh, as he puts it. Patterson's most important misreading, however, is of the old woman's "aged but unabated sexuality." Nothing in the poem suggests that Berthe is a lecherous old woman. She says nothing to indicate that she experiences sexual desire and the text is explicit that she is a virgin, a withered up old flower unplucked until this time, as Ovid puts it. The trade is her virginity for the girl's.

These are Patterson's foundational misreadings; many more follow from them. What could prompt such a series of errors? Have expectations about old women in the Middle Ages infected the imaginations of contemporary medievalists so that they too, like the audiences of the Middle Ages, expect old women in medieval texts to be lascivious go-betweens? Surely something of that sort must have happened in this case, bearing witness in its own perverse way to the strength of this misogynistic tradition.

Five Fourteenth and Fifteenth-Century Go-Between Stories

In England and Western Europe in the fourteenth and fifteenth centuries, the Old Woman figure dominated stories about going between for lust and sexual conquest. The French version of De Vetula, for instance, was written in the mid-fourteenth century,[136] and Pamphile et Galatée, which retells the Pamphilus story in French, dates from the early years of the fourteenth century.[137] Pamphile et Galatée features Houdée, a formidable, lengthily developed Old-Woman figure who, while flooding her dialogue with colloquialisms and proverbs, oversees the capture and rape of Galatée. The *Libro de buen amor* [*The Book of Good Love*], the great Spanish medieval go-between poem, also dates from the early fourteenth century,[138] and from start to finish it abounds with Old Women who go between. Sometimes they are called Trotaconventos (convent-trotter), sometimes "Urraca," but it hardly matters whether the poet is writing about one woman or several since they are so consistently traditional Old Women figures who nag to be paid, complain about their poverty, lie about themselves and the men who hire them, play tricks on the women they are trying to procure, and are denounced as whores. The *Libro* incorporates several episodes of their going between, including the Pamphilus story, this time reworked with Pamphilus and Galatea as Sir Badger and Lady Sloeberry.[139] In addition to full-scale retellings of the Latin comic tales such as these, the tales themselves continued to be copied, referred to, and imitated, attesting to considerable continuing interest in them and in their go-betweens. In the mid-fourteenth century (1348–51),[140] for instance, Boccaccio rewrote *Lidia*, the tale about the lustful duchess, as the Seventh Day, Ninth Story of the *Decameron*, and in 1385–86, Geoffrey Chaucer used *Pamphilus* as the basis of the central episodes of *Troilus and Criseyde*.[141] The fabliaux of the thirteenth century also remained well known. In *Pamphile et Galatée*, for instance, when Houdée is denouncing a neighbor for trickiness, she calls her " 'fille dame Aubree' " (2347) ["Dame Auberee's daughter"]. During the fourteenth century, Jean de Meun's late thirteenth-century *Roman de la rose*, with its spectacular portrait of the Old Woman, was well on its way to winning its place as one of "the successes of world literature," as Sarah Kay describes it.[142] Not only is the Old Woman Geoffrey Chaucer's principal source for his Wife of Bath's monologue in the late fourteenth century,[143] she also supplies details for his portrait of the Prioress in the *General Prologue to the Canterbury Tales*.[144]

Important as the Old Woman figure was in fourteenth and fifteenth-century literature, go-betweens of other types also appear in these stories. Four of them are of interest less for their go-betweens than for the issues they raise for feminist medievalists. Gender-sensitive readers of medieval literature search text after text, looking for the absent medieval woman. Twenty-first century readers persist in hoping that, male-authored though these texts are, they cannot altogether silence women. Story after story, however, yields glimpses of what might be a woman's perspective, only to retreat from them. Sheila Fisher and Janet E. Halley summarize Elaine Tuttle Hansen's view of the likelihood of finding women in these texts: "for a male author to write women in these periods was to refer not to women, but to men—to desire not relationship with women, but relationship to the traditions of male textual activity, and, by extension, of male social and political privilege."[145] The women in two of John Gower's exempla in his Middle English *Confessio Amantis* [The Lover's Confession] (1390) typify this way of writing about women. They are monolithically idealized: pitiful, dutiful, passive, vulnerable, long-suffering, chaste, violated women, and one of them is portrayed exclusively as the property of the males in the story.

Go-between stories involving sex tricks—*Auberee* and *Dame Sirith*, for instance—typically stress either the plot or the characterization of the go-between to divert attention from the actual rape. Gower, like the author of Jehanne's story, instead foregrounds the rape and the woman's misery and disgrace. Since the point of his exemplum is to teach lovers not to court by deception, he focuses on the suffering brought about by the deception. A duke named Mundus lusts after Pauline, a happily married noblewoman who refuses his repeated advances and offers of money. Despairing of success on his own, Mundus hires two priests of Isis to go between for him. They convince the devout wife that the god Anubus has come to them in a vision and promised to appear to her if she will spend a night in the temple of Isis. The priests hint discreetly at the sexual aspects of this meeting— the god has chosen her " 'For love he hath to thi persone' " ["because of his love for your body"]—but they stress that it is her character, " 'chaste and ful of feith' " ["chaste and devout"], that has won this great honor for her.[146] Dutiful, submissive Pauline has her husband decide what she should do, and he sends her off to spend the night at the temple since her encounter with a god will be a shared honor for them both. There, Duke Mundus, disguised as the god Anubus, awakens her, calms her fears with assurances that she is destined to give birth to a god, and has sex with her for the rest of the night. As Pauline leaves for home the next morning, she discovers the duke's deception and is appalled and overcome by grief.

Weeping and deathly pale, the innocently unfaithful Pauline denounces herself to her husband:

> "Helas, wifhode is lore
> In me, which whilom was honeste,
> I am non other than a beste,
> Now I defouled am of tuo." (974–77)

> ["Alas! Formerly I was chaste, but now I have lost my virtue as a wife. I'm nothing but a beast now that I have been fouled by two men."]

Pauline's husband negotiates the punishment of the deceivers with the emperor, who singles out the go-betweens for his harshest sentence. Since they betrayed this good woman out of avarice rather than passion, he has them put to death. The pleasure of such an exemplum must come from

Pauline's much stressed virtue and dutiful submissiveness. Instead of a clever sex-trick story, which it surely could have been, it is the story of a good woman's abuse.

The woman in Gower's second go-between exemplum is equally dutiful and submissive, and even more pathetic since the go-between is her husband. He is the king's steward, and he prostitutes her to the king. When doctors prescribe a night of sex with a fresh, young, lusty woman to save the king's life, the steward "sette his honour fer behynde. /. . ./ The gold hath mad hise wittes lame" [turned his back on his honor;. . .the gold had lamed his wits].[147] He knows where such a woman could be found, he tells his king, and then, like an Old Woman bargaining to raise her price, he whispers in the king's ear that he will only succeed if the king gives him a great amount of gold. The king tells him to take a hundred pounds to pay for the woman, and, "Ayein love and ayein his riht" (2729) [against love and against morality], the steward resolves that he will have the money and his wife will lie with the king.

The steward's wife is the well brought up, attractive daughter of a rich merchant. An innocent, wronged, pitiful figure, she throws her husband's corruption into relief by her response to his proposition. Kneeling before him, blushing with shame, she pleads that she will do anything that is right and fitting, anything honorable, " 'Bot this thing were noght honeste, / That he for gold hire scholde selle' " (2742–43) ["But this would not be honorable—for him to sell her for gold"]. With harsh words, threats, and "his gastly contienance" [his terrifying looks], the steward silences his wife and forces her submission. Once the king discovers the identity of the woman he has had sex with, however, he exiles the steward under threat of death and marries the wife himself.

There is no narrative complexity to this exemplum. The king's bed and its occupants are at the center of the plot and might be expected to add some sensual moments, but Gower barely mentions them. Neither they nor anything else distracts the reader's attention from the point about the go-between and his greed. And when the king rescues the pathetic wife from her prostituting husband by marrying her, the listener accepts that the wrong done to her is happily resolved, not pausing to notice that the young woman is so entirely the property of these males that they are passing her between them at will.

These are formidably clichéd characterizations. Anne Laskaya, writing about medieval legends of long-suffering women, comments, "[B]ecause they often encode females as vulnerable, helpless, weak, and most heroic when they accept grief and extreme violation with Christlike forbearance, these narratives further the naturalization of women's subordination, thereby contributing to the culture's violence toward women."[148] Gower's submissive, violated women indeed "further the naturalization of women's subordination." They are summary figures of male notions of what women should be—man speaking to man within the textual tradition. No sign of other aspects of these women emerges from these stories.

In support of the idea that, despite male dominance of the medieval textual tradition, women's voices must somehow be audible in this literature, Adrienne Munich urges that feminist readings should try to find women's implied power in texts that submerge it.[149] One would expect to find women's power explored in stories about women forcing men to do what women want them to do, and that is what happens in two other stories that involve go-betweens. The men in these stories have abandoned their wives and vowed to return to their marriages only if their wives fulfill a number of impossible demands, one of which is that the wives give birth to sons fathered by the husbands who have left them. Working through go-betweens, the discarded wives reel their husbands back into their marriages, conceiving by repeatedly tricking their husbands into believing that they are the women their husbands currently desire. The go-betweens operate as double agents; the husbands believe they have hired the go-betweens or won them over to their causes while in fact the go-betweens are serving the wives.

Boccaccio tells the first of these stories in the *Decameron* (1349–51),[150] and it ultimately yielded the plot of Shakespeare's *All's Well that Ends Well*. The go-between is a widow from Florence who is too poor to provide a dowry for her very attractive daughter whom a French count named Bertrand is trying to seduce. Bertrand refused to consummate his marriage to a young woman named Gillette because the king of France had forced him to marry her and he considers her beneath him. Gillette and the widow trick the count into repeated intercourse with Gillette, while all the time he believes she is the widow's daughter. Gillette conceives twin boys, provides a large dowry for the widow's daughter, and is accepted by Bertrand as his wife.

Gillette is a dangerous woman as she fights back from being a discard. Her husband has already rejected her sexuality, her prime weapon for reclaiming him, so by successfully substituting in bed for the woman Bertrand craves, Gillette tricks him into desiring her and acting on his desire, whether he knows what he is doing or not. Then by becoming pregnant with twin boys, she asserts her worth as a fertile woman, and it is the "due così be' figlioletti" ["two such handsome sons"] that finally persuade Bertrand to acknowledge Gillette as his wife.

The much longer mid-fifteenth-century French prose narrative *Le Roman du comte d'Artois* (1453–67)[151] works with these same issues in more obvious ways. Its go-between is the governess of a princess with whom the count of Artois is desperate to have an affair, and the count's wife enlists the governess to help her trick her husband into having intercourse with her while believing she is the princess. The count left the countess after two-and-a-half years of marriage because she had not conceived and he wanted a more adventurous life. She then disguised herself as a man, Phlipot, and followed her husband, and at this point she is his confidante and most trusted servant. As such, she listens night after night while her husband moans and groans from desire for the princess.

The bed trick depends on a room with two entrances. As Phlipot, the countess brings her husband to the governess's room where he expects to meet the princess. The countess then goes into a dressing room via a second entrance, takes off her male clothes, and joins the count in bed. The next morning she exits through the dressing room door, and hurries back to the count's lodgings to seem asleep before he returns. The trick works on several occasions, and the countess becomes pregnant. Once the count succeeds in having sex with the woman he believes to be the princess, the countess, as Phlipot, is the audience for her husband's ecstasy over his consummated affair. He is nearly overcome by emotion as he thanks Phlipot for going between for him. Entirely by Phlipot's efforts, the count tells his disguised wife and actual sex partner, he has won the single blessing his soul desires.

Neither of these stories comments on the irony in these husbands' finding their discarded wives so immensely satisfying, but it is present for every listener. When is a desired woman not a desired woman? When a man has rapturous sex with a woman who is not the woman he believes her to be, what is the meaning of his fulfillment? The count, who left his wife because she bored him, is described in bed with her thanking her a thousand times over for her "gracieuse courtoisie" [gracious courtesy] and assuring her in the clichés of romantic loving that she alone can cure him of his suffering (133). Is the old joke about all cats being gray in the dark lurking somewhere behind these scenes? If so, that is a sure deflation for the pretensions of passion.

Gillette and the countess succeed in reestablishing their marriages and reclaiming their self-indulgent, irresponsible husbands from their sex fantasies, but would women identify with these characters and their successes? Are they an answer to Munich's appeal to feminists to find woman's implied power in texts that submerge it? These are certainly strong, clever women, but their power—sex and pregnancy—remains very limited, and their stories have more to do with men's fear of women than with women's power. All is well at the conclusions of these episodes, but in fact all is only well for the triumphant wives. Both husbands left their wives in search of more exciting sexual experiences and more interesting lives.

Their wives, however, using sex and pregnancy, woman's trump cards, followed, trapped, and exposed them, forcing both husbands to return to the situations they tried so hard to escape. The principal concerns, even in these stories of triumphant women, remain misogynistic and male.

Ironically, the most flamboyantly misogynistic speeches in these go-between stories occur when female speakers give straight-from-the-shoulder lectures on women and their lives. Lusca denounced women for their lasciviousness in the most vicious of the Latin comedies. Similarly, one of Boccaccio's old go-betweens spells out the misogynists' grim view of the worth of women and the worth of life for a woman. Boccaccio begins the *Decameron* with a proem explaining that he has written his collection of stories especially for women, but when his Old Woman speaks here, her voice is entirely that of the male writer addressing the male textual tradition.

Go-betweens appear in several of Boccaccio's *Decameron* stories. In one, a go-between's regular work is luring men to her mistress, who then steals their money.[152] In another, a rich merchant sends a go-between to ask his friend's beautiful wife for sex.[153] Boccaccio's most outspoken *Decameron* go-between[154] elaborates the seize-the-day theme that most of the Old Women go-betweens develop: Baucis in *Baucis et Traso*, Dame Hiersent in Jehanne's story, La Vieille in the *Roman de la rose*, the Old Woman in *Pamphilus*, and many others. A woman should fill her bed with lovers while she can, Boccaccio's Old Woman preaches. Before long, everything worth having and doing will be out of reach, and no grief can compare to thinking you have wasted your youth. Age has no consolations for a woman: " 'E da che diavol siam noi poi, da che noi siam vecchie, se non da guardar la cenere intorno al focolare?' " (318) [" 'And what the devil are we women good for when we are old anyway, only to sit around the fire and stare at the ashes?' "] (371). All age brings a woman is the pain of looking back on lost sensuality and desirability: " 'Di che quando io mi ricordo, veggendomi fatta come tu mi vedi, che non troverei chi'mmi desse fuoco a cencio, Dio il sa che dolore io sento' " (318) [" 'Yet, when I think of the things I could have done and see myself reduced to the state in which you see me now, where no one would ever deign to give me so much as a light, only God knows the agony I feel' "] (371). When you grow old, the go-between warns, see to it that your soul has no cause to complain against your flesh for not having made use of your youth: " 'per ciò che tu puoi vedere, quando c'invecchiamo, né marito né altri ci vuol vedere, anzi ci cacciano in cucina a dir delle favole con la gatta e ad annoverare le pentole e le scodelle.' ") (318) [" 'For as you can see, when we get old, no husband or anyone else cares to look at us; on the contrary, we are chased into the kitchen to tell stories to the cat or to count the pots and pans.' "] (371) Being desirable is woman's only source of power. That is why age limits and afflicts women so much more than men, the Old Woman explains. Men are excellent in many ways, and they have many sources of power, but women have only their sexuality:

> "Degli uomini non avvien cosí: essi nascono buoni a mille cose, non pure a questa, e la maggior parte sono da molto piú vecchi che giovani; ma le femine a niuna altra cosa che a fare questo e figliuoli ci nascono, e per questo son tenute care." (318)

> ["It's not the same with men: they are born fit to do a thousand things, not just this one [have sex], and the majority of them are better at it when they're old than when they're young; but women are not good for anything but doing that one thing and giving birth to children, and for this reason we are held so dear."] (371)

The Old Woman bolsters up her point with differences in female and male sexual resilience. Women are always ready for sex, she argues, and a woman can wear out many men while many men can't wear out a single woman (318). A woman's first duty to her spirit is to see to it that her flesh is well satisfied when she is young.

Fear of women's lust obtrudes here, but what is most painfully and aggressively stressed is women's limited worth: sex and pregnancy, exclusively sex and pregnancy, with no redeeming scrap left for an old woman.

The mid-fourteenth-century Spanish *Libro de buen amor* lists the forty-one terms you should never call your go-between, among them sledge hammer, knocker, shoe-horn, halter, currycomb, hook, sheath, file, bridle, fishhook, bell, clapper, spur, trap, cord, and snare, including the go-between's special noun: "nunca le digas trotera, aunque por ti corra" (926) ["do not call her trotter although she trots for you"]. As sexual metaphors, these are a sinister lot, folk wisdom's insight into the grim comedy of going between. Here, from fifteenth-century London legal records, is a case brought by a nine-year-old, Agnes Turner, against Agnes Smith, a bawd, who

> with enticing words fraudulently drew her into her house. . .secretly concealing a certain young man named Robert. . .the said Agnes Turner knowing nothing about it, and then, the door of the said house being falsely and damnably closed, the said Agnes Turner would have been damnably deflowered by the said youth except for the people who came running at the cries of the said Agnes Turner.[155]

This is the trick that was played on Galatea in *Pamphilus*, and it is a lot like the tricks played on the young women in *De nuntio sagaci* and *Auberee*. The Old Woman who goes between is a literary type figure, but her stories are rooted in medieval men's attitudes toward going between and toward women, and in medieval women's lives.

A clear pattern emerges from the very substantial collection of medieval Latin comedies, fabliaux, allegories, exempla, and stories about going between discussed in this section. In nearly all of them, someone's consent to have sex is violated. Going between for lust and sexual conquest is about violating consent, and the work of the go-between is to set up a situation in which consent can be violated. The amount of sexual violence found in these stories follows from that fact, as does the very large number of tricks they include and their sinister portraits of the Old Women who go between.

PART II

CHOREOGRAPHING LOVE: IDEALIZED
GO-BETWEENS

Go-betweens for lust and sexual conquest appear in a variety of genres, but go-betweens for idealized love are found nearly exclusively in romances. They are a radically different figure from the go-between for lust, and they play an altogether different role. Whereas the go-betweens for lust routinely create situations in which people are tricked, trapped, or coerced into sex, these romance go-betweens never violate one person's consent in the service of another person. Love is the theme of most of their episodes and consent is essential. They go between in stories that transfigure desire into passionate, ecstatic, mutually idealizing romantic love. Although one of the episodes discussed in this section depicts the beginning of an adulterous affair, the rest concern courtships, and their typical joyful finale is the lovers' marriage.

The go-betweens in idealized stories are usually members of the lovers' immediate social circle: the man's best friend and closest comrade-in-arms; the woman's lady-in-waiting, who is ordinarily her confidante and sometimes her relative; and cherishing family retainers such as nurses, governesses, and tutors. In two of these episodes, the go-between is a queen. The statures of these go-betweens, however, do not capture the largest difference between them and the peddlers, beggars, retired prostitutes, and servants who go between for lust and sexual conquest. The go-betweens who serve lust are profiting from arranging sexual encounters, and they distance themselves from the couple's relationship to calculate how to make the most from it. Since the idealized go-betweens are friends, relatives, and devoted servants, they are typically very nearly part of the relationship. Most of them are affectionate, caring, and self-sacrificing, and they are intimately involved with the lovers, ordinarily bound by love to one of them, or sometimes to both of them. The lovers themselves are most often the principal characters in the romance: squires, knights, unacknowledged heirs to thrones, princes, princesses, a chatelaine, queens, and an empress.

These young people love each other, and the role of the go-between is to dramatize, celebrate, and idealize the power and mutuality of their love. Throughout the twentieth century, medievalists argued over the nature of love in medieval literature. In 1936, C.S. Lewis presented the most extreme of those positions, contending that courtly love was an adulterous relationship in which a love-stricken man worshipped a cold, distant, powerful woman.[1] Lewis's most important evidence for his claim was a prose book that he cited extensively and described as a "professedly theoretical work" on love, *De arte honeste amandi* [*The Art of Courtly Love*], by Andreas Capellanus.[2] The claim for the adulterous nature of courtly love has been repeatedly discredited from a variety of critical perspectives.[3] By 1965, E. Talbot Donaldson was calling courtly love a myth;[4] in 1970, A.R. Press argued that even the original troubadour poems that formed the basis for Lewis's account of courtly love were not about adultery;[5] and in 2000, Sarah Kay described Andreas's *Art of Courtly Love* as a "clever and ironic text" that medievalists had long mistaken for "a serious treatise on love."[6] The romances involving go-betweens considered in this section contradict at every turn the idea that an adulterous relationship between a worshipping male and a cold, distant, dominating female constitutes ideal courtly love. Only two of these romances concern adulterous love, most of them end with marriages, and most of the women and men in them love equally. Even Guinevere, who in Chrétien's *Charrette* is the classic instance of the egregiously unreasonable, demanding, adored woman, in this account of her story welcomes Lancelot and admits to loving him. The fact that emerges from all this controversy is that love took many different forms in medieval literature. The form initially described as courtly love is only one among many, and not an important one for these romances.

Although love is rarely adulterous in these episodes, it still consciously distinguishes itself from less extreme heterosexual affection. It is intense, demanding, and highly idealized, a desperate risking of the self and spirit. It strikes the lovers dumb or leaves them dying from emotion. They adore the other person, and the women are as love-stricken as the men. Both suffer the classic symptoms of love; they cannot eat or sleep and become highly agitated or depressed. The men perform military exploits as they court the women or defend their right to them, and the women are also willing to risk death for love, and sometimes do. Hazarding parental wrath and the loss of familial love, worldly status, and wealth, both women and men imperil their everyday lives for their loves. These are sublime relationships, at once spiritual and erotic, elevating and noble. There is no trace of Ovidian playfulness and mockery in this loving, and no hint of love as an exploitative game. Love is not entertainment. It yields suffering and ecstasy. And while consummation is its goal—a mutual goal for the man and the woman—love is never reduced to sex.

These men and women love each other despite the fact that six of these unions are extreme misalliances. In one instance the man is an heir and the couple believes the woman has no family or wealth, and in five others the woman is an heiress and they both believe the man is a propertyless knight or squire. While these couples are courting and falling in love, then, one of them is flouting all the obligations of family and society that require a young person to marry for the family's social, political, and financial profit. In most of these cases, by the end of the story the other member of the couple turns out to match or exceed the first in wealth and birth, but the story itself is about young people defying marriage conventions in the service of passionate love. Moreover, even the stories that do not involve gross disparities of wealth and position are nearly all about mutual attraction that yields love. The propertied members of the highly hierarchical courtly society of the twelfth century, then, were patronizing fiction that undercut essential societal customs: the dowry and the parents' right to choose a mate for their child. These patrons and audiences, as they supported the men who wrote these texts, must have been responding to needs their society was not fulfilling.

In fact, a significant change in thinking about the nature of marriage was taking place in medieval Europe during the twelfth century, and it stressed the aspects of marriage these stories emphasized. Land, wealth, and politics were not the only critical factors to be considered in making marriages. This society was elaborating "a sophisticated ideology of marriage as a framework for the relationship of two individuals."[7] Since early in the twelfth century, the church had been struggling to redefine marriage "as a momentous act of consent."[8] Bishop Ivo of Chartres, for instance, disregarded traditional emphasis on a transferred dowry, the parents' blessing, and consummation, and took the position that the "sacramentality of marriage lies essentially in the consent of the individual."[9] Marriage became a sacrament in the twelfth century, and the church compared newly sacramentalized marriage to the religious calling of virginity. Since marriage was "an absolute and lifelong commitment just like a religious vow," it could only be entered into with the spiritual consent of the marrying couple.[10]

At the same time that free consent was becoming the ideal basis of marriage in medieval Europe, it was gaining importance as a commercial concept. Writing about mercantile discourse's invasion of theological thought and the importance of merchants in twelfth-century northern France, Eugene Vance maintains that the church's insistence that free consent be the sole basis of marriage grows out of the transformation of the feudal barter economy into a profit-motivated economy. In a feudal system, exchanges occur between hierarchically related unequal partners, and these exchanges are based on custom. Commercial exchange, however, "demands both the legal *freedom* of partners to negotiate a contract and *equality* as they do so. As the scholastics knew, mutual consent is the basis of true commercial exchange."[11] Commercial exchange, characterized by equal free partners, was becoming an important aspect of the lives and thinking of Europeans, particularly the French of northern France where six designated fair towns "made Champagne into nothing less than the commercial center of northern Europe."[12] Vance does not claim that this new conception of economic relationships produced the church's new insistence upon consent-based marriages; nevertheless, the aspects of individuality stressed in the one mode of thought clearly parallel the other and would have supported it. As Vance writes, "There obviously *was* a specifically mercantile discourse in the twelfth century, and the *oratores* obviously *heard* it, if from a distance."[13]

These romances with their episodes of going between are a parallel literary response to the mercantile and theological discourses Vance describes. Stories about the making of free commitments, often in opposition to family and society, they explore the self-consciousness required to undertake such a relationship, and they would have provided spiritual and emotional support to men and women imagining themselves in these new ways. As Neil Cartlidge writes, twelfth-century literature explores "the subtle and complex process by which an individual recognizes in himself or herself the existence of a compelling link with another individual."[14] While superficially these romances with their princesses and disguised heirs seem to be sheer fantasy, they address central spiritual concerns of their society— obliquely and tangentially, as literature tends to speak.

The stories of lust, violation, and rape in the first section of this book appealed to their audience's misogyny and their satisfaction in seeing woman's subordination exploited. For women, they are mightily disempowering stories. Since the romances offer such different scenarios of mutual loving and consent, could it be that they also reverse the misogyny of the stories of lust and sexual conquest and empower female audiences? We will return to this crucial question throughout this section, once again trying to hear the voices of medieval women filtered through texts written by men.

The fourteen romance episodes discussed in this section comprise all the major dimensions of and important variations on the role of the go-between who facilitates idealized love. The heyday of romance was in France during the last third of the twelfth and the early thirteenth century, and most of these go-betweens appear initially in Old French works from that period. Later, from the thirteenth through the fifteenth century, similar go-betweens are found in Anglo-Norman, Middle English, Italian, and German romances inspired by French romances. Most Old French fabliaux also date from the thirteenth century, and the Latin comedies were written from late in the eleventh century to late in the twelfth century. The go-betweens for lust and sexual conquest and the go-betweens for idealized love, then, flourished during the same time period. No difference in time explains their extreme differences in attitude toward the relationships between men and women.

It may well be that no difference in audience explains their differences either. Manuscript compilations often include a variety of genres: romances appear beside fabliaux and didactic texts, saints' lives and deaths, and *chansons de geste*—epical tales of heroic warriors.[15] This repeated mixing of texts certainly suggests that the same audiences that enjoyed misogynistic material enjoyed these romances.

It is difficult to gauge how widely these romances circulated. As will become clear even when only the episodes involving go-betweens are considered, motifs reappear from romance to romance. Also, many of these stories were adapted or translated into several European languages, which certainly suggests popularity. However, most of them have not survived in large numbers of manuscripts. Chrétien de Troyes' *Charrette*, the Old French romance best known to twenty-first-century medievalists, for instance, exists in only eight medieval copies.[16] On the other hand, the Prose *Lancelot* in its various forms, another of these romances, was copied repeatedly and became enormously influential.[17] To put these facts in perspective, fabliaux also rarely survive in large numbers. *Auberee*, which is the most often copied fabliau, only exists in eight copies,[18] exactly the same number as Chrétien's *Charrette*, while *Pamphilus* survives in 170.[19]

When most of the French romances were being written, even aristocratic audiences would have been unable to read them, despite the fact that they were composed in the vernacular. In this respect too they would be no different from the fabliaux. Clerical readers typically would have read romances aloud to groups of courtly listeners. Although evidence of medieval literacy is very hard to interpret, as Sylvia Huot notes, she nevertheless concludes that "while some twelfth-century aristocrats may have been capable of reading romances, their numbers would have been small." During the thirteenth and fourteenth centuries, however, more and more aristocrats learned to read vernacular writings[20] and solitary reading of romances became possible, though the custom of reading as a community activity may have been so engrained that it prevailed.

In England, romances were initially written in Anglo-Norman. They do not appear in quantity in Middle English until nearly the end of the thirteenth century, and are not widespread until the fourteenth century. In the fourteenth and fifteenth centuries, however, many French romances were translated into Middle English.[21] I have therefore included two twelfth-century Old French romances in their Middle English translations to suggest that dimension of the go-between's diffusion.

Conventional Go-Betweens

Guinevere—*Cligés*

Guinevere, King Arthur's queen, illustrates the essentials of the idealized go-between's role in Chrétien de Troyes' *Cligés* (*c.* 1176).[22] She intervenes for Soredamors, her lady-in-waiting, and Alexander, the heir to the throne of Constantinople, who love each other desperately but who are unable to confess their love without her aid. Guinevere does not cause their love in any way; they are mightily in love before she even suspects that they love each other; and yet they must have her to translate their feelings into action. Her going between transforms two suffering, yearning, separated, immobilized individuals into a married couple.

Soredamors and Alexander fall in love at first sight so overwhelmingly that they turn pale, sigh, tremble, and sweat, and Guinevere thinks they must be seasick. They love mutually and equally, tossing and turning in silent lovesickness, and Chrétien lavishes 600 verses on their suffering. But their idealization of each other makes their loving impossible because they cannot imagine that the other person might return their love. When they are together, they can hardly bring themselves to look at each other, and they cannot conceive of admitting to another person that they love. Much as they both love, their relationship is doomed because they can only think of themselves as unworthy and the other person as hopelessly out of reach.

It is Guinevere who declares this couple's love for them. Their paling and blushing in each other's presence alerts her to their state and she cautions them about the dangers of trying to hide love, counsels Alexander to begin boldly as a lover, and then announces that she knows that he and Soredamors love each other:

> "Qu'aparceüe m'an sui bien
> As contenances de chascun
> Que de deus cuers avez fet un." (2256–58)
>
> [" For I've clearly seen from the behaviour of both of you that of your two hearts you have made one."]

By concealing your feelings, she continues, you are killing each other and will murder love. The best way to preserve love is to marry, and she promises to arrange their marriage.

Even with Alexander's love announced so openly for him, he cannot bring himself to speak to Soredamors, and, with Soredamors beside him, he addresses Guinevere instead. He admits to loving Soredamors, swears that he never wants to stop loving her, and describes his pain from concealing his love. Even if she never loves him, he vows, he will remain her true lover. Soredamors, however, says nothing about loving Alexander, despite Chrétien's lengthy earlier descriptions of her passion, despite Alexander's declaration of love, and despite the queen's announcement that Soredamors returns his love. Trembling, Soredamors says only that Queen Guinevere controls every aspect of her being. Nothing about her is her own; "Ne volanté, ne cuer, ne cors" (2298) ["her will, her heart and her body"] are in the queen's power, and she will do whatever the queen wants her to do.

Given all that has passed, these lovers might be expected at least to speak to each other, but they do not. Guinevere remains the single source of action in this scene. She embraces the couple, announcing:

> "Je t'abandon,
> Alixandre, le cors t'amie;
> Bien sai qu'au cuer ne fauz tu mie.
>
> .   .   .   .
>
> L'un de vos deus a l'autre doing.
> Tien tu le tuen, et tu la toe." (2304–09)

["Alexander, I make over to you the body of your sweetheart—I know you are not lacking her heart. . . .I give you each to the other: each of you take what is hers or his!"]

And they marry that very day at Windsor.

Guinevere's going between is one of Chrétien's principal means of depicting Soredamors' and Alexander's love. What is most remarkable about her contribution is how much of their loving she must do for these helpless people. By the convention of this literature, the more immobile the lovers are, the more they show their love. The convention itself requires a go-between.

Would a medieval woman find this episode empowering? Guinevere is the single wise, perceptive, and effective figure in it. Although her expertise is limited to emotional matters, she is very competent in them. As for the young couple, the woman's life is noticeably constrained compared to the man's. Soredamors is beautiful and mannerly, and she embroiders with her golden hair as thread, but Alexander heads a company of warriors, triumphs in battle, and wins major prizes. In sensitivity and capacity to love, however, Chrétien describes them as equal. And yet when they reply to the queen, only the man sounds like someone who loves. Soredamors submerges her passion beneath the timid, modest, self-effacing response of a dutiful maiden, never sharing the truth about her passionate feelings. Very probably this constrained voice is an idealized representation of a young, aristocratic medieval woman. It is surely not an empowering voice.

Alexandrine—*William of Palerne*

Guinevere is a figure of authority and power in *Cligés*. Alexandrine instead is the best friend of both William, the hero, and Melior, the heroine, in *William of Palerne*,[23] a mid-fourteenth-century Middle English translation and reworking of an early thirteenth-century French romance.[24] The three young people have grown up together and, compared to Guinevere's formal intercession, Alexandrine's going between is intimate, loving, and interventionistic. Melior is the 14-year-old daughter of an emperor, and Alexandrine, Melior's cousin and confidante, is a duke's daughter. The situation Alexandrine deals with is much like Guinevere's with Alexander and Soredamors. William and Melior are about to die of love. Melior is so wasted from not eating or sleeping that her father's physicians have given up hope for her life, and William is immobilized, so love-stricken that he has spent the last seven days sitting under an apple tree staring at Melior's bedroom window without eating or drinking.

Melior is so innocent that her lovesickness mystifies her, but Alexandrine tends her cousin in her illness and helps her talk about love. Once Alexandrine understands Melior's situation, she intervenes aggressively on her behalf with William. In the Old French *Guillaume de Palerne*, Guillaume first learns he is in love through a dream in which Melior, weeping, tells him she loves him and begs him to make love to her or she will die (1118–270). The English *William of Palerne*, however, attributes William's dream to Alexandrine's magical powers. This story is full of magic—a werewolf carries off William as a baby to protect him from a wicked relative, for instance—and the translator extends the magic to Alexandrine. Confronted by her cousin's fatal lovesickness, she sends William his dream about Melior, and he awakens overwhelmingly in love.

As in the original Old French romance, the dream permits William to recognize forbidden feelings. He ultimately turns out to be the heir to several thrones, but when he falls in love with Melior, he is a shepherd who does not even know what country he comes from, and his only friend at court is Melior's father. As William acknowledges, it is madness for him to imagine that an emperor's heiress, adored by neighboring princes, could love him. Alexandrine's magic allows William his first conscious thoughts about loving Melior, and from that night on, he is as desperately lovesick as the emperor's daughter.

This magical English go-between uses her powers again to help William and Melior confess their love to each other. One brilliant spring morning when every bush is crowded with singing birds and the garden is full of flowers, Alexandrine leads Melior to William, asleep under his apple tree. Melior's modesty overpowers her, however, and she stops herself at his side. Left to their own devices, despite the fact that they are together in an ideal setting for love, William—convinced with good reason of his ineligibility for this emperor's daughter—and Melior—shy, naive, virginal, sometimes aware and sometimes unaware of the cause of her pain—might never have discovered that they are dying of love for each other. Alexandrine therefore sends William a second dream in which Melior gives him a rose, sign of the woman, and once he has it in his hand, his pain vanishes (865–68). Comforted, he awakens to find Melior beside him.

At this point the audience expects a love scene but, like Soredamors and Alexander, William and Melior speak only to the go-between. William recounts his sickness—fever and chills, depression and elation, sighing and singing at the same time—but refuses to explain its cause. Melior, who recognizes William's pains as her own, for the first time realizes that he too is in love and she prays to God to help them both. "If only William knew how I'm suffering!," she laments silently, but she cannot bring herself to speak: " 'for y dar nou3t for schame schewe him mi wille, / but 3if he wold in ani wise himself schewe formest' " (938–39) ["because I'm too ashamed to show him how much I desire him unless he first somehow shows me how he feels."]

Now Alexandrine is in the usual position of these go-betweens, literally between Melior and William, both of whom are dying of love for each other but cannot act on their feelings. Alexandrine terrifies William by telling him outright that his sickness comes from being battered in the lists of love, and he throws himself on her mercy, begging for help. When she pretends not to see how she can help him, he confesses to loving Melior. His life and death are in her keeping, he warns Alexandrine.

Alexandrine is now doubly pledged—to intercede for the man with the woman and for the woman with the man; the declaration of love is made not by the man to the woman but by the man to the go-between and through her to the woman. Alexandrine goes through the motions of begging Melior to take pity on William, near death for her sake, and Melior pretends not to understand how she might have harmed William, which lets Alexandrine describe his loyal love and nearly fatal lovesickness; unless Melior loves William, he will die by the next morning. Now Melior, tormented by love since the episode began, can safely play the reluctant lady yielding to her lover's impassioned pleas. "Smyland a litel" [smiling a little]—as well she might—she admits she would rather save a man's life than kill him (991). Since William has endured so much for her sake, she swears to love him forever, and William falls to his knees praising God for this miracle. Then, kissing and embracing, they talk together about how long and how dreadfully they have suffered for love. And Alexandrine, who guessed "þat hire maistres and þat man no schuld hire nou3t misse" (1016) [that her mistress and that man would not miss her], spends the day walking through the garden picking flowers and protecting the lovers from discovery, confident that in her absence, "William wold fonde / for to pleie in þat place þe prive love game." (1019–20) [in that place, William would discover how to play the secret game of love].

The translator adds one more element, and it underscores Alexandrine's intimate role in this couple's loving. The English Alexandrine makes the single joke about sex in all these fourteen romance episodes. When Melior first describes the terrible sickness that is destroying her, Alexandrine assures her that she can cure her and promises to find "a grece," an herb, that will make Melior well. When Melior experiences " 'þe savor and þe swetnesse þat sittes in þe rote' " (638) ["its root's flavor and sweetness"], Alexandrine promises, they will take away all her sorrows. This conversation quiets Melior, only half aware of the nature of her problem and even less aware of the meaning of Alexandrine's solution, and she begs her lady-in-waiting to secure this healing herb as quickly as possible. When the English Alexandrine returns after the couple has spent their afternoon making love in the garden, she coyly underscores the sexual meaning of her earlier metaphor: "and mekly to Meliors, 'Madame,' þan sche seide, / 'have 3e geten þe gras þat I 3ou geynliche hi3t?' " (1029–30) [And she then courteously said to Melior, "Madame, have you gotten the herb that I promised you in friendship?"] Erik Kooper, in "*Grace*: The Healing Herb in *William of Palerne*," analyzes the translator's punning on gras/grace with their double meanings of "herb" and the "grace" a lady grants her lover, and shows their place within the rich metaphors for lovesickness in the English translation.[25] But surely the "gras" needed by Melior in Alexandrine's comment is more specifically William himself, phallically imagined. No remark in all these idealized stories approaches a sex joke as nearly as Alexandrine's gentle little joke here.

Alexandrine acts a usual go-between's part, helping the couple comprehend what they are feeling, standing between them as a conduit for their emotions, and finally serving as the medium by which they can reach out to each other and become lovers. She is part of this relationship from its inception and the lovers' extreme dependence on her idealizes how much they love each other. Later in the poem Alexandrine will disguise William and Melior as white bears so they can run away together to escape Melior's being forced to marry someone else. To love each other, they turn their backs on family, society, worldly position, and wealth, and Alexandrine, who is so intimately part of their courtship that she even guards their first lovemaking, makes their love possible.

Played out against the backdrop of medieval marriage customs, the love story in *William of Palerne* celebrates free commitment in the face of extreme societal pressure. A daughter was her father's possession and an emperor's daughter would expect to be married to an heir for the advantage of the empire. William and Melior, choosing each other so inappropriately, with only their valuing of the other person as motive, defy their society's social structures. Their extravagant disregard for custom and reasonable behavior meets with providential romance-style good fortune when William turns out to be the king of Sicily and Apulia and so a proper match for Melior, but their story celebrates this couple's daring choice when they had no idea William was more than a foundling. These romances are as unrealistic as fairy tales, but the audience's satisfaction from listening to them must have come from pleasure in the ideals they developed. The early thirteenth-century Old French *Guillaume de Palerne* would have been written during the church's struggle to redefine marriage as an act of free, mutual consent, and so, instead of matching a societal reality, the romance's celebration of daring marital commitment would have appealed to a sufficiently widespread societal ideal to make its story satisfying. Melior defies being controlled and exchanged, chooses her own love, and then fights for it and for him.

Alexandrine is clever, effective, witty, and devoted, easily the strongest person in this love story, but that is because she is not in love. Melior's passivity and ineffectiveness match William's, but both are merely conventional portrayals of ideal loving. The woman speaks as enthusiastically about her feelings as the man, and her passion and loyalty match his. She is one of the more potentially empowering romance heroines in these episodes.

Galehot—The Prose *Lancelot*

Romances deal in superlatives. Soredamors, Alexander, Melior, and William all love superlatively, but Lancelot loves Guinevere so superlatively that he is the most stunned into wretchedness of all these lovers. It would be unthinkable that he could begin his relationship with the queen without a go-between, and he has a unique go-between: Galehot. A great-spirited man of enormous wealth and power, Galehot falls so much in love with Lancelot that he gives up his most important military achievement as conqueror of King Arthur for love of Lancelot, and finally he gives up his life. Lancelot loves Guinevere but Galehot loves Lancelot. Lancelot will die of love without Guinevere, but Galehot dies of love without Lancelot. The consequences of Galehot's going between ultimately destroy him.[26] The story of this tragic love-triangle is told in the early thirteenth-century Prose *Lancelot*[27] that was "immensely popular" for more than 300 years, referred to frequently, borrowed from widely, read throughout Western Europe, and translated into Dutch and German.[28] According to William Calin, it "had the most decisive impact on the evolution of romance in England" of any foreign romance.[29]

At the point in the story when Lancelot and Galehot become comrades-in-arms, Lancelot is concealing his identity. He is simply a nameless knight in black armor who achieves astonishing feats in battle and then disappears. Guinevere suspects that the mysterious Black Knight considers her his lady and that Galehot knows how to find him, and she offers to do anything she can for Galehot if he will arrange an interview for her (334–35). Technically, then, Galehot is Guinevere's go-between, but Galehot's emotional ties are all to Lancelot. Lancelot has been suffering extravagantly. He moans in such anguish at night that the kings who share his tent cannot sleep and he soaks his bed with tears, but he refuses to explain why he suffers (330–31). When Galehot asks if he would be willing to meet with the queen, the suggestion strikes Lancelot speechless; he sighs, tears run down his face, and he seems to lose all sense of where he is. Finally he tells Galehot to make the decision. Galehot offhandedly replies that he does not see how meeting the queen could hurt Lancelot. " 'Certes, fait li chevaliers, assez i avra anui et joie' " (336) ["Indeed," says the knight [Lancelot], "there will be much grief and joy in it"], and as soon as Galehot hears the paradoxical language of love, he grasps the meaning of Lancelot's despair and his own role as go-between becomes clear.

Guinevere loves Lancelot. She says she loves him, she acts on her love, and later in the story she is honored as a great lover, but she does not weep or yearn or show other symptoms of love, and when she asks Galehot for help, she creates the impression that if she knew the mysterious Black Knight's identity and how to contact him, she would simply summon him into her presence and interrogate him about his feelings for her. She is no idealized lover, and during the meeting Galehot arranges for her with Lancelot, she is dramatically in control both of herself and of the situation. Lancelot, on the other hand, is bizarrely, exorbitantly, nearly pitifully prostrate from love, as if extraordinarily self-abased loving were required to match his extraordinary exploits in battle. He is deathly pale, cannot raise his eyes, trembles so that he can hardly speak, weeps continuously in Guinevere's presence, nearly faints, and has to be supported physically by Galehot. The situation is doubly ironic because his display of extreme weakness is the backdrop for his admission of having accomplished the major military exploits of their time.

Galehot arranges that Guinevere and Lancelot meet while she is out walking at dusk with her ladies-in-waiting. Lancelot trembles so uncontrollably that he can scarcely greet the queen, and when he kneels before her, he is so overcome by embarrassment that he cannot look at her. Guinevere is not subtle. Instead of creating situations that would encourage him to speak, she asks direct questions: "For whom did you accomplish all this? Do you really love me so much?" And even unnerved as he is by love, Lancelot manages to answer her. Although he responds with just a few words each time, Guinevere establishes that he is Lancelot of the Lake and that his exploits have been more extraordinary than any of them have suspected. Most important, he is the knight who stopped Galehot when he was about to conquer King Arthur, and therefore Guinevere and the king owe their sovereignty itself to him. This man, sighing and trembling at the queen's feet, weeping so uncontrollably that his silk garment is soaked to his knees, is the most powerful man yet known to King Arthur's court. Guinevere's new information about the extent of this hero's conquests makes the glory of being loved by him even more precious (340–46).

The second half of Guinevere and Lancelot's interview is nearly entirely between Galehot and the queen. Lancelot can admit to his love when the queen asks him point blank whether he loves her, but timid, humble, subservient, and overcome by awe of his lady, he can only respond to her. It would be unthinkable for him to ask Guinevere to love him. Galehot re-enters this scene playing the go-between's usual part of speaking for the lover silenced by the magnitude of his love.

Galehot first must rescue Lancelot physically. Guinevere is so insensitive to the precariousness of Lancelot's emotional state that she teases him by suggesting that he is actually interested in one of her ladies-in-waiting. This shocks him so much that he starts to faint, and she has to call Galehot to help her catch him (346). From this moment on, Lancelot hangs his head between Galehot and Guinevere while the go-between and the lady talk about love. As Galehot discovers very quickly, Guinevere already loves Lancelot, but loving Lancelot is no life-and-death matter for her. She enjoys seeing him suffer from loving her and she is very proud of his love. When Galehot warns her that teasing his comrade about love could kill him, she protests how much *she* would lose from Lancelot's death: Lancelot is far more distinguished than even Galehot knows, and she inspired all Lancelot's great deeds. She even shares with Galehot what slight attentions made Lancelot love her so desperately. On his first visit to King Arthur's court, her parting words, " 'A Deu, biaus douz amis' " (345) ["Farewell, fair sweet friend"], transformed his existence and inspired him to greatness. Guinevere is not standoffish or reluctant. When Galehot emphasizes that Lancelot has accomplished more in her honor than any other knight could accomplish, she says that even if he had only made peace between Galehot and King Arthur, he would have done more for her than she could ever deserve. " 'Ne il ne me porroit nule chose requerre do je lo poïsse escondire bellemant.' " (347) ["Nor is there anything that he could ask of me that I could properly refuse him."] Love, here, is a reward she owes this hero for his great deeds, and this is Guinevere's attitude throughout the long conversation with Galehot that follows. Repeatedly Galehot asks her to take mercy on Lancelot and she replies that she should and she will; Galehot must tell her what mercy he is asking of her. Guinevere does not love Lancelot because of her personal feelings for him; she loves him because he is best, mightiest, and devoted to her. Galehot then asks her to declare her love formally, take Lancelot to be her knight forever, promise to be his loyal lady all the days of her life, and kiss him to signify " 'comancement d'amors veraie' " (348) ["the beginning of true love"]. Guinevere offers some gentle objections: this is neither the time nor the place for kissing, and the ladies of her court and Galehot's seneschal will see them; but her reassurances are far stronger than her cautions: " 'N'an dotez pas que ge ausi volantiers n'an soie desirranz com il an soit' " (348) ["You must not doubt that I am as willing and desire it as much as he"]. Lancelot is so overcome by emotion that the only reply he can manage is " 'Dame, grant merciz' " ["Great thanks, my lady"], and these are the first words he has spoken since he nearly fainted and Galehot took his place in this conversation. It is Galehot who suggests that the three of them should draw together as if they were discussing something, at which point Guinevere breaks in: " 'De quoi me feroie ge or proier?. . .Plus lo voil ge que vos ne il.' " (348) ["And what favor would I have him ask of me?. . .I want it more than either you or he"]. Seeing Lancelot's fear, she lifts his face in her hands and kisses him, with Galehot as their witness.

Guinevere is no distant, unresponsive lady in the Prose *Lancelot*. The love of Lancelot and Guinevere is different and unequal, but it is mutual, and Galehot's involvement in it is no more intimate or pressuring than the involvement of Guinevere herself in the love of Soredamors and Alexander. Galehot is a traditional solution to a traditional dilemma: the awed lover, too nearly quelled by love to be bold or even sensible, who must have a friend speak for him if his love is ever to become a reality.

Of all these romance relationships, Lancelot's and Guinevere's would be most likely to dishonor the go-between since it is adulterous, and yet no trace of disapproval of Galehot appears anywhere in the Prose *Lancelot*. This work exists in two substantially different versions. The original non-cyclic version treats Lancelot's and Guinevere's adultery very gently, deliberately drawing attention away from it and even praising Guinevere for being both Lancelot's lady and King Arthur's wife (557). As Elspeth Kennedy, editor of the Prose *Lancelot*, writes, throughout the non-cyclic version, the love of Lancelot and Guinevere is presented "as a source of inspiration and an ennobling force."[30] The non-cyclic version never criticizes Galehot's going between and would not be expected to. The second version, the cyclic version, treats the lovers as sinful and adds considerable material developing their sinfulness; nevertheless, it never criticizes Galehot's going between.[31] It is foreign to these romances to think of going between as dishonorable.

Most romance go-betweens are minor characters, but Galehot has a story of his own that parallels Lancelot's and Guinevere's stories. Generally, there is no conflict for comrades-in-arms between their going between and their mutual affection; the one expresses the other. For Galehot, however, going between is self-sacrificial and ultimately life-destroying. He sees Guinevere as his rival and is forced to yield first place with Lancelot to her. Several episodes dramatize the self-destructive desperation of Galehot's loving. The most moving of these develops his loss symbolically. Galehot takes Lancelot to a marvelous castle set high on a rock in a lush meadow with a tall forest beside it, a deep river flowing around it, and flocks of birds in its battlements. Struck by the castle's beauty, Lancelot exclaims: " 'Com fu fermee de grant cuer' " (1: 574) ["With what a high heart it was built"]. It is Galehot's most important and most treasured castle, and he recollects his sense of himself when he ordered its construction. He built it to be the stage for his coronation, just before their first meeting, he tells Lancelot. He had already conquered thirty kings and was overlord of all their lands, but he was still uncrowned himself. He was waiting to conquer King Arthur and add the kingdom of Logres to his territories, after which he planned an extraordinary coronation that would be remembered for generations. All his thirty-one conquered kings, including King Arthur, would be present, crowned to do him honor. On each of the turrets of this splendid castle would be a silver pillar the size of a man, supporting a great candle; and on the tower in the middle of the castle would be a pillar of gold larger than any of the rest, topped by an even larger candle. All night long the candles would burn so brilliantly that the coronation would be ablaze with Galehot's glory.

This is Galehot's conception of himself at the moment of his meeting with Lancelot: " 'li plus viguerex hom del siegle et li plus redotez' " (1:574) ["the strongest man in the world and the most feared"]. As Galehot tells Lancelot the history of the castle's construction, the man he was and his dreams for himself become the tragic backdrop for the man he has become. Mysteriously, his castle incarnates his metamorphosis. Before their eyes, with no known cause, one of its walls falls to the ground, and at that same moment every castle in Galehot's land crumbles.

Galehot's loss of Lancelot to Guinevere leaves him with so little interest in his own position that he never has himself crowned, and finally his love of Lancelot determines his death. Not only does Galehot give up his worldly honor for love, he dies of love. No ordinary causes of death— fevers or chills or old battle wounds that fester—divert attention from the meaning of his dying. He dies because a young woman brings him a false report that Lancelot has been killed. Galehot's grief is so devastating—"si grant duel que nus hom ne porroit greignor avoir" (1:612) [such great grief that no one could suffer greater]—that within three days he is dead. Galehot wins Lancelot's happiness for him, but the price he pays for it is his own capacity for life and joy. His final significance is as a sacrificial figure, sacrificed to Lancelot and the love of Lancelot and Guinevere, and his destruction is one measure of the extraordinarily high value of that love. Lancelot and Galehot are the two great lovers of the Prose *Lancelot*.

Kathryn Gravdal, in *Ravishing Maidens: Writing Rape in Medieval French Literature and Law*, comments on "the essence of the power play behind 'romantic love' " in which "male domination and female submission are coded as emotionally satisfying and aesthetically pleasing."[32] This is an excellent description of the way many of the stories of going between for lust and sexual conquest create satisfaction, but the meeting of Lancelot and Guinevere in the Prose *Lancelot* reverses this structure extravagantly. Female domination and male submission are "coded as emotionally satisfying and aesthetically pleasing." Lancelot is passive and vulnerable; Guinevere is active, assertive, and in control. She is never the cold, distant *domna* of the troubadours, however. She does not dominate because she is aggressive or cruel. She dominates because Lancelot is so abjectly submissive that if she speaks rationally, she emerges as dominating. Guinevere fills the void left by Lancelot's silencing.

This inverted gender relationship, however, yields another more important reversal. By showing the woman superior to the man and worshipped by him, the gender relationships here are reversed once more. Guinevere, outspoken about the fact that she loves Lancelot and wants to commit herself to him, nevertheless loves at a usual level of intensity, and Lancelot's abject suffering throws her moderateness into relief. What Lancelot's weakness here expresses is his enormous capacity to love. By the conventions of this loving, the more self-abased and immobilized the lover is, the greater the testimony to his spiritual capacity. And so by showing the woman superior to the man and worshipped by him, the Prose *Lancelot* shows her inferior to him. The woman is an ordinary lover in this episode, but the man has a hero's capacity for love.

Guinevere is a king's wife and her husband's possession. Carefully as the Prose *Lancelot* evades the adulterous dimension of this story, it remains present for every listener. Lancelot's love for Guinevere is immensely idealized, but it is rooted in her status as queen. To a large measure the meaning of his worship and love for her must be that she functions as a homosocial signifier of his own worth. By loving Guinevere, Lancelot competes with, bonds with, and bests King Arthur.

Blancheflor's Governess—*Tristan*

Blancheflor's Nurse/Governess ["ihrer Erzieherinnen" 1200], in Gottfried von Strassburg's *Tristan* (*c.* 1210),[33] is more a moment in a text than a character, but she is worth noting for the trick she plays. The stories about going between for lust are full of tricks—the twin in his sister's clothes, the duke disguised as the god Anubus, and Dame Sirith's weeping dog, for instance—but tricks are rare in the idealized stories of the romances. Most importantly, since these are stories of mutual love, their go-betweens do not trick the other member of the couple into sex. Their tricks typically deceive the outer world of the woman's family and social group, as when Alexandrine disguises Melior and William as white bears.

To conceal and justify Blancheflor's entry into the bedroom of Rivalin, the wounded knight she loves, her governess disguises her as an old woman beggar with healing powers. Since Blancheflor, King Mark's sister, is dying of love for Rivalin, and he is thought to be on his deathbed from a wound, the governess believes she can safely leave this couple together unchaperoned. The disguise succeeds, Blancheflor's kisses bring herself and Rivalin back to life, the couple consummates their relationship, and Blancheflor conceives Tristan.

The nurse/governess is a frequent go-between in romances, and a remark in *Tristan* attests to her conventionality. When Blancheflor, frustrated in love and overcome by despair, laments her situation to her governess, the narrator points out how traditional her choice of helper is. She appeals to her governess, he says, "als sî ie tâten und noch tuont, / den ir dinc stât, als ez ir stuont" (1207–08) ["as those in her position have always done and still do today"] (56).

Cypriane and Delfin—*Florimont*

The principal complications of the governess/go-between role emerge with Cypriane, a much richer version of this figure, who appears in Aimon de Varennes' *Florimont* (1188).[34] She has been the governess of Romadanaple, princess of Macedonia, since the princess was five, but now the princess has fallen in love with a common soldier. Unlike Alexandrine, Melior's cousin, who does not hesitate to defy Melior's parents on her behalf in *William of Palerne*, Cypriane belongs to Romadanaple's parents' generation, and her loyalties are double and conflicting: to Romadanaple whom she loves, and to the king and queen whom she serves and whose point of view on loving she upholds and respects. Cypriane is conservative and commonsensical. She thinks of love as a social act consented to by responsible people who weigh many varied objectives in addition to their attraction to each other. When Romadanaple falls in love with a low-born man, Cypriane berates her to convince her to forget him, and when all else fails, she restrains the lovers as much as possible. Her sensible thinking and down-to-earth arguments strike an unusually realistic note for a romance.

Delfin, who helps her go between, is a unique figure in these romances. He is not a nobleman, knight, squire, tutor, or any of the other usual male go-betweens. He is a bourgeois: the richest merchant in the king's capital city and purveyor to his court. The fact that a romance like *Florimont* would include a bourgeois playing the role of the lover's go-between and best friend is impressive testimony to the importance and stature of merchants in late twelfth-century France. This merchant recognizes and participates in the customs of courtly society. Delfin and Cypriane, for instance, are a courtly couple, and Delfin's relationship with the hero, le Povre Perdu (the Poor Lost One—actually Florimont, son of the king of Albania), replicates the feelings between comrades-in-arms in other romances. When Delfin discovers Florimont lying in bed in agony, protesting that he will die of a pain around his heart for someone he refuses to name, the merchant realizes at once that he is in love and that the lady must be Romadanaple, and Delfin comforts Florimont and listens to his grief. When Delfin begs Florimont to forget Romadanaple, it is in the elegant love-language of wounds and poison. Delfin is attuned to courtly conventions, but his bourgeois status and professional identity are equally important for his role in this story. To bring these illicit lovers together, he and Cypriane must trick Romadanaple's family and court, and they do so with a trick like the one Blancheflor's nurse played. This trick, however, is bourgeois, and it depends on Delfin's position as merchant-purveyor.

Cypriane is triply obligated to keep Romadanaple from le Povre Perdu: by her position as governess and instructor in morality; by her love for Romadanaple herself; and by her duty to the king. King Philip, Romadanaple's father, has set up his daughter as a prize to be rationed out to victors, a few minutes at a time, and Cypriane supports his edict. When the king realized how beautiful his daughter was going to be, he prohibited any man from seeing her until the man had first served King Philip for three years, at which point the man would be rewarded with the sight of Romadanaple and a kiss, and would then leave their land immediately. Florimont has already broken through this prohibition twice. He and Romadanaple fell in love in the most romantic of fashions, sight-unseen, by reputation, but he twice used his excellence in battle to bargain for a moment with her.

Delfin and Cypriane are equally reluctant go-betweens. Both fear King Philip's terrible vengeance if he discovers that a man with neither lineage nor possessions loves his much-guarded only child, and they try to convince the lovers to forget each other. Cypriane belittles love's power and ridicules lovers' helplessness; commonsense and will power should put such feelings in their proper place, says Cypriane. Romadanaple must love her equal: " 'Plus bais de roi ou de conte / Ne poroies ameir sens honte' " (7625–26) ["You cannot love without shame anyone of lower rank than a king or a count"]. She must not choose " 'povrement / Povre home et de povre gent' " (7707–08) ["poorly, a poor man from a poor family"]. For Romadanaple, however, love is an irresistible force unrelated to worldly considerations; it cannot change an iota for any cause or in response to any pressure. She will love le Povre Perdu forever or she will die for him.

Delfin is as torn by divided loyalties as Cypriane, but when Florimont loses consciousness from desperate lovesickness, Delfin succumbs to the immediate need to save his life. As he begs the unconscious Florimont to respond to him, Delfin promises to help him love Romadanaple, though he is risking both their lives to do so. Once Delfin's and Cypriane's affection for these young people takes precedence over every other argument and they agree to arrange a meeting for them, Cypriane spells out precise limits for the sexual content of Romadanaple's hours with le Povre Perdu:

> "Mai plevir t'estuet et jurer:
> Se si le te puis amener,
> Que a toi ne ferait folie
> D'outraige ne de vilonie,
> Se je de riens t'en puis aidier,
> Fors d'acoler et de baissier." (8483–88)

> ["But you must promise and swear that if I am able to bring him to you, that he will not do anything foolish or excessive or dishonorable to you, or go any further than embracing and kissing, if I can be of any help to you in this."]

Cypriane has introduced into romantic love a significantly alien perspective in which consummated sex is "foolish," "excessive," and "dishonorable" for unmarried people.

Cypriane concocts the trick, Delfin carries it out, it is rich in merchant and purveyor details, and it is very dangerous for both go-betweens. They are risking not only their positions but also their lives themselves for this meeting. Delfin dresses le Povre Perdu in the old clothes of a poor tailor and has him carry needles, thread, and a very large pair of scissors for cutting cloth. The final touch is a roll of material that le Povre Perdu balances on his head. The material falls down in front of his face, concealing him from the many members of the court who would recognize him. Then, with the cutting and fitting of a new dress for the princess as their pretext, Delfin and le Povre Perdu proceed to try to spend the afternoon in Romadanaple's chambers.

Their plot courts disaster twice. First, Delfin and his "tailor" encounter
King Philip, who decides to have something made for himself from the
cloth covering Florimont's head. Just as the king is on the verge of unveiling
Florimont, Delfin convinces him to wait to see another more appropriate
piece that he has stored away for him. Delfin and Florimont resume their
progress only to confront the queen who is delighted that her daughter is
planning to have a new dress and who decides to oversee the cutting and
fitting herself. To buy time, Delfin insists the earth must be covered with
cloth before he will put down his precious material. Then, with all excuses
exhausted and Delfin and Florimont awaiting discovery and execution, a
messenger calls the queen to the bedside of the king who has suddenly been
taken ill. Finally, the door to Romadanaple's chamber closes on two couples.
    Initially, Cypriane's role in this scene seems clear; she has no part in it.
Aimon, the poet, subtracts her decisively: she "stayed back" with Delfin
(8929), and the love scene continues without her. She is reintroduced,
however, when the narrator discusses his lack of precise information about
the physical relationship between Florimont and Romadanaple:

> Mout ont baissié et acolé.
> Mai je ne sai por verité
> Se plus firent de lor voloir. (9129–31)

> [They kissed and embraced many times, but, truly, I do not know if they
> satisfied their desires any further.]

The restraining of this love has been Cypriane's concern since the moment
Romadanaple started thinking about le Povre Perdu. It is as if the question
"How much are the lovers loving?" prompts the poet to reintroduce the
character most closely associated with that issue. It was nearly evening, he
explains, and, after watching over the lovers from a distance without inter-
ruption, Cypriane went to their bed:

> "Damoisele, seu que doit
> Que vos avez si tant esté?
> Avez mon comant trespassé?"
> "Non, voir," fet ele, "bele mestre.
> Ovrez les dras, si vairez l'estre.
> Per foi, il ait ses braies mises;
> Andui avomes nos chemises." (9136–42)

> ["My lady, why have you been here so long? Have you broken my
> command?"
> "No, truly, dear governess," she [Romadanaple] replies. "Draw back the
> covers and you will see how things are. In faith, he has his breeches on and
> we both have on our chemises."]

Cypriane, at once the lovers' go-between and sexual guardian, cautions them to keep their desire for each other hidden and praises their restraint: " 'Car se la masons est fermee, / Dedens puet bien estre embrasee' " (9145–46) ["For if the house is closed up, it can still be on fire inside."] They must not act on their desire:

> "Damoisele, de vostre cors
> Ne faites pas tel vilonie
> Dont je por vos perde la vie." (9150–52)
>
> ["My lady, do not do anything so dishonorable with your body that I lose my life on your account."]

The unannounced subject of these lines is pregnancy, which would disgrace Romadanaple and condemn Cypriane to execution. There is a real world just outside the bedchamber of this romance, and consummated love risks consequences. With considerable anxiety, Cypriane tries to convince Romadanaple to get out of bed before she is discovered with Florimont: " 'Vuels nos tu toz livrer a mort?' " (9170) ["Do you want to have us all put to death?"]

No other go-between in these idealized episodes cautions the heroine against getting pregnant. As the voice of the everyday world, Cypriane frames Romadanaple and Florimont's love scene with realistic considerations and common sense just as Delfin grounds it in another social class's concerns with goods and commerce. Reluctant as both Cypriane and Delfin are, they are self-sacrificing and loving go-betweens.

Unlike the stories about going between in the service of lust, romances rarely appeal to voyeuristic interests. Romadanaple's and Florimont's afternoon in bed is the first scene with voyeuristic potential in these romance episodes. Melior and William make love during their garden tryst, but they are never on display as lovers. Alexandrine leaves to pick flowers and the audience follows her. Although Romadanaple's and Florimont's afternoon hugging and kissing in her bed is described, the account seems more nearly hearty, even factual, than sensual. The woman controls the lovemaking. As le Povre Perdu sits on the earth beside her bed, the action stops for nearly a hundred verses while wisdom and love debate in Romadanaple's heart whether she should marry such an inappropriate man. When love wins out, she draws Florimont to her, kisses him a hundred times, commands him to take off his borrowed tailor's helper's clothes and come into bed with her (9074–78), and Aimon describes them hugging and kissing, mouth to mouth. Since the scene is never told from the man's point of view, the audience is not tempted to enjoy the woman's body vicariously, and since the couple loves mutually, there is no aggression in the scene. Its lack of voyeuristic appeal, however, rests principally on choice of detail and tone.

Romadanaple's explanation for Cypriane of the underwear she and Florimont still have on at the close of that afternoon, for instance, is so mundane it is almost comic.

Like *William of Palerne*, and in accordance with late twelfth-century church concerns about the basis of marriage, the story of Romadanaple and Florimont idealizes consent, free choice, and mutual loving. It celebrates two young people striking out against parental and societal constraints to base their choice of mate on love. Both lovers choose daringly; Romadanaple is a forbidden love for le Povre Perdu, and when she decides she wants to marry him, she believes he is a common soldier whom she should never love. Romadanaple is as strong as her choice of lover would suggest. She shows no trace of the diffidence, humility, and reserve that diminish female speakers like Soredamors. Cypriane taught Romadanaple to read and write—unusual accomplishments for men in the twelfth century, and very unusual for women—and she is outspoken, direct, insistent, and determined. In her interactions with Florimont, she is as strong a speaker as he is. Nevertheless, despite Romadanaple's personal strength, by making one look at her and one kiss the prize for three years of martial service, her father has turned her into a trophy, a payoff. The point of this plot twist is to emphasize how extraordinarily beautiful Romadanaple is. But the king's edict reifies Romadanaple; it leaves her as an object to be viewed, kissed, but never courted. And since she must be kept from the sight of men, she lives shut away in her palace chambers. By means of Cypriane and Delfin, Romadanaple breaks through this structure.

Having raised these serious issues about daughters and the misuse of parental control, *Florimont* proceeds to dodge them. Once Romadanaple's father discovers that le Povre Perdu, his most valuable warrior, is heir to the king of Albania, with considerable trepidation as to how his daughter will take to the idea, he concludes that this is the man she should marry. Ably as *Florimont* maneuvers around its central problem, however, it remains fundamentally a story about a locked-up woman trying to break out of her cage. Much as exploring issues of misused parental control may have engaged *Florimont's* romance audience, when they listened to a story about a beautiful heroine, they wanted her at once strong and successfully constrained.

Herland—*Romance of Horn*

Of all the go-betweens of romance, only Herland, in the Anglo-Norman *Romance of Horn* (c. 1170),[35] is bribed into going between. A bribed go-between evokes the fabliaux and Latin comedies in which hired intermediaries trap women for sex. Romance go-betweens ordinarily act out of loyalty, devotion, friendship, sympathy, or love. Like Cypriane and Delfin, their love for the young people is so great that they put aside their own personal and professional concerns to help them become a couple. The usual structure of who goes between for whom and why in an idealized story breaks down in the *Romance of Horn*. Herland, the bribed go-between, has no special attachment to the young woman he goes between for. His attachment is to Horn, a young squire, but he goes between for Rigmel, a princess who has fallen in love with Horn. Herland is Horn's tutor and the king's seneschal. All his loyalty and ancient ties are to the men, not the woman. Instead of counseling supportively as Guinevere does with Soredamors and Alexander, or Alexandrine with William and Melior, or Galehot with Lancelot, this go-between struggles to keep from going between. Finally, as the princess looks forward to her first meeting with Horn, Herland deals with his fear of compromising Horn and his guilt for acting against the king's wishes by substituting another young man and pretending that he is Horn.

Since a bribed go-between is such a major break in structure for the go-between's relationship to the couple, one would expect this romance to stress the impact of the princess's gifts on Herland. The compromising of Herland, however, is neither emphasized nor explored. Instead, the gift-giving scene, a truly courtly extravaganza, is presented as testimony to Rigmel's vast wealth, to Horn's extraordinary worth to her, and to her conception of the difficulty of convincing a member of the court to introduce her to Horn. Herland's bribing is submerged in the scene's lavishness.

When Rigmel summons Herland, she acts as if she were receiving a prospective lover. She does not tell him why she wants him to come, and the news that he is on his way inspires her to arrange her clothing, check her appearance in the mirror, ask her ladies-in-waiting how she looks, and create an intimate atmosphere for the two of them in her rush-strewn chamber. She speaks to him "dulcement, par amur" [sweetly and lovingly], serves him ancient wines fit for a prince, and claims to care about him:

"'Beau sire seneschal,   mut ad grant tens passé / Ke vus ai mult forment   en mun quoer enamé.' " (538–39)["Fair lord Seneschal, for a long time past my heart has been full of affection for you."]. As the moment to tell him what she wants of him approaches, she stresses how close they will become: " '[D]es or m'estrez privé / Plus que nul ki onc fust   encor(e) de mere né.' " (555–56) ["From now on you will be more intimate with me than any other man who was ever born."] Then, to the accompaniment of the seneschal's exclamations of indebtedness and amazement, and his offers of service, Rigmel lavishes a crescendo of amazing gifts on him.

Rigmel's gifts are immensely valuable and associated with far away lands and fabled times, beginning with a heavy gold ring forged in the biblical Daniel's age and ornamented with a sapphire worth a castle. She and

Herland drink a friendship pact with the king's best wine in an enormous gold cup, so beautifully engraved, by techniques descended from King Solomon of Israel, that it is matchless, and Rigmel presents the cup as a gift to Herland. The head groom next leads in by a golden bit a more beautiful horse than could be found in sixty cities. Two greyhounds come next, raised in the palace by the princess. They are white as swans and swift as falcons, and their golden collars are engraved and studded all over with jewels, like precious bracelets. Even their leashes are made of beautifully worked silver. Rigmel's final gift is a goshawk that she herself has brought through the seventh mewing. It is unequaled from here to Spain, she tells Herland, and a better bird than any other knight carries. Now, at last, after gifts that should ransom a prince, Rigmel is ready to ask to see Horn. When Herland protests at the magnitude of her gifts, she replies that all would be repaid if only he would bring Horn to her. He promises to bring him the next day.

Huge as Herland's payoff is, the going between that he is asked to perform is simple and unexceptional. He does not have to save anyone from death, like Alexandrine with William and Melior, or play tricks, like Cypriane and Delfin who disguise Florimont as a tailor's helper, or like Blancheflor's nurse who dresses her up as a beggar woman. He is not asked to pressure or deceive the other person as the go-betweens of the stories of lust and sexual conquest do. All Rigmel wants from Herland is that he bring Horn to her chambers. Herland, however, sees facilitating a meeting between the princess and a man, without the king's blessing, as a dangerous and disloyal act. An unapproved match will disgrace him and Horn and dishonor Rigmel, Herland decides, and he broods over the irresponsibility of women in love. A woman falls madly in love when she sees a handsome young man and she will not leave him for anyone or anything, neither friend nor relative, no matter who is hurt. Punishment is futile. Beat a woman for loving and she will love the man that much more strongly (681–89).

Like Romadanaple with Florimont, Rigmel has fallen in love with Horn from his reputation alone. Since she has never seen him, Herland finally decides to test Rigmel's intentions by substituting Haderof, the second most handsome man in the kingdom. Rigmel welcomes Haderof lovingly before she realizes he is not Horn, and she is livid with Herland for tricking her and mortified that he would imagine her unchaste. She is so angry that she wants him dragged to death behind a horse. Herland fears the king, but he fears this raging princess even more, and, hearing the deadly hatred in her voice, he silences Rigmel's tirade by swearing to bring Horn the next day.

A major part of Horn's fame derives from how desirable he is. Repeatedly, the women of the court discuss how much they wish he were their lover. One night Rigmel, tossing and turning from lovesickness, awakens Herselot, her confidante, to talk about Horn:

"Lee serreit ki l'avreit   suz covertur martrin.
Deu le me dunt encore   e li bier saint Martin!
Pas ne·l chaungereië   pur nul rei palaïn." (726–28)

["Happy the woman who had him under a coverlet of marten pelts! May God and the noble St. Martin give him to me! I wouldn't trade him for any sovereign king."]

When Herselot sees Horn for the first time, she returns to describe him for her lady. After explaining that this angelic young man is so handsome that no queen or countess could resist him, Herselot tells Rigmel that she thinks she should have sex with Horn, and then announces that she herself wishes Horn would rape her:

"Plust a Deu ke de mei   oüst faite ravine
E mei oust sul a sul   en chambre u en gaudine!
Joe fereië sun boen   par sainte Katherine.
Ja ne·l savreit par mei   parente ne cosine." (966–69)

["Would to God he had raped me and had had me alone with him in a chamber or in woodland! I would do his will, by St. Katherine! No kinswoman or cousin would know about it from me."]

And this is a duke's protected young daughter who is savoring the hope of being raped. Rigmel calls Herselot a fool and tells her to be quiet. Rigmel will possess Horn herself, God willing!

Herland accompanies Horn to his first meeting with Rigmel. When Rigmel's household sees Horn, he is so extraordinarily handsome that his beauty fills her rooms with splendor and everyone thinks an angel has come to visit her. Horn and Herland enter hand in hand, and Rigmel's first response as she recovers from the shock of seeing Horn is to promise more gifts to Herland and then to try to detach him from Horn. She sends Herland across the room to keep company with her ladies-in-waiting and invites Horn to stay with her, but Horn is not equally ready to let go of Herland, and he reminds Rigmel that Herland has long been his guardian and teacher. " 'Tuz les biens ke ioe sai   m'ad il endoctriné' " (1073) ["Everything good I know I've learned from him"], Horn tells her, explaining that Herland brought him to her and he now must follow Herland's advice. Power and social class are the immediate issues. Herland tells Horn to love Rigmel. He should grant Rigmel whatever she wants, " 'Kar n'ad taunt franche rein   entre Rome e Paris' " (1082) ["for there's no woman so noble between Rome and Paris"]. If only Horn had already reconquered his own country and reinstated himself as its rightful king, Herland continues, he would immediately advise King Hunlaf to marry the two of them. Rigmel describes the fine position Herland would hold in such a kingdom, smothered with gifts and as honored as any count, duke, or marquis.

Despite Rigmel's openly desiring comments about Horn in her conversation with her lady-in-waiting, once Horn himself takes charge of this couple's relationship, they discuss marriage and only marriage. Horn's requirements are social and political, his improvement in stature and rank to equal Rigmel's. Horn, an orphan, protests that he cannot accept the love Rigmel offers him until he is knighted, accomplished, and worthy of her in every way. Some 3,500 lines later, after adventures, rescues, and escapes, they finally marry, only to have Rigmel stolen from Horn once again before they can settle down to long overdue prosperity. After this meeting in Rigmel's apartments, however, this couple no longer needs a go-between.

Like Romadanaple, Rigmel is a locked-up woman asserting herself in the one way open to her, given her extremely constricted situation. As Judith Weiss points out, discussing the wooing women who appear in six Anglo-Norman romances, Rigmel has neither a mother nor a sister and, despite her royal wealth, lives "in her chambers isolated from the real centre of activity."[36] Her attendants can emerge into public rooms where they can see Horn, but she cannot. Florimont and Romadanaple fall in love mutually, sight unseen, but there is no indication that Horn loved Rigmel before they met. It is Rigmel who must court Horn. When she asserts herself so imperiously to bribe Herland into bringing Horn to her, she is performing the one risky, significant action she can perform by choosing the man she will love.

Rigmel is strong, outspoken, insistent, clever, and passionate. And like so many of these romance heroines, she chooses her man because she loves him, without regard to power and wealth. The poem stresses how much women desire Horn, Rigmel admits her passionate desire to Herselot, and Herland fears Rigmel's irresponsible passion. Weiss describes the poet's conception of women "in the main as creatures of ungoverned appetite."[37] On the other hand, Rigmel is outraged at the idea that she is not chaste, and what Herland considers irresponsible passion sounds like the daring commitment the other romances admire in their heroes and heroines who choose each other for love alone, despite parental anger and difference in fortune. Herland condemns women for refusing to give up the men they love when their love harms a friend or relative, and for loving all the more if they are beaten for loving, but Rigmel's loving, as Herland describes it here, is the kind of love that reappears in romance after romance, shared by men and women alike.

Despite Rigmel's glorious gifts for Herland and her imperious manner with her ladies-in-waiting, she is a needy figure, physically constrained, desperate for Horn's love, and unable to do more than beg him to accept her love. Passionate as this princess is, it seems unlikely that she would have empowered twelfth-century female audiences.

Glorizia—Boccaccio's *Filocolo*

Giovanni Boccaccio's *Filocolo* (c.1336–38),[38] a prose romance in Italian which he wrote early in his career, dates from approximately a century and a half after the *Romance of Horn* and Aimon de Varennes' *Florimont*, and it treats the representation of desire strikingly differently. Herland has no part in a love scene in *Horn* because at this point in the story Horn is too unequal to Rigmel to kiss or embrace her. *Florimont* contains an extensive bedroom love scene, presided over by Cypriane, but the scene is notably unerotic. Boccaccio, on the other hand, creates a love scene that is unabashedly sensual, reads like the prelude to a rape, and seems deliberately designed for the pleasure of voyeurs. To protect the meaning of the scene as consensual love, he makes elaborate use of a nurse/governess go-between. The situation is as sexually exploitative as any pre-rape sequence in a story of lust and sexual conquest—a young man awakens a woman by making love to her. The reader follows the man as, naked, he enters the sleeping woman's bed, embraces her, kisses her a hundred times, pulls back the bed curtains to look at her naked body, kisses and strokes her breasts, and caresses her genitals.[39] In context, however, this apparent prelude to a rape cannot be one because Boccaccio embeds the episode in dramatizations of the woman's enthusiastic consent. As every reader knows by this point in the story, the woman is as full of longing for the man as he is for her.

Florio, the hero, is the son of the king of Spain, but Biancifiore, the heroine, is an orphan of unknown birth. Like William with Melior, she is brought up with Florio until his royal parents discover that the young people have fallen in love and Florio wants to marry her. They then sell her into slavery, and Glorizia, who nursed and raised Biancifiore, accompanies her. Biancifiore is purchased for a harem and imprisoned in a tower of virgins guarded by eunuchs. Florio heroically ascends the tower concealed in a chest full of flowers, and Glorizia finds and hides him. Throughout the day she creates situations in which Biancifiore talks about loving Florio while he overhears her, and in the evening Glorizia hides him behind Biancifiore's bedcurtains where he listens to more discussions of love between the two women as they prepare for sleep. Glorizia's gentle, affectionate questions and suggestions help Biancifiore attest to how very much she loves Florio, and since Florio hears her declarations of love and confessions of desire, although she has no idea that he is present, her conversation with her nurse renews her emotional intimacy with him. Glorizia's questions for Biancifiore establish beyond any doubt the young woman's consent to this night of love. Not only is Florio the only man she loves, Biancifiore swears, she begs the gods to protect her from caring about anyone but Florio, and pledges that her soul will remain his even after death. Through Glorizia, Boccaccio has Biancifiore consent beforehand to Florio's caresses; her vows are the emotional context for his lovemaking to her as she sleeps. When he awakens her, she is dreaming about being embraced by him, and before they consummate their love, they swear marriage vows in front of a statue of Cupid and bring Glorizia to celebrate their joy with them. Biancifiore both is and is not passive in loving. Vulnerable as she is, she is dreaming of reunion with the lover who is embracing her, and part of the voluptuousness of the scene evolves from anticipation of their subsequent ecstatic loving.

The *Filocolo* is another romance about commitment. Florio abandons family and future kingdom to comb the world for his lost Biancifiore, and the two of them risk death at the stake to sleep in each other's arms. The admiral who owns the tower of virgins discovers them together in bed and only the intervention of the gods saves their lives. As with so many of these romances, the couple ultimately turns out to be evenly matched; Biancifiore is an emperor's daughter.

Although Glorizia and Cypriane, from *Florimont*, are both nurse/governesses, Glorizia's relationship to the lovers is quite unlike Cypriane's. Since Florio's parents have wronged the young people so egregiously by selling Biancifiore into slavery, Glorizia has no divided loyalties and never advises restraint or hesitates to help the couple love. She does not even intervene when they risk death by continuing in bed together. Unlike in *Florimont*, no real world encroaches on this romance. It is purely sensational, with the sexual threat of the harem hanging over Biancifiore, and gods who rescue the lovers when they are about to be burned at the stake. These are embattled lovers, not a couple working out a complex relationship like Romadanaple's with her Povre Perdu, or Rigmel's with Horn. The complications for Biancifiore's and Florio's relationship are all external, and Glorizia is their accomplice who celebrates their love with them, not an older woman who, like Cypriane, counsels sensible behavior.

Pity—René d'Anjou's *Le Livre du cuer d'amours*

One final idealized story about a conventionally supportive go-between illustrates this tradition's deliberate rejection of the go-betweens of the stories of sexual conquest. *Le Livre du cuer d'amours* [The Book of the Heart of Love], a mixture of poetry and prose written by King René d'Anjou in 1457,[40] allegorizes a courtship. The young man, allegorized as Heart, deals with Fear, Shame, Jealousy, Refusal, and so forth; his companions-in-arms are Desire and Generosity; the young woman is allegorized as Sweet Mercy, and Heart's go-between is Pity, a wise old nun who is the abbess of the Hospital of Love. She leads Heart through the stages of a responsible courtship, instructing him how to behave with Refusal, Standoffishness, and the Slanderers, and she herself pays a visit to Sweet Mercy to praise Heart and his exploits. In the final episodes of the allegory, it is Pity, Heart's go-between, who leads the way for Love's court's offensive against the Manor of Rebellion (175). Pity reassures Sweet Mercy that she must not fear going to the Castle of Pleasure with Heart because Honor is there with Love (190). Allegorical though she is, then, Pity is an ordinary go-between in the service of idealized love. She counsels the young man about loving, argues his case with the young woman, and then encourages them both as their relationship progresses.

What makes this relentlessly conventional allegory of interest is that King René used the *Roman de la rose* as one of his models,[41] and yet no trace appears of La Vieille, the *Roman*'s retired prostitute go-between who revels in the crowds of men who once flocked to her bedroom, and who counsels Fair Welcoming to fleece his lovers down to their last penny. For La Vieille, King René substitutes his wise old nun and successful abbess who supports both the man and the woman in their attempt to find a respectable, honorable love. Pity is a comfortable, unchallenging figure, and her going between protects the high tone of King René's allegory. There is no place for a go-between for lust and sexual conquest in a work like his, and he turns his back firmly on the *Roman*'s La Vieille.

From Guinevere in *Cligés* to René d'Anjou's Pity, the role of these conventional supportive go-betweens is to dramatize the power of love and the suffering of lovers. Their going between puts love on display, whether it is the immobilized loving of Soredamors and Alexander, William and Melior, and Lancelot, or the daring loving of Blancheflor, Florimont, and Florio, determined to reach their loves no matter what they risk to do so. All these lovers love independent of their go-betweens' efforts; none of these go-betweens pressure the lovers to love. When the go-betweens play tricks, they direct them against the disapproving parents and society surrounding the young people, never at one of the couple. The sole exception to this generalization is Herland's substitution of Haderof for Horn, but Herland is trying to slow down the relationship between Rigmel and Horn, not trap someone into having sex as in the stories of lust and sexual conquest. The devoted and often self-sacrificing women and men who go between in these episodes act exclusively for lovers who consent to love each other and who are nearly all already passionately in love.

Go-Betweens Who Intervene

Unlike these nine conventional go-betweens who support or facilitate loving for men and women who love each other, five unconventional romance go-betweens intervene significantly in the couples' relationships. Their going between is more intimate than conventional going between, and their intervention often raises disturbing ethical issues. To make the couple's relationship possible, they force them to change their feelings or rethink their conceptions, or they persuade them to recognize their own needs or the other person's needs. One of these go-betweens tricks a woman—not the woman's court or her family but the woman herself—into promising to love. Another go-between kisses and embraces the woman his friend loves and wants to marry. A third go-between tries to force a chaste wife to commit adultery. The conventional idealized go-betweens work within clear limits, smoothing love's progress, helping lovers acknowledge that they love, sustaining them through initial meetings, deceiving their families so they can be together, and so forth. But they do not reshape the lovers' feelings for each other. These five unconventional go-betweens instead exceed so greatly the acceptable limits of conventional going between that they bring to the fore the dangers of having a third person interfere in a love relationship. Like the conventional idealized go-betweens, they deal only with consensual relationships, but within that agenda, they force the hazards of going between to surface for testing.

Guinevere—The Prose *Lancelot*

In the most extreme act of going between in all these stories from romances, the man and woman do not love each other at all when their go-between unites them. There is no indication that they are even special friends. Nevertheless, when the go-between asks them to become a loving couple, they agree to do so. The go-between is Queen Guinevere once again, this time in The Prose *Lancelot*, and the couple is the Lady of Malohaut, Guinevere's confidante, and Galehot, Lancelot's comrade-in-arms who goes between for Lancelot and Guinevere and dies from his love for Lancelot. Guinevere asks Galehot if he is willing to love as she directs, since she loved as he directed. She is reminding him of the scene in the meadow when he spoke for Lancelot, overcome by love. Galehot gallantly tells Guinevere that she may do with him as she wishes, " 'et de mon cors et de mon cuer' " (353) ["both with my body and with my heart"]. She then suggests that he love the Lady of Malohaut. Guinevere praises the Lady of Malohaut briefly, but her real attraction derives from her relationship to Guinevere, as the queen spells out for Galehot. When he and Lancelot are in foreign lands together, she tells him, they will be able to lament together, while she and her lady will comfort each other and share their joys. Guinevere then has this new couple take formal vows to love each other as true lover and lady, "et de cuer et de cors" [with body and soul], they kiss at her request, and that evening all four of them, Guinevere and Lancelot and the Lady of Malohaut and Galehot, talk together in the meadow (352–55).

It does not matter that Galehot and the Lady of Malohaut are not emotionally involved when they agree to love each other because only their parallel relationships to Lancelot and Guinevere are important to them. Their union has nothing to do with personal attraction. Its one basis is their love of Lancelot and Guinevere. When the Lady of Malohaut first becomes Guinevere's confidante, she promises, " 'Ge ferai qanque vos voudroiz outreement por si haute compaignie avoir' " (351) ["I will do whatever you wish, unreservedly, to have such a noble companion"], and Galehot subordinates himself to Lancelot's needs from the moment he first sees Lancelot. Galehot and the Lady of Malohaut consummate their relationship the same night that Lancelot and Guinevere consummate theirs, and Galehot is engaged to marry the Lady of Malohaut at the time of his death, but their feelings for each other are never discussed and they are never portrayed significantly as a couple.

Galehot and the Lady of Malohaut both consent to their alliance. Guinevere is not tricking or forcing one of them, or using one of the couple to satisfy the desires of the other one. On the other hand, this relationship is certainly not based on romantic love. It is the equivalent of the medieval arranged marriage. Like a couple marrying to unite two noble households, these two accept the queen's request that they love each other for reasons that have nothing to do with satisfying their own desires.

The person of power in this episode is Guinevere, just as she was when she went between for Soredamors and Alexander in *Cligés*. There she was wise, perceptive, and effective. Here, instead, her power expresses her stature rather than specific personal strengths. As Lancelot's lady and a beautiful, noble queen with a confidante who shares her life, she can tell these two people to love each other and they will. Would Guinevere's role in this episode be empowering for a medieval woman? Perhaps, to a limited degree. Arranging a relationship is a function typically reserved for fathers. On the other hand, instead of negotiating an alliance involving lands and possessions, Guinevere exercises her power only within woman's social and emotional sphere.

Urake—*Partonope of Blois*

Urake, who goes between in *Partonopeu de Blois*,[42] a late-twelfth-century Old French romance, tests painfully and dramatically the dangers of a third person's involvement in a love relationship. She is essential for this couple. Although they were lovers in the past, they have broken apart, and their situation is so greatly altered that for them to love again the man must mature and the woman must change her feelings about him and her way of relating to him. Through aggressive intervention with both the man and the woman, Urake helps them forge a new relationship. In the process, however, she becomes so caught up in the drama of controlling their lives that she very nearly destroys the marriage she is working so hard to build.

Partonopeu de Blois was very popular, Anthime Fourrier ranks it with the *Tristan* and *Grail* stories in popularity,[43] and there are many versions in several languages.[44] The Middle English version, *Partonope of Blois*,[45] which the *Middle English Dictionary* dates c.1450, is a close adaptation of the Old French romance and gives Urake the same role she had in the original. As with *William of Palerne*, I will substitute the Middle English translation for the Old French original to suggest the Middle English go-between tradition.

Urake goes between for her sister Melior, the magical queen of Chef d'Oire and empress of Byzantium. Melior's magic depends upon her never being seen. At night, in an unlighted room, she makes love with Partonope, future Earl of Blois and nephew of the king of France, but she is invisible during the day. Since the members of her court are similarly enchanted and invisible to Partonope, he lives in what seems to be an empty castle and is waited on and loved in isolation. After two years of this life, Partonope shines an enchanted lantern on his lover, discovering the fairest woman ever born, but his lack of faith destroys Melior's magic and suddenly she, he, and her court become visible to each other. Melior denounces and reviles him, leaving him so sick at heart that he looks forward to dying at the hands of her lords, who will avenge her lost honor when they find him in bed with her. It is at this point that Urake begins going between.

Urake first tries to preserve this couple's love straightforwardly. Melior's other attendants are mortified at the sight of Melior in bed with Partonope, but Urake draws the obvious conclusion: " 'Thys man ye loue, we all well se' " (6198) ["We all see perfectly well that you love this man"]. And she tells Melior to marry this very appropriate choice of hers: wise, manly, and handsomer than anyone from India to Chef d'Oire. Although Melior is too furious to listen to Urake's good sense, Urake saves Partonope's life by leading him through a crowd of menacing knights and squires to the ship that will take him back to Blois.

Urake saves Partonope from death again a year later when she discovers him in the Ardennes forest eating roots and grass and hoping a wild animal will kill him to prevent his suicide. Grief, guilt, and his conviction of worthlessness have left him so haggard that Urake does not know who he is, and so full of shame that the only name he admits to is "traytour" (7367). When he realizes he is with Melior's sister, he faints, and Urake recognizes and embraces him. She sees he is dying, but none of her efforts to save him have any effect until she lies to him. She claims to be Melior's emissary and to have been combing France seeking him because her sister has forgiven him and wants him to be " 'Hir love, hir lorde, hir souerayngne' " (7422) ["Her love, her husband, her sovereign"]. Partonope does not believe Urake until she describes Melior's "gentilnesse" that could not let him suffer long. Then, word tumbling over word in his elation, he praises his lady's kind heart, " 'full of pite and rouþe' " ["full of pity and compassion"], and he recovers (7469).

Urake does not change Partonope's nature or restructure his feelings for Melior. Once Urake convinces him that Melior has forgiven him, his life is saved and Urake can nurse him back to health, from a skeleton too weak to walk to the strong, handsome young man that Melior first loved. The lye Urake uses to rejuvenate his prematurely gray hair and the herb baths and good food she provides are incidental to the healing process. Her effective medicine is love letters she forges from Melior.

Urake heals Partonope with a single lie: Melior has forgiven him. The fantasy Urake creates for him of a gentle-hearted, merciful, loving Melior matches his image of her, and all he needs to become himself again is time and faith in Melior's love. For Melior, on the other hand, no such easy coincidence of fiction, reality, and ideal is possible because Melior's ideal relationship with Partonope is irrecoverable. When they were lovers in her magical castle, he was completely in her power. She chose him, acquired him, and kept him. She fell in love with him when she heard that he was the handsomest young man of his time, and she brought him to her by luring him by magic into a ship which then, without a crew, sailed to her land. In her empty castle, torches carried by invisible hands led him to her sumptuous bedroom, and in the middle of the night, Melior, naked, joined him in bed. Throughout their relationship, she remained the mysterious, magical queen he could never see, and he was a powerless dependent living luxuriously in her kingdom and at her pleasure. In the relationship she chose for him, Partonope was Melior's kept lover, not her husband, and while she had promised that she would become visible and marry him after two-and-a-half years, that marriage too would have been entirely on her terms.

Urake must transform Melior to function in a new reality. To love without magic, Melior must learn to accept a lover with independent power, to imagine life from another person's point of view, and to risk herself in emotional commitment to a person she cannot control. To prepare for all these, she must learn to forgive Partonope. Urake is the vehicle for these profound changes. She torments Melior into becoming a woman who can love in a world she no longer controls. This love story works itself out not between the lady and her lover, but between the lady and her go-between.

To break down Melior's pride and force her to recognize her own feelings and needs, Urake attacks her with lies. Urake had left Melior's kingdom in outrage a year earlier when Melior ignored her pleas to forgive Partonope. Now Melior summons her sister to her aid. To force Melior to marry, her nobles have announced a three-day tournament with their queen as prize. Judges will select the tournament winners, and Melior will be required to choose one of them as her husband. When the first of these conversations begins, Melior remains furious with Partonope despite her misery over losing him. In fact, Partonope is on Urake's island in excellent health, but Urake describes him as she first found him, near death in the Ardennes forest, insane, running in the woods like a wild animal, neither eating, drinking, nor sleeping. Before Melior lured him to Chef d'Oire, Urake reminds her, Partonope was a happy, successful young man, living on his lands in France. It is Melior's love that has reduced him to such a pitiful state. Urake pressures Melior to rethink her love affair from Partonope's point of view. His great betrayal, which she resents so implacably, was a reasonable response to an unreasonable situation (7896–905). What was treasonable about wanting to see the woman he loves?, Urake asks. Clearly, Partonope loved Melior far better than she ever loved him. As Melior protests again and again her love for Partonope and her resolve to love only him, Urake insists that the situation is beyond all help since Melior must take the tournament winner as her husband. At the close of this conversation, when " 'Of nought it serveth all my repentyng!' " (8240) ["All my repenting is useless!"], Melior forgives Partonope completely and accepts her responsibility for their situation. Nevertheless, Urake persists relentlessly, summarizing all the worst aspects of Melior's situation. Partonope, reduced to madness, will not be at the tournament; Melior can no longer choose her own husband; much as it may pain her, Melior must give her heart to the man the judges choose: " 'They shull chese, but ye moste love' "(8259) ["They shall choose, but you must love"]. By deceiving Melior about Partonope's condition, Urake forces her sister to experience how deeply she loves him, how much she wants to forgive him and needs to be forgiven by him, and her responsibility for the pain they are both suffering.

When Melior and Urake meet next, Urake intensifies the seriousness of her lies, pushing her sister to suicide threats. Her pitiless treatment is in response to a Melior quite unlike even the repentant Melior of their previous conversation. This time Melior is bemoaning her pride and her merciless reviling of Partonope, and she wishes she had died when she sent him away. Urake's final blow is to announce that Partonope is dead. Melior faints, but before she faints she takes responsibility for Partonope's death and swears to kill herself rather than marry anyone else. Melior is no longer a controlling figure. She is a woman so overpowered by love that only the man she loves makes her life worth living. Emotionally, Melior is now as subdued by guilt, despair, and love as Partonope was when Urake rescued him in the forest. Urake, the lying go-between, has succeeded in reducing the dominating, all-powerful woman of that couple to beneath the level of the man who will now assume power over her, and the narrator of *Partonope* bursts in to denounce Urake: "Lorde God! what herte hadde she?" (8669) [Good Lord! What kind of heart did she have?].

Urake has orchestrated a grand finale for this story, and it features a dramatic role for herself. After Melior has given up all hope, Urake will bring Partonope to win the tournament and be awarded Melior as his prize and his bride. For Urake, controlling other people's lives has taken precedence over helping lovers love. But chance overturns Urake's plans. Partonope mysteriously disappears, taken prisoner while out on a pleasure trip, and Urake must sail to the tournament for Melior's hand without her champion. This is the price Urake pays for having driven Melior to swoons and suicide vows. Urake is overwhelmed by grief and repentance, and she sees herself as guilty of the final destruction of the love of Partonope and Melior through Melior's forced marriage to another man. Partonope is absent from the lists because Urake lied so much longer than was necessary.

The real change this episode dramatizes, however, is Urake's loss of power. Since her first introduction, she has taken charge of Partonope and Melior. She fed and nursed Partonope and saved him twice from death, and she tormented Melior into a new sense of herself and her lover. But now Partonope is regaining control of his life and his relationship with Melior. He maneuvers his way out of prison and comes to the tournament as the Knight of the Silver Shield, a mysterious challenger unknown to them all, even to Urake. At last, going between yields place to courtship and marriage.

Urake never explains why she lied to Melior for so long, but with the decision about the winner of the tournament still in doubt, Urake realizes that the Knight of the Silver Shield who is fighting so brilliantly must be Partonope, and she tells Melior the true story of Partonope's recovery and disappearance. A single couplet suggests that Urake's conscience is hurting her. She "thought þo she wolde tell euery dele, / For to hir suster she had not quytte hir wele." (10216–17) [thought she would tell her sister everything because she had not done well by her].

After repeated brushes with disaster, the judges finally agree that Partonope should become the new king of Chef d'Oire and Melior's husband. He is no longer simply a handsome young man chosen as her lover by a magical queen. He has become a knight who has won his wife in tournament against the most powerful princes of his time and according to the conditions established by the most important people in his wife's kingdom. And his wife has grown into a woman willing to love a man with power and identity of his own.

Urake is unique. No other go-between in these idealized stories intervenes in lovers' lives to the degree Urake does. She manipulates Partonope and Melior and takes control of them until she becomes so involved in her own scheme for the renewal of their relationship that she nearly destroys them as a couple. Her lie to Partonope simply inspires him to heal, but the suffering she subjects Melior to catalyzes major changes in her nature. Urake forces her to give up her exclusively dominant role in her relationship with Partonope and to accept him as an independent person. No other idealized go-between restructures the lovers' way of relating to each other as Urake reshapes her sister's relationship with Partonope.

More than any other romance, *Partonope* explores the dangers of going between. When Urake lies to Partonope to save his life and to Melior to make the lie to Partonope a truth, she exercises perilous power. She is not merely uniting lovers as conventional go-betweens do; she is making critical decisions about what their lives should be like and how they should lead them, in particular about what kind of person her sister should become. Finally, when Urake conceals Partonope's recovery, she falls prey to the temptation of orchestrating a significant episode in other people's lives, and she fails. The Old French *Partonopeus* poet took a hard look at the privileged position of the romance go-between who stands between two people, armed, for better or worse, with truths about them and their feelings that the other member of the couple does not know.

The woman of power in *Partonope*, however, is Melior, not Urake. As the poem begins, Melior is so sexually self-assured that once she chooses the man she wants, she straightforwardly imports him into her bed. The temptation is to argue that she retains this self-confidence and power as the romance progresses. Matilda Bruckner, for instance, contends that "What we may observe in *Partonopeu* is not just a shift from female to male in the balance of power, but rather a dynamic interplay between the two."[46] But as Urake breaks down Melior into a guilt-ridden, suicidal, despairing woman in love, and as Melior waits in her tower to see whom the men of her land are going to make her marry while Partonope rides in triumph in the bride-winning tournament to win the right to be Melior's husband, it is hard to imagine that this poem is not about a shift in power along conventional gender lines. The man begins powerless and dominated but wins power; the woman begins powerful and dominating but gives up power. Melior grows into acceptance of her lost control of Partonope, and a conventional marriage ensues.

Lunete—Chrétien de Troyes' *Yvain*

Chrétien de Troyes' *Yvain (Le Chevalier au lion—The Knight of the Lion)* (*c.* 1177–81)[47] is paradoxical, ironic, oblique, and populated by characters who can be read in opposed ways. Lunete, its go-between, is ambiguous, like the rest of the major characters, and can only be understood through her relationship to two other highly equivocal figures, the knight, Yvain, and his lady, Laudine. At first glance, Yvain appears to be an idealized romantic lover, the central figure of a courtly love story like Soredamors's and Alexander's, or William's and Melior's. He falls wildly in love at first sight, suffers extravagantly, risks death to remain where he can feast his eyes on his lady, and goes mad and runs naked in a forest, starving, when he realizes he has broken faith with her. Nevertheless, despite Yvain's stylized courtly passion, important factors suggest that he is not very deeply in love, or at least that many aspects of life take precedence over love for him. He leaves his wife a week after they marry, promises to return in a year, and then forgets her altogether. Moreover, his emotional interactions with his lion occupy more of the story than similar encounters with his wife.[48] Stephen Knight, who sees in Yvain a landless young man out to marry a propertied widow, dismisses love as "one of the major euphemising and legitimising elements in this and other romances," a cover-up for the real motivations of Yvain, "the upwardly mobile travelling murderer."[49] Yvain, then, both is and is not an idealized courtly lover.

Laudine too can be read as an idealized lady of romance. Chrétien occasionally writes as if she loves Yvain, and Philippe Ménard[50] and A.R. Press[51] claim that she falls passionately in love with Yvain before their marriage. There are strong indications, however, that Laudine marries out of political necessity, not love. Robert Hanning writes of Laudine's "coolness" toward Yvain,[52] and Joan M. Ferrante, discussing the "emptiness of the fantasies of honor and love, which the hero pursues," sees Laudine marrying Yvain because she needs "a knight to defend her land."[53] Laudine's land is magically vulnerable to attack by a single knight. When a challenger spills enchanted spring water on an emerald in the forest that surrounds her principal city, his action provokes a tremendous thunderstorm, wind and lightening tear at the forest, and rain, snow, and hail pelt down at the same time. The storm is considered an attack on Laudine's domain, and she must have a champion to answer these challenges or she will lose her land. Since Yvain defeats and kills her protector-husband, she must have a new champion. She marries Yvain to defend her spring and many indications suggest that that is her exclusive reason for marrying him: she agrees to the marriage before ever having seen him; before their marriage she shows no interest in his personal qualities, only his martial prowess; and throughout the romance, few verses deal with her feelings for him.

Tony Hunt describes *Yvain* as "allusive and critical, rather than affirmative and explicit,"[54] and Lunete concocts and engineers the two episodes that undercut most decisively the story's romance affirmations: the beginning of the love relationship and its resumption. She goes between aggressively in both these episodes, and the meaning of her going between depends crucially on whose agent she is, the man's or the woman's. As would be expected in such a paradoxical poem, Lunete seems to be both.

Lunete plays conventional go-between roles for Yvain, and the audience initially assumes she is his go-between. After fighting Laudine's husband at her spring, Yvain pursues his dying opponent to his castle and becomes trapped between two portcullises that drop around him like a cage. In gratitude for Yvain's kindness to her when she once visited King Arthur's court, Lunete saves his life with a magic ring that makes him invisible, and she gives him food and clothing. When he falls in love with Laudine, Lunete comforts him and convinces Laudine to marry him—her husband's slayer. Finally, after Yvain has destroyed his initial relationship with Laudine, Lunete tricks Laudine into resuming her marriage. For Yvain, then, Lunete is a traditional go-between: consoling, encouraging, supportive, and so dedicated to his cause that, to help him, she risks losing Laudine's trust and even her own life; indeed, when Yvain fails to return to Laudine, Lunete narrowly misses being burned at the stake for having advised Laudine to marry him.

Nevertheless, while Lunete performs a go-between's actions for Yvain, the person she actually serves is Laudine. Both lady and lady-in-waiting consider her the woman's go-between rather than the man's. Lunete feels gratitude toward Yvain, but she is Laudine's confidante and companion, an incomparably older and deeper relationship. Laudine stresses her absolute trust in Lunete, appeals to her for advice whenever difficult situations arise, and ordinarily takes her advice. One of Laudine's reasons for marrying Yvain is her conviction that Lunete would never have argued his case "Que por loiier ne por desserte / Ne por amor, que a lui et" ["for reward or profit or for any love she felt for him."] (1743–44). And while awaiting execution at the stake for counseling Laudine to marry Yvain, Lunete tells Yvain himself that when she advised Laudine to marry him, " 'par la sainte Paternostre, / Plus por son preu, que por le vostre / Le cuidai feire et cuit ancore' " [" 'by the holy Paternoster, I thought and still think I was doing it more for her benefit than for yours' "] (3655–57).

It is Laudine, not Lunete, who violates most extremely the usual pattern of romance relationships. Idealized go-betweens typically unite people who are passionately in love. Several of these couples abandon possessions and status for love—Melior and William, Florimont and Romadanaple, Biancifiore and Florio—and none of them enter into a relationship with the other person just because they need him or her. But Yvain is not a love match for Laudine. Her problem is political, not romantic: she must have a man as powerful as Yvain to defend her spring. J.M. Sullivan, describing the Laudine/Lunete relationship as that of a sovereign served by her "active and effective counselor," argues that "it is in that capacity that the narrative's noble auditors would have identified with her (Lunete's) character."[55] Because the couples served by the other idealized go-betweens need help with loving, not with politics, none of their go-betweens are in a counselor/ sovereign relationship; Laudine alone needs political advice.

To deal with Laudine's problem, Lunete convinces her to marry—three days after her husband's death—Yvain, the man who killed her husband. Lunete does not trick Laudine in any way. When Laudine, grieving, contends that there are no men equal to the husband she has lost, Lunete points out that the man who defeated him must be more worthy than he. Lunete's humanly shocking argument ignores altogether the personal element in marriage, but if the purpose of this marriage is to find someone capable of defending Laudine's spring, then it follows that Laudine should marry her husband's slayer. As Hanning writes, "Our response to this episode is highly ambivalent. We sense the difficulties not resolved, the coolness of Laudine, and the deficiencies of prowess, kept before us by the references to Laudine's dead husband."[56] Readings of the episode tend to polarize between disapproval and admiration. Donald Maddox characterizes Lunete's position as "shallow" and describes it as "an absolute valorization of physical strength" such that "superior might is repeatedly valorized as a determinant of right," although he acknowledges that primitive and courtly figures alike hold this position throughout the poem, and it is "the operative assumption behind the fountain custom."[57] Karl D. Uitti, on the other hand, admires "the freedom and the suppleness inherent in her [Lunete's] practicality and living wisdom."[58]

After first forgetting Laudine and then suffering spectacularly for love of her, Yvain returns to her spring determined to force her to come to terms with him by keeping up his challenge until she relents. He causes such a storm that her town rocks at its foundations. Walls shake, her tower nearly falls, her subjects are terrified, and Lunete and Laudine agree that no knight of hers is brave enough to defend the spring. Lunete convinces Laudine to secure a defender for her spring by swearing to help the Knight of the Lion win back his lady in exchange for his aid, and the knight, of course, is Yvain. Lunete is not tricking the woman on behalf of the man, as a go-between from the stories about lust and sexual conquest would; she is tricking her on her own behalf. Laudine has only two options: resume her marriage or see her city destroyed. Because of her political situation, she must take back Yvain as her husband. Lunete's trick makes it possible for her to accept Yvain with such honorable justification that she can save face before both her court and herself.

Lunete's first act of going between was simply an argument: which is the better warrior, the winner or the loser? It was up to Laudine to decide whether to act on the implications of the argument. Lunete's second act of going between is a trick; she tricks Laudine to forge a way for her lady to move beyond her fiercely hurt pride and her publicly sworn word never to have anything to do with Yvain. In both cases, Lunete makes it possible for Laudine to do what pride and convention say she cannot do, but she must do to save her city: first, marry the man who killed her husband; second, take back a husband she swore never to take back. For Yvain (when he has not forgotten Laudine altogether while tourneying), their relationship is a passionate love match fired by desperate and unreasonable love at first sight, but it was never anything of the sort for Laudine. For her, from first to last, it is primarily a matter of political necessity. Ambiguous as Lunete's double relationship with Yvain and Laudine leaves her, in the last analysis, Lunete fits the basic requirements for a romance go-between: an aristocrat and a noblewoman's lady-in-waiting who goes between out of love and loyalty. Appearances to the contrary, she serves her lady more significantly than she serves the man who desires her lady, and her persuasion is political counseling, not sexual pressuring. The figure who undercuts the idealization of this story most decisively is not Lunete but Laudine because when she accepts Yvain as her lover and husband, she does not do so for love.

In an exceptionally flamboyant reading of Lunete, Roberta Krueger argues that the "underlying reality" of woman's status in romance is as "an object of exchange," and Yvain's "conquest of his rival's wife and possession of her domain resembles a marriage by capture in early Germanic society."[59] Lunete, Krueger writes, "primarily serves Yvain and the system of knightly honor," and "in the terms of the romance's structure of exchanges, she acts as a relative who hands a daughter or sister over for marriage, to honor a peer or appease an opponent."[60] "Beneath the fiction of Laudine's and Yvain's mutual desire," Krueger says, "the text inscribes coercion and possession."[61] But no father or sovereign arranges Laudine's marriage. It is Laudine who exchanges herself for martial protection for her estate. When a woman exchanges herself, the power relationships Krueger is discussing apply very differently. Lunete is Laudine's counselor, but it is Laudine who strikes the marriage bargain.

As Tony Hunt observes, "Chrétien is a dialectician who juxtaposes rather than harmonizes, who is committed to no single belief, and who *experiments* in each of his romances with various combinations of contemporary debating points."[62] The courtship story in *Yvain* is built from outrageous actions and debating points. Lunete, convincing Laudine to marry her husband's killer and to take back a husband who has failed her, breaks out of the expected behavior of a romance go-between. At the close of the romance, in her double role of at once the woman's and the man's go-between, she tricks her lady into a sexual relationship with a man who desires her. No other idealized go-between plays such a trick. Lunete's trick recalls the stories of the old women who trap their victims in the tales about sexual conquest, and Chrétien may well have been deliberately alluding to this alien material to introduce another layer of ambiguity into his romance. The ambiguity, however, remains under control, first because so much of Lunete's story shows her going between for her lady, not Yvain, and second because Lunete tricks Laudine into resuming her marriage, not into being raped or seduced. Nevertheless, when Lunete tricks Laudine, a new, discordant note is struck in romance going between. As Robert Hanning points out, "Chrétien does not allow real joy at the end of this difficult romance."[63] Neither does he allow unalloyed satisfaction with any of the characters, including Lunete. It is ironic that this least straightforwardly developed of all the idealized go-betweens, playing the least typical role in the most paradoxical romance, should also be the go-between that twenty-first-century readers know best.

Claris et Laris

Claris, a duke's son, and Laris, son of the king of Germany, young knights who go between in the last of these unconventional romances (Old French, 1268),[64] have none of the complexity or subtlety of a Lunete or a Urake. They are guileless and aboveboard, and the audience never doubts their allegiances or their word. Nevertheless, their actions as go-betweens either are, seem to be, or attempt to be dishonorable, unethical, sinful, and treasonous. Together, the knights violate more crucial conventions than any other romance go-betweens. Sworn brothers and comrades-in-arms, their passionate mutual devotion fuels their highly irregular going between and erupts in acts of love that defy morality. Nevertheless, even when Claris and Laris are violating the conventions of romance going between most egregiously, their situations vindicate their actions and the audience continues admiring them and trusting their honor and motives.

Going between is a structural device in Claris et Laris. Claris's love story appears in the first half of this immense romance, and Laris goes between for him. Laris's is in the second half, and Claris goes between. To underscore the parallelism of these widely separated episodes, the author reproduces the circumstances of the first going between for the second. In both, as one of the lovers nearly dies of love, one of the knights rescues him or her from a faint that appears to be death.

Claris's going between for Laris is so outlandish that it borders on comedy. Nothing else in romantic literature approaches it. Claris enters the bedchamber of Marine, the woman Laris loves, finds her unconscious, takes her in his arms, tells her he loves her, and kisses and embraces her until she regains consciousness. His justification for making love to Marine in apparent gross betrayal of Laris is that Marine has fainted and is near death because she saw Laris wounded and believes he has died. Claris's deception saves her life. To complicate the scene further, neither Laris nor Marine realizes his or her love is returned, so when Marine regains consciousness and is enraged to find Claris making love to her, he struggles with a double explanation: Laris is in fact alive and Laris loves Marine.

When Laris and Marine recover sufficiently, Claris takes Laris to Marine's bedchamber, and as they hug and kiss—each other this time— Claris plays the role of social conscience and restrainer. " 'Compainz. . . ceste pucele / Avez vioant moi fianciee' " (19454–55) ["Companion, in my sight you have just engaged yourself to this young woman"], he tells Laris, and he cautions him to guard Marine's honor and protect her from blame. Claris is very specific about what he has in mind:

"De l'acoler ne du baisier
Ne vous doit faire nul dangier,
Mes que ce soit celee[ment];
Du seureplus entierement,
Je vous en proi, vous soferrez,
Tant que espousee l'avrez." (19459–64)

["She should not deny you embraces or kisses, so long as it is done in private; but I beg you to forgo altogether anything more until you have married her."]

He sounds as down-to-earth and realistic as Cypriane with Romadanaple and Le Povre Perdu.

Claris lies to Marine and tricks her, but he does not trick her to change her feelings or to take control of her; he tricks her to convince her of a truth, that Laris is alive and in love with her. Marine decides when, how, and whether she will love. Claris succeeds so easily with Marine not because he deceives her, but because she already loves Laris as much as Laris loves her. Despite making love to his comrade's beloved, Claris remains within the conventions of idealized going between.

Laris, on the other hand, breaks the most basic rules of idealized going between for Claris. Claris is so devastatingly in love that on two occasions he nearly dies of love, but the woman he loves is Laris's sister Lydaine, and she is his king's wife. The non-cyclical Prose *Lancelot* treats Lancelot's adulterous affair with Guinevere as an honorable love, but adultery is a sin in *Claris et Laris*, no matter how fueled by passion it is, and adultery with the king's wife is both sinful and treacherous. When Claris realizes he has fallen in love with his king's wife, he vows never to act on such guilty desires. Other knights are inspired to great deeds by love, he muses sadly, but his love is treasonous and evil. Even if Lydaine wanted to be his entirely, "Cuer et cors debonairement" (330) [body and soul, willingly], he would not betray his lord by accepting her love. Lydaine is equally uncompromising about adultery. She is livid when Claris tells her he loves her. Surely he must not love her at all, she rages, if he asks her to do something as monstrous as break her marriage and dishonor her lord and king. She had always loved Claris and been his friend, but now she never wants to see him again (7975–90). *Claris et Laris* celebrates conventional values: the sanctity of marriage, a knight's fealty to his lord, and the love of comrades-in-arms for each other. Both Laris's going between and Claris's love for Lydaine are dishonorable and unethical by this poem's morality.

Laris goes between for Claris to save his life. He first promises Claris Lydaine after rescuing him from a deadly faint: " 'Car je croi bien a ce mener / Ma seror, (ne m'en cuit taisir), / Que l'avrez a vostre plesir' " (3970–79). ["For I truly believe—and I don't intend to keep quiet about it—that I'll be able to persuade my sister to let you have her at your pleasure"]. " 'Que l'avrez a vostre plesir' "—of all the idealized go-betweens, Laris most nearly promises the lover sexual possession of the woman: his sister and Claris's king's wife.

In the short run, however, nothing comes of Laris's promise. Nearly 4,000 verses pass before Laris finally intervenes for Claris with Lydaine. It is Claris, not Laris, who initially asks Lydaine to love him, but when she rejects him so angrily and tells him she never wants to see him again, he faints and Lydaine believes he is dead. She grieves for him as the best knight who ever mounted a warhorse, but her strongest emotion is her fear of her brother Laris; she expects him to kill her when he learns the cause of Claris's death.

With Claris lying unconscious between them near death from love, Laris alternately coaxes and bullies Lydaine. She admits that Claris fainted after she refused to love him, and Laris becomes so furious that he threatens to have her burned alive if Claris actually dies. He had promised her to Claris, he tells her: " 'Car je li promis leaument, / Que tu a son comandement / Seroies par la moie amor' " (8099–101) ["For I promised him loyally that you would be at his command because of your love for me"]. Lydaine must choose between killing or saving both himself and Claris, Laris tells her, and if she wants to save them both, she must hug and kiss Claris. Lydaine, however, is as unbending and as certain of the justice of her position as her brother is. How could he expect her to commit such a crime, dishonor her king, break her faith with her husband, and disgrace herself on Laris's account?

With the likelihood of saving Claris's life seeming bleaker and bleaker, Laris asks Lydaine to kiss Claris and accept him as her "ami" and then if King Ladon should die, Claris would look after her (8121–26). Lydaine agrees to this proposal but remains concerned for her honor, and Laris promises to take Claris to England immediately and remain there until Lydaine invites them to return.

Laris dominates the love scene of Lydaine and Claris. Following Laris's orders, Lydaine rouses Claris from his faint by kissing him a hundred times, and when Claris praises her for saving him from death and promises her a rich gift, she tells him that the gift belongs to Laris; she acted on his orders. The couple's agreements about loving are more contractual than romantic. Lydaine spells out carefully that she will let Claris hug and kiss her, but he must agree to forgo the "seurplus" [consummation], and at the close of this episode Claris and Laris leave for England.

As long as Lydaine's husband, the king, is alive, despite Laris's demands and Claris's suffering, Lydaine is convinced of the shamefulness of infidelity and the disgrace of lost chastity. Widowed, she changes her mind. With King Ladon dead and the king of Spain laying siege to Lydaine, she wishes she and Claris had been lovers, or at the very least that she had not sent him away, so that he and her brother could defend her. She repents her chastity in a long monologue, denounces her mad response when Claris first said he loved her, and acknowledges the importance of Laris's going between:

"Et lors oi ge trop vilain tort,
Quant du tou(l)t ne fis son voloir;
Certes, bien m'en doie douloir,
Quant li miens freres m'en pria
Et le baisier li otria." (13683–87)

["And it was very wrong, and uncourtly, of me then not to do his [Claris's] will completely; certainly I deserve to grieve over it since my own brother asked me and granted him the right to kiss me."]

She continues regretting that she has sent away Claris and Laris—she ought to have danced for joy so long as she knew they were in the country—and she bewails her undervaluing of the perfect love and service of Claris, the flower of the world. Finally she vows to cut off her hair like a nun and take the veil: " 'Maudite soit ma destinee, / Qui tant est mauvese et maudite!' " (13705–06) ["A curse on my destiny, which is so wretched and accursed!"]. Lydaine wishes she had loved Claris in the past to be protected personally and politically in the present. Her feelings have nothing to do with either romantic love or desire.

Does Lydaine love Claris? She apparently finds him appealing. She kisses him more than a hundred times to bring him back from his faint, and she is eager to marry him after King Ladon's death. There is no indication that Laris has pressured her into an undesired relationship. On the other hand, Lydaine certainly does not love Claris the way he loves her, or the way Biancifiore loves Florio, or Melior William, or Soredamors Alexander, or any of the rest of these idealized women and their men. Lydaine's love arises from a collection of varied motivations. Claris is a handsome, distinguished knight who loves her; her brother wants her to love him; and she needs political protection. She does not love Claris because he is the most amazingly marvelous human being on earth and she will die if he does not return her love. On Lydaine's part, this is an ordinary relationship in which a marriage fulfills many needs. It is not idealized love.

Laris promises to make his sister love his best friend, even though she is married to his king. This is as extreme and unethical going between as can be found in the idealized stories. However, the ethics of both Laris's going between and Claris's loving are significantly complicated by Lydaine's marital situation. Lydaine is fifteen years old, an ideal age for a medieval wife. King Ladon, her husband, however, is one hundred, and the poem suggests very strongly that he is impotent. When Claris thinks about him in bed with Lydaine, he admires her equanimity in accepting her sexual situation:

> "Et s'est ce merveillouse chose,
> Que vous, qui estes flor de rose
> Et eslis de droite nature,
> Lez si ancienne faiture,
> Con mes sires vostre mari,
> Gesez sans avoir cuer marri,
> Qui est sanz deduit de jonece." (3792–98)

["And it is an extraordinary thing that you, who are the rose blossom and chosen one of nature, lie without feeling sick at heart side-by-side with such an ancient creature as my lord your husband, who lacks all youth's delights."]

King Ladon himself advises Lydaine to marry Claris. While the royal couple watches Claris and Laris distinguish themselves in a tournament, the sight of Lydaine inspires Claris to remarkable feats, and King Ladon praises his fierceness and strength and then tells Lydaine that he wants her to marry Claris after he dies. You could not make a better choice, he recommends, and she says nothing (7511–26).

Potentially, the Claris, Laris, and Lydaine story raises more ethical issues than any other of these idealized episodes. How guilty is Claris for desiring his one-hundred-year-old king's fifteen-year-old wife? Is it admirable or shameful for Laris to save his comrade-in-arms' life by promising to win his married sister's love for him? How significantly does Lydaine break faith with her late husband when, besieged by the king of Spain, she laments sending Claris out of the country and wishes she had taken him as her lover? All these questions remain undebated and unanswered since they work themselves out situationally through Lydaine's chastity and King Ladon's death. They are never confronted as ethical issues.

Similarly, the story of Claris, Laris, and Lydaine seems to be on the verge of violating the most essential mandate of idealized going between. When Laris offers to win his sister for his comrade-in-arms and then rages at her for not being willing to love Claris, he is trying to force her to love. As with the rest of its moral problems, however, *Claris et Laris* finesses the issue of the go-between who forces a woman into a sexual relationship. Laris acts against his society's values to save Claris's life, but Lydaine's conventional morality triumphs over him. Even in *Claris et Laris*, no one succeeds in forcing anyone else to love. Laris and Lydaine work out their compromise; she will become Claris's "ami" but not his lover and they will marry after King Ladon dies. The contrast here is with a work like Chrétien's *Yvain* that foregrounds its outrageous actions and keeps its potential allusions to going between in the stories of sexual conquest within unsettlingly easy reach. *Claris et Laris* instead, by solving so blandly the issues it raises, leaves them sensational rather than difficult and provocative. Similarly, its portrayal of Lydaine is cloyingly conventional: the beautiful, dutiful, obedient, faithful young wife who fulfills honorably and resolutely her place in the patriarchy's support network, despite the pressures the young man who desires her brings to bear on her.

Protheseläus: Dating Romance Going Between

Go-betweens are clearly a minor structural feature of romance. For the romance writer, they provide a convenient vehicle for uniting lovers, testing relationships, and displaying all aspects of love. As confidant figures for both the man and the woman, go-betweens are supportive audiences for discussions and debates about loving, and, depending on the kind of go-between at issue, they can either echo the lovers' attitudes toward love or contrast with them.

These go-between figures became important impressively quickly in the romances; nine stories involving them have survived from the last third of the twelfth and the beginning of the thirteenth centuries. Surely these writers were building on each other's work, but who was imitating whom remains much debated. Chrétien de Troyes may have created the first such figure. Philippe Ménard identifies Guinevere in *Cligés* as the first go-between to unite paralyzed lovers.[65] On the other hand, Penny Simonds and Penny Eley date *Partonopeus de Blois c.* 1170,[66] which places it before both *Cligés* and *Yvain* and would make Urake the first idealized go-between. It seems probable that Lunete and Urake are related somehow, but did Urake inspire Lunete or vice versa? *Florimont* introduces further complications. It is internally dated, 1188, and scholars have argued that *Partonopeus* influenced *Florimont*, which places *Partonopeus* before 1188. Laurence Harf-Lancner and Sarah Kay, however, claim that *Florimont* instead influenced *Partonopeus*, which moves *Partonopeus* to the end of the century.[67] Urake then becomes a descendant of Cypriane as well as of Lunete. Thomas's Anglo-Norman *Romance of Horn* (*c.* 1170) in which Herland goes between for Rigmel also figures into this time frame, not to mention whatever stories have been lost. A cluster of romances using go-betweens—intertexts for one another—appeared during this period, but with current knowledge, little can be concluded about specific source relationships.

One impressive point about dating and the go-betweens of romance, however, is undebatable. By 1185–90, a mere fifteen to twenty years after the first suggested date for these figures, going between was so well established as a romance narrative ploy that it yielded a burlesque. Hue de Rotelande, the Anglo-Norman author of *Protheseläus*,[68] lavishes go-betweens on his romance. Five of his characters go between: a confidante, two comrades-in-arms, a servant, and a nobleman of the lady's court; and two of these characters go between for two different people. Much of their going between is bizarrely inappropriate and turns the conventions of romance inside out.

Evein, for instance, lady-in-waiting to La Pucele de l'Isle, the exceedingly beautiful ruler of eighty castles, defies the most fundamental rule of romance going between. She and her lady attempt to force the hero to love. Evein tricks Protheseläus into dismounting and disarming and then lures him into La Pucele's tower where she locks him up. Although both Evein and La Pucele know that Protheseläus is in love with another woman, La Pucele tells him that the price of his freedom will be marrying her. He of course remains true to his love, Medea, queen of Crete, which infuriates La Pucele.

Another comic going-between episode in *Protheseläus* involves four go-betweens and a second broken tenet. Instead of serving lovers and love, the honored work of romance go-betweens, Evein, La Pucele's lady-in-waiting, and Latin, La Pucele's constable and a king in his own right, use going between as a means to another end. To free Protheseläus from La Pucele's prison, they coax her into falling in love with Melander, who is Medea's constable and Protheseläus's comrade-in-arms, and who heads a huge army sent to rescue Protheseläus. As Melander covers himself with glory on the battlefield, Latin and Evein praise him lavishly to La Pucele, stressing his wealth, youth, and distinguished ancestry. Evein adds arguments about the futility of loving a man who doesn't care anything about you, and before long La Pucele forgets her passion for Protheseläus and substitutes Melander. All aspects of this development violate romance conventions grossly. Go-betweens support lovers' love. They do not pressure lovers to change their minds about whom they love in order to bring about another result—in this case the freeing of Protheseläus.

Evein and Latin continue their enthusiastic going between until La Pucele and Melander marry. Evein is repeatedly at her lady's side detailing Melander's accomplishments and virtues: "Look how elegantly he sits on his horse!" "Watch him joust!" Moreover, if La Pucele is interested in Melander, they keep urging her, she must free Protheseläus. He is Melander's comrade-in-arms, the man he loves best. She cannot love one while holding the other one prisoner (8850–83).

Although La Pucele now loves Melander, Evein and Latin believe their problem is only half solved. Melander must love La Pucele, and so they add a third go-between to their group, Protheseläus himself. They present Protheseläus with the advantages of such a marriage for Melander—no woman on earth is richer, more beautiful, or of higher birth than La Pucele—and they then send Protheseläus off to go between. As a go-between, Protheseläus is not serving lovers; he is serving himself. He has a huge personal motive for going between. If Melander marries La Pucele, then it follows that she must set Protheseläus free.

Protheseläus never reflects upon the morality of asking another man to marry because it will be useful to him, any more than Evein and Latin reflected upon the morality of convincing La Pucele to fall in love on Protheseläus's behalf. Protheseläus instead reckons up Melander's obligations to him as his comrade-in-arms who can be counted on for any service. With considerable and unqualified enthusiasm, "haitez et joianz" [delighted and joyful], Protheseläus tells Evein and Latin that if they can convince La Pucele to love Melander: " 'De meie part mult sëur sui; / Ren que jo voille vers celui, / N'ert pur ren laissé, ne seit fait' " (9420–22) ["As for my part, I am very confident; nothing will prevent him from doing whatever I may want of him"]. Surely Hue is writing comedy here, and his joke requires a sophisticated audience that knows what go-betweens do and do not do in idealized stories.

Protheseläus flouts another rule of romance going between. Only people who care about the lovers go between in romances. Going between is never turned over to professionals. In *Protheseläus*, however, a paid professional goes between, Jolif, a "lechere" (10013) [minstrel], "enveisez de bels deduiz" (10017) [who enjoys good sport (sex and minstrelsy both)]. Jolif is not an honorable intermediary. The base meaning of "lecheor" in Old French is "lecher," "a man given over to debauchery," and it could be used as a general insult.[69] La Pucele sends Jolif to the battlefield to test Melander's interest in her, and Jolif describes her unctuously for him—her fairy-white skin, lovely eyes, wide forehead, beautiful shape: "By heaven, who could keep from loving her?" "Mult sot Jolif de cel mester, / L'esp[iri]t lui vot [en]gregier" (10026–27) [Jolif knew this trade well; he wanted to inflame his passions], the narrator comments. Comically fortuitously, Melander has just caught a glimpse of La Pucele and fallen in love with her. He tells Jolif how much in love he is and then assumes that he owes Jolif money: " 'Sacez que grant ert li löers!' " (10048) ["You can be sure that you will be well paid!"]. It is Jolif, "lechere," who carries Melander's love declaration to La Pucele.

Hue layers episodes of going between on top of each other to underscore their comic excessiveness. As Melander negotiates with Jolif, Protheseläus searches the battlefield for Melander to convince him to love La Pucele. When they meet, before Protheseläus mentions La Pucele, Melander appeals to him to go between with her for him. He begins by alluding delicately to his own going between when Protheseläus fell in love with Medea. Once Protheseläus understands Melander's plea, Protheseläus realizes his own petition has become a source of joy, and he explains his mission and very tentatively suggests that Melander can have him released from prison if he really loves La Pucele. In a blatant burlesque of the mutual devotion of comrades-in-arms, Melander responds with extravagant vows of self-sacrifice: "If there were no other means of getting you out of prison,

> "Il n'ad el mund [në] en nul regne
> Si vil garce ne si vil femme
> Que ne prëisse volenters;
> Tant m'estes [vus] amis et chers." (10160–63)

> ["there is no girl so base, or woman either, anywhere on earth, in any realm, that I would not willingly marry; you are so much a friend and so dear to me."]

Instead of self-sacrifice, of course, Melander is to have just the marriage he most desires, and Protheseläus's going-between for this couple degenerates into pretending to plead Melander's suit with La Pucele when in fact Protheseläus knows that La Pucele loves Melander.

Protheseläus also burlesques minor aspects of romance going between. One of the most dramatic ways for a future go-between to learn that the

lover loves is by overhearing him lamenting his torment, usually in the
night when he is supposed to be sleeping. The friend then begs him to
explain his grief. This was how Laris learned that Claris loved Lydaine, for
instance (3843–981), and Lancelot kept two kings awake as he moaned in
the Prose *Lancelot*, although he then refused to explain his grief. Characters
in romances also occasionally fall in love before they see each other:
Florimont and Romadanaple, for instance, and Rigmel. Hue combines
these motifs comically. Melander initially learns prosaically about
Protheseläus's love for Medea. Protheseläus sighs in despair as he and
Melander ride through a wood, and in response to his comrade's inquiries,
Protheseläus admits that he has loved Medea for five years. Melander, who
is Medea's subject, asks Protheseläus whether he has seen Medea. Melander
asks the question as if he expects him to say that he has not, and when
Protheseläus admits that he never has, Melander reassures him calmly that
he will take him to see her, and the episode ends (2553–58). Medea also is
in love with Protheseläus sight-unseen (276–79), and Judith Weiss points
out how "comically improbable" this non-relationship is for both of them
since Medea loved Ipomedon, Protheseläus's father, in Hue's earlier poem,
Ipomedon, and consequently must be twenty years older than Protheseläus.[70]

Less than 250 verses after this unprepossessing episode, the traditional dramatic scene of overheard secret love occurs. All night long Protheseläus tosses
and turns, laments, and vows his unwavering fidelity to Medea until finally his
desperate sighs rouse Melander. Melander questions him about his suffering
and argues that their friendship obliges Protheseläus to confide in him:

> "Ne m'estes pas bon cumpaignon,
> Sire, si jo l'osoue dire,
> Quant vers mei celez la matire
> Et le grant dol que vus menez." (2805–08)

["You are not a good companion to me, my lord, if I dared say it, when
you conceal from me the reason for the great grief you are suffering."]

Protheseläus replies within the same conventions:

> "Amis, si deus joie me dunt,
> A vus ne dei jo ren celer:
> Jo mor, certes, pur trop amer." (2815–17)

["Friend, as God may give me joy, I should not conceal anything from
you. Indeed, I am dying because I love too much."]

He continues describing his deadly love for Medea that would be half
cured if only he could see her, and Melander responds by promising to take

him to her. This episode is so deliberately anticlimactic that it must be parody. There is no secret left for these two to share. The earlier scene has preempted this one entirely. Protheseläus has already told Melander that he loves Medea, and Melander has already promised to take his comrade to the queen. Surely Hue de Rotelande is burlesquing these conventions.

Hue violates as well the decorousness of this genre. The only sex joke in these idealized stories of going between is Alexandrine's gentle teasing of Melior when, after her afternoon of lovemaking with William, Alexandrine asks if Melior has found the herb that will cure her lovesickness. Hue, however, has Evein elaborate a military metaphor full of sexual double meanings when the two women trap Protheseläus in La Pucele's tower and she is about to rush to him (6512–18). La Pucele should not be too open about her feelings for Protheseläus, Evein warns. Punning on "covering" and "uncovering," she observes that the wise person "covers himself," but La Pucele desires Protheseläus so much that as soon as she sees him she will show him just what she feels:

"Ja tost serrïez descoverte
Vers cel chevaler qu[i]'st läenz,
S[e] trop nen est laner [ne] lenz." (6527–29)

["Indeed, you would quickly be 'uncovered' for this knight who is inside, if he is not too cowardly or slow."]

Finally Evein warns La Pucele to remember that Protheseläus loves another woman. La Pucele should not imagine that this knight lacks the ability " 'De vus covrir ne descovrir' " (6532) ["To cover or uncover you"]. In fact, he desires someone else. These voyeuristic word games reduce passion to carnality: the woman sexually assaulted, stripping for sex; the man having sex. Hue's jokes leave no room for the idealizing perspective of romance.

By 1185–90, then, going between was so firmly established as a conventional element of idealized romance that when Hue de Rotelande violated its tone, ridiculed its traditional episodes, and turned inside out its portrayal of how and why knights and ladies go between, he could expect his burlesquing to be understood and enjoyed.

A Go-Between for Lust in an Idealized Story: *Éracle*

As *Protheseläus*'s comic parody confirms, early in the development of romance as a genre, its writers and audiences were aware of the idealized go-between's role and the actions and meanings associated with it. A second anomalous work establishes romance's early recognition of the opposed tradition of the go-between for lust and sexual conquest. *Éracle* (1165–80),[71] by Gautier d'Arras, a contemporary of Chrétien de Troyes, imports a go-between for lust into an idealized story. She is a poor, greedy Old Woman, the most frequent avatar of the go-betweens for lust. By the time of the writing of *Éracle*, she had been known in Latin since the beginning of the twelfth century from *Pamphilus* and the *Disciplina Clericalis*, both of which were widely read and repeatedly copied. *Éracle*, however, contains the oldest surviving literary instance of this figure in the vernacular. A professional arranger of love affairs, she brags about her skills in enticing and trapping women, and she is paid by everyone in the story who deals with her. When Paridès, the young man who is dying from lovesickness, manages to drink a little eggnog after the Old Woman counsels him, his overjoyed mother gives her a good cloak and then adds enough money to make her rich for the rest of her life. The young woman's payment is more covert. She is Athanaïs, an empress, who is imprisoned in a tower and guarded night and day by twenty-four old men and their wives who watch her every move. At the end of her meeting with the Old Woman, Athanaïs promises to send her a gift the next day and instructs her to keep the gift for herself but give "le sorplus" [the "extra"] to Paridès. Athanaïs hides a letter for Paridès under the crust of a meat pie that she sends to the Old Woman in a silver dish. The go-between is infuriated at being given nothing more than a meat pie. What could a nobleman like Paridès want with silver?, she rages. He has as much silver as the empress has! But once she breaks the pie crust and finds the letter, she is beside herself with glee:

> "Biaus sire Dius, merci!
> C'est li sorplus que je voi chi,
> c'est li sorplus que il i a!
> Cil Damedius qui tout cria
> doinst a l'empereïs grans biens!
> Je prent cest argent qui est miens." (4443–48)

> ["Thank you, dear Lord! This is the 'extra' that I see here; this is the 'extra'! May the Lord who created everything grant the empress great blessings! This silver is mine and I'm taking it!"]

The Old Woman's long-honed mastery of love matters sets the tone of her one professional conversation with Paridès, whose family is preparing his grave. "Molt voiseuse et sage" [very sly and wise] (4023), she appraises his symptoms and lectures him about what women want from men. Every woman turns proud and standoffish when she sees a young man languishing for her love, she argues. What women really want is to be dominated and overpowered, seduced and kept under a man's heels. When she was a girl she tormented all the men who loved her and never loved any of them. She then promises to trap any woman he desires: " 'tant sai de barat et de gile / que vostres bons ert acomplis, / se c'ert nes li empereïs.' " (4178–80) ["I know so much about trickery and guile that you will have your way, even if she were the empress herself"]—" 'De barat et de gile,' "—the traditional methods of the Old Woman go-between. When Paridès faints at the empress's name, the Old Woman understands at once that he loves her, and while Athanaïs is the most important, most heavily guarded woman in Rome, the Old Woman is not daunted in the slightest. With all the professional arrogance of her type, she guarantees him success.

The Old Woman is a typical figure from a story of sexual conquest. Paridès and Athanaïs are equally typical figures from romance. He is the most handsome, graceful, and talented of all the young noblemen, she is as perfect a young woman as nature can produce, and they fall in love at first sight, cannot eat or sleep, and both seem about to die of love. Athanaïs's perfection is attested to by Éracle, a seer with divinely guaranteed judgment of women, who chose her from all the women in Rome to be the emperor's wife. For seven years she was as perfect as Éracle predicted until the emperor, Laïs, imprisoned her and set guards to watch her for fear she would be unfaithful while he was away on a military expedition. Éracle warns Laïs that if he locks up Athanaïs, she will curse her high position and riches a hundred times a day and no matter what Laïs contrives to contain her, she will find a way to be unfaithful to him. After months of imprisonment and resentment, Athanaïs falls so desperately in love with Paridès that she risks death for a moment with him.

The Old Woman of *Éracle* promises Paridès to act the part of a traditional go-between from a story of sexual conquest: she will get the woman for the man, never mind the means. But *Éracle* is an idealized story: the man and woman already love each other equally. Eager as the Old Woman is to lie, trick, and trap, she is relegated to carrying a message from one yearning lover to another. Moreover, the account of the nature of women that she gives when she is trying to hearten Paridès—women never love men who love them—turns out to be false in every way for the woman he loves. Athanaïs loves Paridès just as much as he loves her. With Athanaïs's announcement that she loves Paridès, the need for a go-between for sexual conquest disappears. Athanaïs takes charge of her love affair herself.

Éracle would be expected to idealize love; nevertheless, Athanaïs and Paridès become lovers by playing a trick that by atmosphere and implication belongs in a story about lust as decidedly as the Old Woman does. And yet this trick performs the function of a trick in an idealized story. It is played against the hostile outer world of Laïs's guards, not against the woman to trap her sexually for the man, and Athanaïs herself concocts the trick. The Old Woman lives in a windowless, single-room house. In the letter hidden in the meat pie, Athanaïs tells Paridès to dig a hole in the Old Woman's floor big enough to hold both of them, camouflage the entrance to the hole, fill the ditch outside the house with water, and get the Old Woman to build a huge fire in her fireplace. Athanaïs then rides to the house on a skittish horse, makes the horse rear, falls into the water in the ditch, pretends to be injured, and is carried by her guardians to the Old Woman's cottage to dry off before her fire, after the guardians assure themselves that the Old Woman is alone. While some of the guardians watch the single door and others ride back to the palace for fresh clothes for the empress, Athanaïs and Paridès become lovers in the "sousterin." And when Athanaïs is freshly clothed, she leaves her wet cape behind for the Old Woman. "Rique loiier de son feu; / elë ara bien fait son preu!" [Handsome payment for her fire; she will have done very well for herself!] (4675)

This is not an idealized scenario. Athanaïs falls into ditch water, and the lovemaking takes place in a hole in the ground, lower even than the floor of the Old Woman's house. This is the kind of trick one expects from an Old Woman in a fabliau. Similarly, lovers do not make off-color jokes in idealized stories, but after Athanaïs falls into the ditch water, she dismisses her guards in lines full of innuendoes. The double meanings in her first image are appropriately elevated:

> "Signor, mal me vait!
> Une goute ai qui mal me fait,
> je l'ai molt longement celee;
> orendroit m'est renouvelee
> al caoir que je fis a terre." (4547–51)

[["My lords, I am suffering! I am afflicted by a rheumatism which I have hidden for a long time; now the pain has been reawakened by my fall."]]

Athanaïs's long-hidden pain is a standard idealized image for love. Loving conceived of as a fall to earth, however, suggests the values and judgments of a story about lust, and her second group of double meanings becomes nearly overtly sexual. Athanaïs proposes to treat her "goute," her rheumatism, with heat and rubbing: " 'Signor, dist ele, ales vos ent; / caufer me voel priveement.' " (4567–68) ["Leave me, my lords," she says, "I want to warm myself privately."] What her pain needs, she continues, is to be warmed and rubbed, " 'caufer et froiier.' "

Éracle, then, is a mixture of contradictory elements and attitudes toward love. On the one hand, there is Athanaïs's too knowing language about sex, the low trick played at the Old Woman's house, and the Old Woman herself, who boasts she can trap any woman at all. On the other hand, there is an idealized empress and nobleman who are stricken by love at first sight and are willing to give up their lives for their love. When Athanaïs and Paridès make love, she tells him that at that moment Éracle, who is always right, will be informing the emperor that they are committing adultery. She has thrown away both God and his earthly world to love Paridès, Athanaïs announces. In answer to her pronouncement of their doom, Paridès pledges his body and soul into her keeping. Athanaïs and Paridès assert the absolute value of their love by accepting death as love's price.

This unique mixture of idealized elements and elements from tales of lust—an Old Woman figure in a story of romantic love—allows *Éracle* to sustain two values in opposition: idealized love and marital fidelity. Athanaïs and Paridès love passionately, absolutely, and romantically, but they are committing adultery. Athanaïs agonizes over her infidelity before she and Paridès become lovers, and she sees the face of God turned against her when they are in each other's arms. When Éracle chooses Athanaïs as the most perfect woman of her time, one aspect of her perfection is her capacity for fidelity. And when Laïs hurries back to Rome after Éracle tells him that his wife has committed adultery, Athanaïs and Paridès expect to be drowned, burned alive, or hanged, and Laïs denounces his wife furiously.

On the other hand, passionate love does not overpower marital love for Athanaïs. Laïs kills her love by imprisoning her. Trapped in his tower, surrounded by his guards, Athanaïs thinks of herself as a caged bird, and by the time she first sees Paridès, her love for her husband is dead. According to Éracle, Laïs is more to blame for his betrayal than either Athanaïs or Paridès, and Éracle interrupts Laïs's tirade against Athanaïs to spell out the emperor's accountability. Athanaïs would have remained as perfect a woman as Éracle had found her, and as loving and faithful a wife as Laïs had always known her to be if only Laïs had treated her with the dignity and trust she deserved,[72] Éracle tells him, and Laïs, deeply grieved, admits he has justly lost Athanaïs, gives up his right to her to Paridès, and she and Paridès marry.

By introducing a go-between from the stories about lust and sexual conquest, *Éracle* passes double judgment on the love of Athanaïs and Paridès. They are idealized, noble lovers, as they show in their devotion to each other and their absolute valuing of love, but they are also adulterous and ignoble lovers, and this judgment of their love is carried by the Old Woman's role in the story, the fabliau-style trick Athanaïs concocts, and the consummation of their love in the hole in the Old Woman's floor. Nevertheless, despite the intrusion of this figure from an ideologically opposed tradition, the lovers never lose control of the essentials of idealized loving. The trick played at the Old Woman's house dupes Athanaïs's guards, not one of the lovers, and both lovers enter into their relationship with fully informed consent about the consequences of their act.

The anomalous Old Woman and the adulterous lovers of *Éracle*, then, enact the contradictory meanings associated with going between in the two traditions. The threat of the go-between for sexual conquest is that she or he will destroy the integrity of the love, reduce it to lust, and bring about possession of the woman or the man by force or trickery. At the heart of the difference between going between for idealized love and going between for lust and sexual conquest is the lovers' control over their loving. As is clear from Gautier d'Arras's complex use of the traditional Old Woman figure and the meanings attached to her, these distinctions guided him in the late twelfth century as he constructed this story in which idealized love remains ideal and yet is tarnished both by adultery and by its association with a go-between for lust and sexual conquest.

The Two Traditions

Idealized go-betweens such as Alexandrine, Guinevere, Galehot, Cypriane, Blancheflor's nurse, and Glorizia dramatize romantic lovers' extreme feelings for each other and help them trick the families and societies that threaten their love. The lovers these go-betweens serve all love mutually, and their go-betweens uphold their relationships without intervening in them. The unconventional idealized go-betweens play the same roles as the conventional go-betweens, but in addition they push against the ethical limits of going between. Claris hugs and kisses the woman Laris loves; Laris tries, unsuccessfully, to force his married sister to commit adultery with Claris; Lunete tricks Laudine into promising to love the husband she has vowed never to love again; and Urake torments Melior with lies until she forces her to change. The conventional go-betweens' stories are straightforward because both members of the couples already love each other. The unconventional stories tackle more complex situations: separated lovers who have lost the magic that makes their love possible; people who love unavailable people; people who are not romantically in love.

Nevertheless, unconventional and conventional idealized go-betweens alike never behave like the go-betweens who serve lust and sexual conquest. In the usual stories of lust and sexual conquest, men act out their power against women, and the go-between is their means of violation. No one is violated in idealized loving, and mutual consent nullifies sex as male power. Idealized go-betweens do not trap people into sexual acts; they unite consensual couples. Unmotivated by self-interest or greed, their going between is idealized just as their knights' and ladies' loving is idealized, and they act out of personal and emotional commitment to the lovers: loyalty, devotion, friendship, sympathy, and love.

The go-betweens who serve lust and sexual conquest, on the other hand, typically care nothing about the lovers' feelings. Clear-eyed and clear-headed, they stand outside the charmed circle of desire, scheming to get as much as possible out of the situation. Instead of validating the lovers' passion, they underscore their own alien perspective by making sex jokes or leering. Sometimes they ridicule lust, as when Herselot sets fire to the bedroom in which the priest believes he is possessing a twelve-year-old, or when Baucis sells the prostitute she is turning into a virgin to Traso, the soldier, again and again. Routinely, they treat love exclusively as lust and tackle winning physical possession of whatever woman or man their employers desire. The idealized stories concern emotions and loving relationships; the stories of lust and conquest are about sex.

Idealized stories portray many aspects of their characters' lives and relate them complexly to each other. Lancelot, Yvain, Partonope, and Claris and Laris, for instance, are all extraordinary knights as well as lovers. The stories about lust instead typically focus on a single sexual episode or problem. The characterization of Pamphilus, for example, is as limited as a fabliau characterization; Pamphilus desires Galatea and has less money than she does, and that is the limit of its complexity.

The most important difference between the go-betweens for idealized love and the go-betweens for lust and sexual conquest is their ways of going between. The go-betweens that serve lust are ordinarily hired to trap the other person with bed tricks, identity tricks, deceptions of all sorts, and, most often, straightforward lies about who is or is not where. Dame Auberée presides over a whole fabliau of tricks, from the surcoat hidden under the bed quilt to the wife lying in front of the altar in the middle of the night, surrounded by candles. The old nurse in *Alda* operates in the same tradition when she dresses Pyrrhus in his twin sister's clothes to seduce his sister's best friend. In the most standard trick, the go-between— Dame Auberée, Davus, the Anus, Houdée, or Trotaconventos—lures the woman into a room with a bed where she is joined by a man who proceeds to rape her. These tricks and deceptions are exactly the actions that are never allowed to intrude into the stories of idealized love. In the idealized stories, the woman and the man must both consent to love each other. One cannot be trapped into serving the other's desires. The essential difference between the going between of the idealized stories and the stories of lust, then, is mutual consent, and it makes romantic love possible.

PART III

CHOREOGRAPHING LUST AND LOVE: CHAUCER'S PANDARUS

Like a matrix, or the warp and weft of a tapestry, or the streets and avenues of a city laid out on a grid, the go-betweens for idealized love and the go-betweens for lust and sexual conquest underlie Geoffrey Chaucer's *Troilus and Criseyde* (1385–86). As Chaucerians will recognize at once, Chaucer's Pandarus is an anomalous aberration from this sharply bifurcated Western medieval tradition. Differentiated as these two types of go-betweens had been for nearly three centuries, Pandarus belongs to both types at once. He is as deeply rooted in the rich intertextuality of the go-betweens for idealized love as he is in the equally rich intertextuality of the go-betweens for lust—a virtual contradiction in terms. The Latin comic tale, fabliau, novella, and exemplum, the genres in which the go-betweens for lust are most often found, participate in wholly different views of the world than the romances, and yet Pandarus is the outgrowth of both.

The two traditions diverge most insistently in their conceptions of the meaning and worth of sexual relationships. In the romances, being capable of extraordinarily intense, idealizing love is the sign of a great soul. Men and women risk their lives and fortunes to love because nothing else conceivably equals its worth. Probably in the late twelfth century these notions amused court ladies and scandalized their husbands, Larry Benson hypothesizes, but by the late fourteenth century, love as a "source of chivalric virtue" was such a commonplace idea that it appeared in nonfiction conduct handbooks as well as in fiction.[1] In the tradition of going between for sexual conquest, on the other hand, love is lust, usually predatory lust, and its goal is physical possession of the other person rather than the winning of love. Some of these stories are little more than extended dirty jokes, many are comic, and those that are not comic are raw and sour.

When Chaucer wrote *Troilus and Criseyde*, he used this double go-between tradition as one of its essential components, as fundamental to the making of the poem as Petrarchan lyricism and Boethian philosophy. Conventionally lovesick and idolizing as Troilus is, he would never have hired a professional go-between to help him woo Criseyde, and yet the consummation of his extravagant passion is made possible by a figure whose actions come out of that second tradition that translates loving into the entrapment and procuring of women. This mingling of the two traditions, carrying with them such opposed conceptions of loving and relationships, leaves *Troilus and Criseyde* without a genre. What is this poem's genre? What kind of poem is it? This most basic question about a work of literature cannot be answered for *Troilus and Criseyde* because it participates in different genres at once and simultaneously and contradictorily sustains the meanings that accompany those genres.

Although we do not know which French romances Chaucer read—there is no strong evidence, for instance, that Chaucer knew Chrétien de Troyes' masterpieces[2]—no one questions Chaucer's immersion in the French romance tradition and so in the idealized go-between tradition. As Charles Muscatine's *Chaucer and the French Tradition* developed so richly, Chaucer's poetry grows directly out of French twelfth and thirteenth-century literature. Chaucer's familiarity with the go-betweens for lust and their tradition is also indisputable. He used two of its most important works as sources, Jean de Meun's *Roman de la rose* for *The Canterbury Tales*,[3] and *Pamphilus* and its descendants for *Troilus and Criseyde*.[4] How well Chaucer's audience knew the literature he read is uncertain, of course, but if Chaucer was as steeped in French romance as he seems to have been, probably so were a number of the people who heard and read his poetry, and *Pamphilus* and the *Roman de la rose* were among the most frequently copied and referred to works of the European Middle Ages.[5] Moreover, an unrecoverable popular tradition also very probably lay behind these text-based go-betweens. It seems likely that characters such as the Old Woman who goes between in the fabliaux and exempla appeared as well in oral stories that have left no trace. An unusual piece of evidence suggests strongly that a far less sophisticated audience than Chaucer's court ladies and gentlemen recognized the connections between Pandarus and the disreputable go-betweens for lust. This evidence is a poem called "The Chance of the Dice" that, as early as 1440, uses "pander" as a common noun to mean "procurer". The poem is the text for a fortune-telling game and an entertainer might well have carried it from town to town. Each stanza has a number, the players throw dice, and their fortunes are then read, depending on which stanzas match their dice casts.

> Ey prut auaunt / for shame why cast ye soo
> Vpon thys dyse / ne koude ye fynde no chaunce
> Sauf oonly this / syth ther be many moo

More fortunat to ioye / and to plesaunce
Your destanye hath shapen / your penaunce
Ther is no beter pandare / as I trowe
ffor al this londe throgh out / suche be ye knowe[6]

[Hey, (the noise of a fart), get out of here! You should be ashamed of yourself! Why do you throw these dice so badly? Couldn't you find any chance except this one since there are many others that lead to joy and pleasure? Your destiny has shaped your penance. There is no better pander, as I believe, for you are known as such throughout this whole land.]

According to the *OED*, it was not until 1530 that Pandarus's name produced the common noun "pander," but here it is, nearly a century earlier. Furthermore, the context of this stanza does not supply the meaning of "pandare," implying that the writer expected his audience to know the word. Ordinary people, then, apparently understood "pander" as a common noun for a disreputable person within fifty years of Chaucer's writing *Troilus and Criseyde*.

The strongest argument for Chaucer's audience's familiarity with the double go-between tradition, however, is that *Troilus and Criseyde* is so clearly written for an audience who is aware of it. In its central relationships and impact, *Troilus and Criseyde* depends on an audience whose literary experience includes both go-betweens for idealized love and go-betweens for lust and sexual conquest. Such an audience would have responded doubly to *Troilus and Criseyde*—as if watching its action through alternating panes of colored glass. Or, to use a contemporary analogy, imagine an opera set with two scrims. As the first scrim is lighted, the audience sees the outline of a glorious castle. Red and blue flags, glittering with gold, fly from its battlements and knights and ladies, resplendent in fur cloaks, elaborate head-dresses, and jeweled robes, gather beside it. But when the lighting changes and the second scrim appears, an ancient woman wrapped in shapeless brown wool, bent into a bow from age, loaded down with baskets of linens and trinkets, hobbles along a rutted town road, her sparse gray hair escaping from beneath a frayed kerchief. Like a fourteenth-century audience hearing *Troilus and Criseyde*, the opera-goers view the scene on stage first before one scrim and then before the other, shifting back and forth, again and again.

Pandarus as Idealized Friend

Pandarus appears initially as an ordinary figure from romance: the lover's best friend who goes between for him. This aspect of his characterization is so engaging that even in the twenty-first century an article can appear treating Pandarus exclusively as Troilus's friend,[7] despite the energy with which current criticism labels him an incestuous procurer. Like the majority of romance go-betweens and their friends, Pandarus and Troilus are from nearly the same social class. Although Troilus is a prince, Pandarus socializes easily with Troilus's relatives, and at one point he seems to be part of the king's high council (V, 281–86).[8] As in several romances, Pandarus is related to one of the couple; Alexandrine is Melior's cousin in *Guillaume de Palerne* just as Pandaro is Troilo's cousin in Boccaccio's *Filostrato*; and Laris in *Claris et Laris* and Urake in *Partonope de Blois* both go between for their sisters, just as Pandarus goes between for his niece. The most richly traditional aspect of Pandarus's role in *Troilus and Criseyde* is his part as confidant. Like Galehot and Lancelot, Claris and Laris, Lunete and Laudine, and Alexandrine and Melior, Pandarus is Troilus's dearest companion and loving, supportive friend who consoles, encourages, and cherishes him. As the good confidant should be, Pandarus is both a shoulder to weep on and a loyal comrade to share joy with. Troilus's great speeches about the nature of love are so uncolloquial and formal that the reader remembers them as soliloquies, but in fact Pandarus is the audience for some of the finest of them. "Love, that of erthe and se hath governaunce," Troilus's magnificent Boethian hymn at the end of Book III, for instance, is presented as a piece of habitual action. During the blissful time when Troilus was Criseyde's lover, the narrator tells us, Troilus would frequently lead Pandarus into a garden where Troilus would praise Criseyde and "synge in this manere" (III, 1743–44).

Traditionally, the confidant listens to intimate secrets and has privileged access to the soul of the lover, which is masked for everyone else. Sharing of this kind is the loving core of Pandarus's relationship with Troilus. The typical scene between these two occurs in Troilus's bedroom, and while the most memorable of these is the first long one in which Pandarus rallies Troilus from his depression and badgers him into admitting whom he loves, there are also several others. For instance, Pandarus's announcement that he has seen Criseyde and won her "love of frendshipe" for Troilus takes place in Troilus's bedroom as the two prepare to sleep. And after the first night of love between Troilus and Criseyde, Pandarus and Troilus spend the next day together in Troilus's room in a strikingly intimate scene of shared joy. Troilus marvels at his new feelings toward Criseyde now that they have become lovers:

> "I not myself naught wisly what it is,
> But now I feele a newe qualitee—
> Yee, al another than I dide er this." (III, 1653–55)

And Pandarus supportively echoes and clarifies his thoughts: "I dare say a man who has experienced the bliss of heaven feels differently from the first time he heard heaven talked about." Until nightfall, Troilus alternates between thanking Pandarus and praising the bounty of his lady: "This tale ay was span-newe to bygynne" (III, 1665). These scenes recall many similar bedroom scenes of shared confidences between lovers and go-betweens from idealized stories as different as *William of Palerne* and *Florimont*.

Although only these limited aspects of Pandarus match the idealized go-betweens securely, for most of the first half of the twentieth century, Chaucerians thought of him as legitimated by the romance go-between tradition. Impressed both by scholarly studies that uncovered a large number of romance go-betweens, primarily in French and Italian texts, and by contemporary critical notions about the ways of loving allegedly authorized by the rules of Courtly Love, Chaucerians stifled their initial alarm at finding a procurer in a love poem. Karl Young's 1908 monograph on effective friends and lovers' helpers from romance opened up an extensive continental tradition of figures like Boccaccio's and Chaucer's Pandaruses,[9] and the idea quickly took hold that medieval literary norms sanctioned Pandarus's going between. By 1913, in *Courtly Love in Chaucer and Gower*, W.G. Dodd did not bother to document his description of Pandarus's role as one of "the conventional ideas" of the period, "for the intermediary between the lover and his lady was a recognized figure in mediaeval love affairs."[10] This dictum became standard fare for Chaucer students. As late as 1963, A.C. Baugh was still confidently cautioning readers of his edition of Chaucer's poetry to judge Pandarus's behavior by Courtly Love standards: "The rules permitted both the lover and his lady to have a confidant. . . . However we may condemn his [Pandarus's] conduct by modern standards, his efforts in behalf of Troilus were sanctioned by the tenets of Courtly Love."[11]

This idea that the go-between tradition exonerated Pandarus actually had its beginning in a misreading of a passage from *Claris et Laris* that had been taken so far out of context that its meaning was reversed. Paolo Savj-Lopez, writing at the end of the nineteenth century about lovers' friends who go between in romances, quoted the speech in which Laris promises Claris to convince Lydaine to accept Claris's love: " 'Que l'avrez a vostre plesir' " ["to let you have her at your pleasure"] (3970–79; speech discussed on pages 120–21 above).[12] Laris is Lydaine's brother and Lydaine is married to Claris's king. As Savj-Lopez presented this speech, it seemed to show that romantic love and going between for a friend were valued so highly that they took precedence over all other obligations—marital, feudal, familial, and professional. W.W. Lawrence reproduced Laris's speech and translated it into English in 1916 as part of a discussion of the moral climate of opinion that made possible Boccaccio's and Chaucer's poems.[13] But neither Savj-Lopez nor Lawrence mentioned that Lydaine is fifteen and her husband the king is one hundred years old; nearly 4,000 verses pass before Laris acts on his offer, and then only to rescue Claris from a second nearly deadly faint; Lydaine is outraged when Laris finally proposes on Claris's behalf; and on and on so that it is Lydaine's shocked rejection of Laris's proposal, far more than the proposal itself, that mirrors the conventional morality of the period.

Edging Away from Romance

The go-betweens of romance are so intimately a part of the lovers' loving that their relationships to them pose dangers at every turn. To create Pandarus, Chaucer draws back from the conventionally conceived idealized courtly go-between to explore the treacherous potentials for illegitimate intimacy and power that the courtly go-between's role opens up. To suggest the breadth of those potentials, he develops Pandarus with homoerotic, heterosexual, and incestuous proclivities—disguised so that they can always be denied, but nevertheless unsettlingly present. Chaucer then gives him active, aggressive parts to play with both the man and the woman. Love in romance takes its stand on the idea that passionate, ecstatic, erotic love is also spiritual, elevating, and noble. Chaucer uses his newly reconceived go-between to generate disturbing currents of opposed conceptions of desire that swirl about and undercut this central concept of romance. As Chaucer opens up Pandarus's character to more and more alien possibilities, he moves him further and further away from the romance go-between.

If *Troilus and Criseyde* is read against a backdrop of romance, from the beginning of the poem the relationships seem slightly askew. Charles Muscatine identifies Troilus as the problem: "It is difficult to think of a single hero of French romance who is quite so prostrated by love, so removed from the actual business of courtship, who depends so completely on an intermediary."[14] But in fact French romance is full of prostrated heroes—and heroines too—incapable of courting and initially altogether dependent on intermediaries. William, in *William of Palerne*, for instance, sits day after day under an apple tree gazing up at Melior's window, unable to eat or sleep and dying of love. Lancelot has to be led to Guinevere, nearly faints when she speaks to him, and weeps until his garment is soaked to his knees with his tears. Claris brings Laris to the bedside of his lady where Laris is then struck dumb and has to be prompted to speak at all. Alexander is too self-effacing to betray any sign of his love to Soredamors, and these are just a few of the paralyzed lovers of the idealized stories.

Since the lovers served by the idealized go-betweens are often immobilized by their emotions, the go-betweens quite regularly supply the action for their brief plots, concocting a way to bring lover and lady together and carrying it out. Alexandrine takes Melior to the garden where William is dying of lovesickness; Galehot arranges Lancelot's first interview with Guinevere; Claris tells Marine that Laris loves her; and Guinevere announces to Soredamors and Alexander that they should marry. The generically inappropriate character in *Troilus and Criseyde*, then, is not Troilus. His paralysis enacts his humble despair at the thought of the unattainable excellence of the woman he loves—" 'She nyl to noon swich wrecche as I ben wonne' " (I, 777), and paralysis is one of romance's standard ways of expressing emotion. The inappropriate character is Pandarus.

Although the go-betweens contrive the beginning of the courtships and produce situations that allow the lovers and ladies to find each other, once their plots are in motion they do their best to get the lovers to take charge of the actual courting. Alexandrine absents herself as soon as William and Melior realize that they both love each other; Galehot leaves Lancelot with Guinevere until Lancelot faints and Galehot has to rush back to catch him; Claris only stops the kissing of Marine and Laris to make sure they realize their responsibilities as an engaged couple; and Soredamors and Alexander marry the very day that Guinevere tells them they love each other.

The go-betweens of romance support the lovers in their loving; Pandarus instead overpowers Troilus and slyly, deviously, and duplicitously attacks Criseyde. As Jill Mann describes, he "manipulates, coaxes, threatens and deceives with unflagging energy."[15] When *Troilus and Criseyde* begins, Troilus is as emotionally paralyzed and as resigned to dying of love as William and Melior. But Pandarus, unlike Alexandrine, excludes Troilus so radically from the courting of Criseyde that when Troilus presumes to ask Pandarus how he will proceed, Pandarus tells him to mind his own business:

> "Whi, entremete of that thow hast to doone!
> For Goddes love, I bidde the a boone:
> So lat m'alone, and it shal be thi beste." (I, 1026–28)

The traditional idealized go-between would have eased Troilus out of his paralysis and helped him become a lover. Pandarus instead reinforces Troilus's paralysis and reserves the courting of Criseyde for himself.

Even early in the poem, Pandarus's courting has disquietingly sexual overtones. His interactions with Criseyde are uncomfortably cozy and intimate. He moves from playful flirtatiousness—Take off your widow's veil! Let's dance!—to what looks very much like a pass camouflaged as a joke: thrusting Troilus's letter between Criseyde's breasts. John Fleming describes Pandarus's move as "a symbolic sexual aggression—if not a sexual violation."[16] Laura Hodges reminds us—as medieval hearers would not have needed to be reminded—that Pandarus would first have had to lift

Criseyde's widow's wimple to access her low-cut bodice, "an additional level of titillation."[17] Troilus could never have played such a trick but it typifies Pandarus's interactions with Criseyde, as does his arch taunt that closes the scene, telling her to throw the letter away so everyone will stare at them. As Richard Fehrenbacher describes Pandarus's "oddly overfamiliar behavior" with Criseyde, "their relationship is troubled by a scarcely concealed incestuous desire."[18] Chaucer added Pandarus's sex play to his source. There is nothing indecorous about this episode in Boccaccio's *Filostrato*: no comedy, no inappropriate familiarity, no forcing of Criseida, and no flirtatious relationship between the go-between and the lady. Once Pandaro suggests that Criseida is only pretending not to want Troilo's letter, she accepts it and tucks it between her breasts herself (2.113).[19]

Although Pandarus's intimacies with Criseyde create a more suggestive climate than any aspect of his initial conversations with Troilus, Richard Zeikowitz argues that they too trace a seduction. Zeikowitz casts Troilus as the too weak younger man who cannot resist his male friend and is ultimately "unwillingly seduced" by him into revealing whom he loves. Zeikowitz traces the "heightened eroticism" as Pandarus closes in on Troilus's secret. Once Troilus confesses Criseyde's name, Zeikowitz points out, Pandarus as know-it-all advisor dominates Troilus, taking total control of his pursuit of Criseyde.[20] Ultimately, Zeikowitz argues, "The text depicts mutual pleasure, yet also a politicized, sodomitical scenario: Troilus's pleasure with Pandarus comes as a result of his complete submission to Pandarus's schemes and manipulation. . .while Pandarus reaps the pleasurable rewards from having taken full charge of Troilus's personal life."[21]

For most readers, the most confounding development of the opening books of *Troilus and Criseyde* is the extent to which Pandarus usurps the initial relationship between the lovers. The sexual energy behind Pandarus's enthusiasm for both Troilus and Criseyde expresses itself less in attempts to possess either man or woman than in open maneuvers designed to let him share in their love. The double pronouns begin in Book I before Pandarus even knows what woman Troilus loves: " 'thow myghte after swich oon longe, / That myn avys anoon may helpen us' " (I, 619–20). By the end of Book I, they are coming thick and fast. It is " 'oure labour' " that will be wasted if Troilus is not patient enough, and Pandarus expects success unless " 'drerinesse / Or over-haste oure bothe labour shende' " (I, 971–72). As he dedicates himself to the service of Troilus and his lady, he imagines the time when they will love each other, no one else will know about it, " 'And so we may ben gladed alle thre' " (I, 994).

Pandarus channels Troilus's desire through himself to such a degree that he becomes part of the lovers' possessing of each other. Privacy was not articulated as a concept in the Middle Ages, and Steven R. Guthrie, discussing

Troilus and Criseyde as struggling toward a concept of privacy, characterizes Pandarus as an "invasive" go-between, "a go-between who comes between, surrounds, and overwhelms the two lovers," "the embodiment of invasion of privacy" in a plot that has no need for such an invasion. As Guthrie says, "Pandarus does not just intrude on the circle of lovers' intimacy, he takes up residence within it, dissolves both circles, and redraws them as a single circle around himself."[22]

This undercurrent of sexual sharing—Pandarus's flirtatiousness with Criseyde, the homoerotic dimension to the pressures he places on Troilus, and his attempt to join the couple in their loving—is altogether absent from the interactions of the romance go-betweens and their lovers. The go-betweens of the idealized stories maintain a decorous distance from the lovers' feelings. They are happy for them when their relationships succeed, but they never become so emotionally involved in the lovers' loving that they seem to be sharing their experiences vicariously. Urake in *Partonope of Blois* is the one idealized go-between who tries to manage a couple's relationship independently. She nearly derails it in the process, but her involvement with the lovers is not emotional like Pandarus's. None of the romance go-betweens identify so intensely with the couple and their pleasure that they intrude on their loving.

Pandarus's jokes are also not to be found in the romances. None of the idealized go-betweens are comic characters or make jokes like his, and most of his jokes are about loving. When he arrives at Criseyde's house, for instance, she greets him with:

"Tel us youre joly wo and youre penaunce.
How ferforth be ye put in loves daunce?"

"By God," quod he, "I hoppe alwey byhynde!"
And she to laughe, it thoughte hire herte brest.
Quod Pandarus, "Loke alwey that ye fynde
Game in myn hood." (II, 1105–10)

Pandarus, hopelessly in love, sounds like a family joke, " 'game in myn hood,' " and " 'I hoppe alwey byhynde' " must be lewd on some level. Similarly, when Criseyde invites Pandarus to a meal, he replies: " 'Nece, I have so gret a pyne / For love, that everich other day I faste.' " (II, 1165–66), and she nearly dies laughing. Or again, Pandarus pokes fun at romantic love's masochistic and paradoxical relishing of its pain by talking about his own " 'lusty sorwe.' " The major characters relate very differently to jokes like these. Pandarus makes them and enjoys them thoroughly; Criseyde laughs at them and sometimes contributes to them; and Troilus has nothing at all to do with them.

Like Pandarus, Boccaccio's Pandaro has loved the same woman unsuccessfully for some time, but his lack of success is mentioned solemnly, with
due respect, and his loving reinforces his role as a parallel figure to Troilo.
Pandaro sympathizes with Troilo's feelings and acknowledges their importance. In contrast, Pandarus's jokes about his hopeless loving match his
usual cynicism about idealized love. When Troilus first tells him he loves
Criseyde, as Pandarus leaves after promising to speak with her, Troilus
hastens to assure him that all he wants is an honorable relationship with her.
Pandarus replies: " 'Fy! No wight doth but so' "—["That's what everyone
says"] (I, 1038). From the start, Pandarus sees lust behind love, undermining
Troilus's elevated spiritualizing of desire.

As the lover's best friend and confidant, the lady's relative, and their social
equal, Pandarus clearly belongs among the idealized go-betweens, but they
are not cynical about love. It is the go-betweens for lust and sexual conquest
who smirk at the lofty claims of lovers, and the contrast between lover and
go-between appears in many of their stories. Since they are hired, for the most
part, the relationships they arrange mean nothing to them beyond their fees.
Ordinarily from a lower social class than the couple, most of them dismiss love
as meaningless lust. They make sex jokes, like Davus's tantalizing of the young
woman with "pignus" [pledge] and "factum" [the act] in *De nuntio sagaci*. Or
they savor the sex act, as Dame Sirith does when she gives Wilekin advice on
how far to stretch the thighs of the chaste wife she has trapped for him with
her trick of the dog and the mustard. If they speak the language of love, they
do it to seduce the woman, as the Old Woman does in *Pamphilus* when she
tells Galatea about Venus's flames and the delights of love. Or they use idealized language satirically or to deceive someone, as Hercelot does when she
refers to the priest as " 'saiges et cortois' " ["wise and courteous"] and
describes the twelve-year-old he believes he is buying as " 'plus blanche que
flor d'espine' " ["whiter than the thornbush flower"] to help lure the priest
into the bedroom where she will trick him into having sex with a prostitute
instead of the young virgin. The would-be lovers in these stories talk about
dying for love and cannot eat or sleep, but the go-betweens have no use for
their exalted conception of desire and deal only with what they see as its basis.
The difference between Troilus and Pandarus is a more subtle version of this
blatant contrast between the lovers in the stories about lust who lament their
breaking hearts, and their socially inferior go-betweens who laugh behind
their backs at the seducers' all too easily intelligible and unelevated desires.

Trafficking in Women

The usual idealized go-between works on behalf of both the man and the
woman, uniting two people who love each other, but the go-between

from the stories of sexual conquest is the agent of one of the couple and the adversary of the other. That is Pandarus's role. He is trafficking in women. From the moment Pandarus discovers that Troilus is in love, even before he knows who the woman is, his objective is to provide an affair with her for Troilus. Procuring for Troilus, Pandarus is Troilus's agent and Criseyde's adversary. As Pandarus instructs Troilus: " 'Lo, hold the at thi triste cloos, and I / Shal wel the deer unto thi bowe dryve' " (II, 1534–35). This is their shared conception of Pandarus's going between. Criseyde is a deer to be driven by the beater, Pandarus, to the hunter's station where Troilus will be waiting in hiding to shoot down his prey. At first Pandarus works to interest Criseyde in Troilus, praising his prowess on the battlefield and his friendliness, stressing her power over this prince—if she doesn't love him he will die—and bringing her to her palace window to watch Troilus ride past. Ladies in romances often admire their knights from castle towers, but only Pandarus stages such an episode.

One of Pandarus's weapons against Criseyde depends on the idealized stories for its impact. When Pandarus found Troilus ill in his room in Book I, he gave no indication that he already knew what was wrong with him, but when Criseyde inquires, " 'Kan he wel speke of love?' " Pandarus, with a little smile, describes a romantic event in an ideal setting, the palace garden in springtime. One day when Troilus was napping in the garden, Pandarus says he returned to overhear him confessing his sins to the god of love and bewailing his broken heart, wounded by one who stood in black (II, 523–25, 533–39). Pandarus claims to have tiptoed away unnoticed, leaving Troilus unaware that he had been overheard, and only later with great difficulty was he able to persuade Troilus to admit to being in love.

This is a traditional episode from the idealized stories: the comrade-in-arms's discovery of his comrade's suffering. Galehot lies awake all night listening to Lancelot weep and groan in his sleep. Laris awakens to hear Claris lamenting his hopeless love in such an extreme emotional state that he nearly dies. This episode is so conventional that *Protheseläus* burlesques it. As Melander tries to sleep, he overhears Protheseläus groaning about how much in love he is. Melander forces him to confide in him and promises to help him win Medea, but the episode is a comic anticlimax because Protheseläus has already told Melander that he loves Medea.

Pandarus's little tale for Criseyde is deliciously emotive, in part because it harks back to this repeated scene from idealized story, but, as always, it is a weapon. This archetypically romantic image of a desperate young knight lamenting his suffering alone in a spring garden arouses a whole different set of responses from Pandarus's first practical arguments about Troilus's rank and martial excellence. It would never occur to a reader that Galehot,

Melander, or Laris was lying to Guinevere, Medea, or Lydaine about their overhearing, but they are not trafficking in women. This episode is such an effective tool for Pandarus at this point and he is so much Criseyde's adversary that surely he is concocting this story to manipulate Criseyde.

R.W. Hanning describes Pandarus as a "fabricator, rather than decoder, of the poem's discourse of desire" and stresses that Pandarus "largely ignores the possibility that Criseyde might desire Troilus on her own."[23] Pandarus's fabricating is primarily manipulation of Criseyde, working her over to create the responses needed for Troilus's satisfaction. How unrelievedly and cleverly adversarial Pandarus is emerges in all his conversations with Criseyde. What seems most innocent turns out to be another tool for pressuring her to desire Troilus. This is Pandarus's most insidious form of trafficking in women, the mind-warping, brain-washing side of his pandering.

Pandarus swears for a whole stanza that he would rather have all three of them publicly hanged, hanged so high that everyone could see them, than do something as shameful as help someone destroy Criseyde's honor (II, 351–57). With so much to conceal and so much to accomplish, he balances in a high-wire act. His impact on Criseyde depends as much on timing, changes of tone, movement of argument, and modification of perspective as on his arguments themselves. The following undistinguished passage from the speech in which he first tells Criseyde that Troilus loves her throws Pandarus's usual methods into relief. He has already talked for six stanzas, Criseyde has yet to say a word, and the preceding stanza is his promise to guard her honor. He continues:

> "Now understonde, for I yow nought requere
> To bynde yow to hym thorugh no byheste,
> But only that ye make hym bettre chiere
> Than ye han doon er this, and moore feste." (II, 358–61)

The evident purpose of these lines is reassurance. The structure of their argument is not-A-but-B, where even A is not very threatening. Criseyde is not being asked to promise anything to Troilus, but only to be nicer to him. A brief version of Pandarus's usual threat follows: Troilus's despair is potentially deadly; Criseyde must show Troilus more favor " 'So that his lif be saved atte leeste' " (II, 362). And Pandarus then repeats his assurances that Criseyde's increased friendliness is all he or Troilus ever had in mind: " 'This al and som, and pleynly, oure entente. / God help me so, I nevere other mente!' " (II, 363–64). Pandarus underscores doubly how reasonable what he is asking is: " 'Lo, this requeste is naught but skylle, ywys, / Ne doute of resoun, pardee, is ther noon.' " And then, as if all were still in order, he hurries to cope with an imagined objection from Criseyde that

carries the action of the story several months—and much elaborately overcome reluctance—into the future:

> "I sette the worste, that ye dreden this:
> Men wolde wondren sen hym come or goon.
> Ther-ayeins answere I thus anoon,
> That every wight, but he be fool of kynde,
> Wol deme it love of frendshipe in his mynde." (II, 365–71)

To appreciate what a great deal Pandarus is presuming here one must keep
in mind that only seven stanzas earlier Criseyde first learned that Troilus
was in love with her. It will take another lengthy episode before the couple exchanges letters, several letters will pass between them before Pandarus
arranges their first face-to-face meeting, and yet here is Pandarus talking
about Troilus paying visits to Criseyde and Criseyde worrying that people
will notice she has a lover. After coaxing Criseyde along from one easily
accepted point to another, Pandarus has shaken off caution to leap to the
future. His next move, " 'What? who wol demen, though he se a man /
To temple go, that he th'ymages eteth?' " (II, 372–73), is one of his least
persuasive analogies: believing that Troilus's visits to Criseyde's home
mean he is her lover is like believing that a man who goes to a temple is
eating the statues in it. Its outlandishness and the sudden change in tone
from Pandarus's usual lecturing distract attention from how much he has
slipped in without comment. Pandarus then pulls back to safer ground,
reminding Criseyde of Troilus's character and circumspection, and how
universally his qualities are admired (II, 374–76), and as he continues,
Pandarus takes visits from Troilus to Criseyde for granted. Why would it
matter if everyone in town saw him coming?

> "Swych love of frendes regneth al this town;
> And wre yow in that mantel evere moo,
> And God so wys be my savacioun,
> As I have seyd, youre beste is to do soo." (II, 379–82)

Pandarus has moved from pressuring Criseyde to take pity on Troilus to
advising her about how to hide a love affair. And then equally suddenly, as
if nothing incongruous had been said, he reverts to his original unobjec-
tionable argument that Criseyde should save Troilus's life by being a little
nicer to him: " 'So lat youre daunger sucred ben a lite.' " (II, 384).

By the close of his four stanzas—leaping ahead, pulling back, leaping
ahead, pulling back in a typical procedure that allows him to cover far more
ground than he then admits to having covered—Pandarus has returned

Criseyde to their starting place. Since they end as they began, she can acknowledge as little as she pleases of what has been said, without either commitment or self-compromise. And yet the rest of Pandarus's unconfronted and unacknowledged suggestions continue to exert their influence on Criseyde's perception of her situation and its possibilities. Although she lets them pass without comment, the scenario Pandarus has sketched of Troilus's visits shielded by "love of friendship" functions as part of the pressure Pandarus brings to bear upon her to persuade her to love.

Nothing remotely like Pandarus's conversations with Criseyde occurs in the idealized stories. Since they typically concern couples who already love, their go-betweens seldom find themselves in situations in which they are trying to win love for someone. For the most part, they are arranging meetings, as Galehot does for Lancelot and Guinevere, and Alexandrine for William and Melior, or they are helping desperate young people declare themselves to each other, as Guinevere does with Soredamors and Alexander. On the rare occasion when they do try to convince someone to love, the few who do, Laris and Lunete, do not act like Pandarus with Criseyde. They are adversarial, but they are not subtle and sly, and they do not manipulate the other person with half-hidden suggestions. Laris and Lunete are winning wives for the men they go between for, or, in the case of Laris, winning the promise of a wife in the future. They are not engineering seductions, and their persuasion sounds tame and direct beside Pandarus's.

Laris's attempts to persuade his sister Lydaine to promise to love Claris are neither subtle nor seductive. Laris never mentions Claris's desirableness, or any of his attractive attributes. Instead, with Claris lying in a dead faint in the room where Laris and Lydaine are arguing, Laris announces that he promised Claris that Lydaine would love him, and if Claris dies of love, he, Laris, will burn Lydaine alive. This angry badgering has nothing at all in common with Pandarus's cunning tempting of Criseyde ever more deeply into a relationship that he promises will not turn into a love affair. Lunete's offensive against Laudine, in Chrétien de Troyes' *Yvain*, is no more like Pandarus's against Criseyde than Laris's is. Once again the go-between wastes no time describing the man's attractiveness. Instead of threatening the woman, however, she argues with her. Lunete is tough and relentless rather than tricky and cunning as she forces Laudine to see where her self-interest lies. Laudine must not waste time grieving over her dead husband, Lunete tells her. She must find someone to defend her spring, and God will send her a better husband. When Laudine insists that there could be no better husband than the one she has just lost, Lunete points out that the man who conquered Laudine's husband must be a better man than he, and with that her going between is virtually complete. Pandarus tempts Criseyde with his account of this able, attractive, and powerful young man who desires her. He frightens her with her deadly power over both Troilus and himself. He lies to her about Troilus's intentions, and he coaxes her so slyly into imagining herself in an ongoing relationship with Troilus that she does not even need to admit to herself that that is what she has been considering. This is a different order of going between from Laris's and Lunete's.

Il Filostrato

The go-betweens of romance do not account for Chaucer's Pandarus, but neither does Boccaccio's Pandaro. Romances typically celebrate idealized love; the *Filostrato*, on the other hand, celebrates shameful but ecstatically desired passion. That is the most basic reason why Boccaccio's Pandaro goes between so differently from Chaucer's Pandarus. Pandaro never conceals the love affair he wants Criseida to enter into with Troilo. He does not pretend to Criseida that loving Troilo like a brother, or just letting him look at her from a distance, or showing him "bettre chiere" will suffice. Taking a lover is always openly at issue. Pandaro is procuring for Troilo. Without knowing who the woman is, he promises him: "-Lascia far me, chè le fiamme amorose / ho per le mani e sì fatti sermoni-"(II, 32) [" 'Let me act, because I have at hand amorous flames and speeches of similar kind. . .' "]. He is Criseida's adversary as intensely as Pandarus will be, and he pursues her for Troilo by congratulating her for having attracted such a man and reminding her repeatedly of the advantages of such a brilliant catch. But he does not lie to her or trick her or lay plots to entrap her. He never tries to maneuver her into an intimate situation or deceive her about anything. His method is sexually candid persuasion; he talks her into the affair.

The easiest way for Pandaro to arrange Troilo's first meeting with Criseida would be to misrepresent his purpose, but Pandaro never takes any of the many opportunities that present themselves to conceal his intentions. Criseida protests that she can do nothing more for Troilo. When Pandaro encourages her to comfort Troilo and talk with him, she objects that she never intends to give him "la corona dell' onestà mea" [" 'the crown of my chastity' "] (II, 134). The obvious dodge for Pandaro is to assure her that comforting and conversation do not require giving up her chastity. Instead, Pandaro offers Criseida nowhere to hide. He dismisses her virtue as of no account. It is priests who praise this crown, he says, but only when they cannot rob it: "-E ciaschedun com' un santo ragiona, / e poi vi colgon tutte quante al sonno-" (II, 135) [" 'And each talks like a saint and then surprises all of you women in sleep' "]. No one will find out about Troilo, Pandaro promises her; Troilo is suffering a great deal, it is wrong to let a good act pass by undone, and being wise means not wasting time.

Criseida protests that she is Troilo's a thousand times over except in that one thing Pandaro wants of her, but, impatient with these last waverings, he asks her outright how and where she wants Troilo to come to her. Pandaro's work is finished because Criseida's resistance collapses, and as she agrees to take Troilo as her lover, she spells out what Pandaro's going-between has accomplished. For the first time, she admits openly to Pandaro that she desires Troilo. She stresses only one aspect of Pandaro's role. He has changed her from a woman who does not desire to a woman who does.

> -Tu hai l' onestà mia spezzata e rotta,
> io non ardisco di mirarti in faccia.
> . . . .
> il sangue mi s' agghiaccia
> intorno al cor, pensando quel che chiedi.- (II, 138)
>
> ["You have shattered and broken my virtue; I dare not look you in the face. . . .My blood turns to ice around my heart, when I think of what you ask."]

This is the essence of his going-between—her broken virtue and the planting of desire in her heart—and she insists that Pandaro is responsible for what she is about to do. She sounds urgent and accusatorial, without a trace of softening coyness in her manner, and she is openly and quite emotionally ashamed of the desire she feels:

> -Tu mi mettesti nel core un disio
> ch' appena credo ch' el n' esca giammai,
> e che mi fia cagion dell' onor mio
> perdere e, lassa, d' infiniti guai.- (II, 139)
>
> ["You put in my heart a desire which I believe will scarcely ever leave it, and which will be the cause of my losing my honor and, alas, of infinite troubles."]

After cautioning Pandaro once more about keeping the relationship secret, Criseida agrees to arrange the rendezvous with Troilo.

Troilo and Criseida begin their love affair themselves, quite independent of Pandaro. They spend the night together at Criseida's home by mutual agreement, and Criseida herself plans their meeting, greets Troilo with a thousand kisses, and then leads him to her bedroom "sí come quei ch' arde-van d' egual foco" ["as those who burned with equal fire"] (III, 30).

Boccaccio's Criseida, then, makes her own decision to love, and in that respect she is like the women of the idealized stories, but none of the romance heroines, deciding to love, speak the way Criseida does. There is no trace in her language of the ennobling spiritual passion that unites Florio and Biancifiore in the *Filocolo*, or William and Melior in *William of Palerne*, or Romadanaple and Florimont in *Florimont*. The lovers of the idealized stories are not at all ashamed of loving and have nothing to blame their go-betweens for. All three of Boccaccio's characters, however, believe that the passion Criseida feels is shameful, and they consider it shameful because they stress its sensuality. Sensual passion is guilty passion in the *Filostrato*; it is also immensely desirable, for both the man and the woman. The aim of this courtship is ecstatically sensual union, and its necessary condition is a woman so passionate that as she awaits her lover, she is as much on fire as he is. The more openly she desires him, the more perfect a lover she becomes.

Moreover, the shamefulness of this love is essential to its excellence. Passion and its intensification are the *Filostrato*'s principal values. Passion is so singularly the primary value in this story that Criseida and Troilo are willing to lose each other rather than lose it. With the exchange looming over them, threatened with separation, Criseida refuses to run away with Troilo because if he could possess her openly and whenever he wished, he would not desire her and she would not desire him: "-Ma se tu m' averai liberamente, / tosto si spegnerà l' ardente face / che or t' accende, e me similemente.-" (IV, 153). [" 'But if you will possess me freely, soon the burning torch will be extinguished which now enkindles you and me likewise.' "] It is the intensity of their passion that they must protect at all costs, not their relationship, and that intensity depends upon secrecy and difficulty, in other words upon shamefulness. The shamefulness of going-between, then, is an outgrowth of the primary, crucial, and desirable shamefulness of the loving itself.

When Pandaro tells Troilo that he has convinced Criseida to agree to an affair with him, he reminds him that if he compromises her reputation, Pandaro too will be disgraced since he is both her cousin and her guardian. With his fears as backdrop, he spells out his conception of the role he has been playing for Troilo.

-Io son per te divenuto mezzano,
per te gittato ho 'n terra il mio onore,
per te ho io corrotto il petto sano
di mia sorella, e posto l' ho nel core
il tuo amor.- (III, 6)

["I have for you become a go-between, for you I have cast my honor to the ground, for you I have corrupted the wholesome breast of my sister and have placed your love in her heart."]

Pandaro announces his view of his shameful role forcefully and unambiguously; he has become a "mezzano." But he then moves at once to a tantalizing glance forward at what lies in store for Troilo:

-Nè passerà lontano
tempo che 'l vederai con più dolzore
che porger non ti può la mia favella,
quando in braccio averai Criseida bella.- (III, 6)

["Nor will a long time pass before you will see her with more joy than my speech can give you, when you will have the beautiful Criseida in your arms."]

Boccaccio balances deliberately the price with the payoff. Troilo counters with his own conception of what Pandaro has done, claiming for Pandaro the traditionally honorable part of a loyal comrade-in-arms:

-Ma per l' amistà nostra ti richieggio
che quel nome villan tu non ti pogni
dove sovvien dell' amico a' bisogni.

Lascialo stare alli dolenti avari,
cui oro induce a sì fatto servigio;
tu fatto l'hai per trarmi degli amari
pianti ov' io era, e del duro letigio
che io avea con pensieri avversari
e turbator d'ogni dolce vestigio,
sì come per amico si dee fare,
quando l'amico il vede tribulare. (III, 16–17)

["But I beg you by our friendship that you do not apply that ugly name to yourself where it is a case of assisting a friend in his need.

"Let that name be for wretched, avaricious ones whom gold leads to such service. You have done it to draw me from the bitter anguish which I was in and from the harsh dispute which I had with adverse thoughts, the disturbers of any vestige of sweetness, as should be done for a friend when a friend sees him in tribulation."]

Although Pandaro's pressuring of Criseida far exceeds the going between in any of the romances, by claiming friendship as his motive, Troilo is fitting him into the idealized tradition. As Troilo continues, however, he under-cuts his previous argument and leaves this love affair as shameful as it has always been:

-E perchè tu conosca quanto piena
benivolenza da me t'è portata,
io ho la mia sorella Polissena
più di bellezza che altra pregiata,

ed ancor c' è con esso lei Elena
bellissima, la quale è mia cognata:
apri il cor tuo se te ne piace alcuna,
poi me lascia operar con qual sia l'una.- (III, 18)

["And so that you may know how much complete good will I bear for
you, I have my sister Polyxena, more praised for beauty than any other,
and also there is with her the most beautiful Helen, who is my sister-in-law.
Open your heart, if either of them pleases you; then let me work with
whichever one it may be."]

This is blatant trafficking in women, a chilling homosocial exchange: in
trade for Criseida, Troilo offers his sister or his sister-in-law, the cause of
the Trojan war. Short of pimping Johns for prostitutes, this is as brazen
trafficking in women as could be imagined. Troilo shows no sign of recognizing the bonds of family and society that he is offering to violate, or how
grossly immoral what he is suggesting is: procuring a woman for sex when
she and the man share no emotional attachment. Troilo has given up arguing that going between is moral. Procuring is Troilo's thank you for his
friend, nothing more or less. Troilo's first response to Pandaro attempted to
defend him by the code of the romance go-betweens, but nothing in idealized literature approaches this second stanza. The counter offer of Helen
and Polyxena is Boccaccio's deliberate move to shock the reader out of any
lingering romance perspective. It is less an argument than a gesture, a par-
rying. Going between in the *Filostrato* is dishonorable and valuable; shameful and indispensable; what must be hidden and what must be
accomplished; procuring and the generous act of a friend. It takes its place
beside the paradoxically valued dishonorableness of the love affair, just as
Boccaccio had moved the *Filostrato*'s love story away from the idealized
love of the romances toward the deliciously titillating, knowing, cynical
delight in sex that would fill story after story in the *Decameron*.

Explaining Pandarus via the Romances

Pandarus's aggressive, overly intimate approaches to Criseyde and his
suspiciously homoerotic takeover of Troilus's wooing of her raise questions
and anxiety levels as *Troilus and Criseyde* begins, but with the party at
Deiphebus's and the consummation night, his going between breaks
through all the limits of legitimacy. Neither of those episodes derives in any
way from the *Filostrato*, and there is nothing like them anywhere in idealized literature. Charles Muscatine, in *Chaucer and the French Tradition*, tried
to ground two aspects of this alien material in the romances: Pandarus's
presence in the lovers' bedroom and his tricks to trap Criseyde.[24] In fact,

go-betweens are often present during love scenes in romances, and even during scenes of consummated lovemaking. On the other hand, they usually have little or no impact on the action of those scenes or their atmosphere. None of the romance go-betweens introduce any of the elements Pandarus adds to Troilus and Criseyde's first meeting and first night together. Typically, nothing in the romances calls attention to the go-betweens. None of them interject themselves repeatedly into scenes of loving, or undercut romance attitudes toward love, or make little jokes like Pandarus's " 'Light is nought good for sike folkes yën!' " (III, 1137). And of course none of them throw the lover into bed. Steven Guthrie, writing about privacy in *Troilus and Criseyde*, describes the lovers' need for a "private" love affair far more than a secret one, and he writes about their "vulnerability. . . to the prying of sympathetic eyes."[25] None of the romance lovers are half-smothered by their go-betweens the way Troilus and Criseyde are by Pandarus. Romances simply do not use go-betweens the way Chaucer uses Pandarus.

Muscatine offers two go-betweens as intruders into love scenes comparable to Pandarus: Cypriane, Romadanaple's governess in *Florimont*, and Alexandrine, Melior's cousin in *Guillaume de Palerne*. Cypriane guards the lovers when they spend the afternoon together in the princess's bed after Florimont has been smuggled in as a tailor's helper, but Cypriane's role is the opposite of Pandarus's. Instead of encouraging the loving, she restrains it, and she never adds comedy to the scene. She arranges this meeting only because she believes Romadanaple is about to die of love, and the princess promises to remain chaste. Cypriane does break into the love scene itself, but not at all in Pandarus's fashion. As evening approaches, she interrupts the lovers to ask if Romadanaple has kept her promise of chastity. Instead of smiling knowingly as Pandarus does, Cypriane warns the couple of the dire consequences if they don't stop hugging and kissing before they are discovered together.[26] Although Cypriane is very much present in the bedroom of romance, she is not present as a Pandarus figure.

Muscatine's second illustration, from *Guillaume de Palerne* (*William of Palerne*), is even less like Pandarus's scenes with the lovers. Although Alexandrine urges Melior to pity Guillaume, there is no connection between her urging and Pandarus's pressuring of Criseyde. Melior is as devastatingly in love as Guillaume. Muscatine writes, "Only when the lovers finally embrace does she [Alexandrine] fade out of the picture, in a manner reminiscent of Pandarus."[27] But in fact, without comedy, without any ambiguity whatsoever about where she is and when she is present—no lights carried to fireplaces, no " 'Swouneth nought now' " issuing from unspecified sleeping quarters—Alexandrine leaves the lovers together in the garden and goes off to pick flowers and keep chance intruders away.

She even has a decisive exit line: "Iluec les laist, si s'en parti." (1720) [She left them there and departed]. In no way is she a hovering presence like Pandarus in *Troilus and Criseyde*.[28]

Muscatine matches a second scene from *Guillaume* with Troilus and Criseyde's first meeting at Deiphebus's house,[29] but this time there is no appreciable connection between the go-betweens. Guillaume and Melior have been secret lovers for some time by this point in the story, and Guillaume falls sick when he believes that Melior is going to marry someone else. Melior then goes to Guillaume's bedroom, accompanied by her retinue, but only she and Alexandrine actually enter the room (2805–08). The couple then reaffirms their love, makes love at length (2870–73), and by the close of this episode Guillaume is well again and the court is astonished at Melior's curative powers. But the important point here is that Alexandrine is never mentioned, neither during the love scene nor when Melior leaves. Alexandrine's only part is to enter with her lady—no poking, laughing, falling to her knees when the lovers kiss, or whatever. The poet effectively forgets her.

Muscatine does not mention the romance go-between whose bedroom activities most nearly resemble Pandarus's. She is Mirabell from the mid-fifteenth-century Middle English *Generydes*, which is believed to have been adapted from a lost Old French original that circulated in England in Chaucer's lifetime.[30] Mirabell's lady, Clarionas, falls ill after convincing herself that her fiancé, Generydes, loves someone else. When Mirabell brings Generydes to her lady to help her recover, Clarionas denounces him for faithlessness and he faints. Mirabell then persuades Clarionas to kiss Generydes to revive him, and Mirabell is present during this love scene. Unlike Pandarus, however, Mirabell is unswervingly lackluster and never says or does anything to differentiate herself from these chaste, conventionally presented lovers (4623–734).

The truth is, like Mirabell, go-betweens in the crowded love scenes of romance are typically ignored when not needed. When Protheseläus and Medea first meet, they are so overcome by emotion that they can only stare at each other, too swept away to speak or respond. Melander, who goes between for his comrade-in-arms, intervenes, suggesting that the queen kiss Protheseläus. She does and they kiss each other a hundred times over. Where is Melander during all of this? Where is Latin, another important nobleman who accompanied Protheseläus to Medea's tent? Far enough away so that both have to be called back when Medea wants to talk to them later, but close enough so that they appear at once when called. Deduction would suggest that they remain in Medea's tent, but their presence during this love scene is never alluded to (10614–727).

Floriant et Florete,[31] a thirteenth-century French romance, illustrates dramatically the problems raised by trying to account for Pandarus's role during intimate scenes by associating him with the similar inclusion of French go-betweens. Floriant loves and is loved by Florete, whose father, the emperor of Constantinople, is fighting against Floriant, and Gauvain, Floriant's comrade-in-arms, loves and is loved by Blanchandine, Florete's lady-in-waiting and daughter of the King of Hungary. Floriant and Florete both fell in love when they exchanged a few words, but neither suspects the other's feelings. Floriant, in the middle of a battle, faints at his next sight of Florete and has to be carried off the field. When Gauvain discovers that Floriant is unwounded, he suspects the cause of his faint and, in traditional confidant fashion, coaxes him into admitting he is in love. Events on the women's side match these exactly. When Florete sees Floriant fall in battle, she too faints, and Blanchandine helps Florete confess her love.

Joli, a young nobleman, goes between for the couples, first carrying a message for Floriant from Florete and then returning with a declaration of love and a ring for Florete and a ring and a parallel love message from Gauvain for Blanchandine with a request that the women meet the men that night. Seduction is never an issue here. These are willing lovers, women and men both, and it is the women who work out the arrangements for the night meeting, not the go-between. They send Joli back to Floriant and Gauvain with the key to the orchard gate and an invitation to the men to meet them there. The lovers spend that first night, and every night following, by moonlight together in the orchard, and Joli's part shifts from messenger to guard, protecting the lovers against intruders. The scenes Joli guards are sexually intimate (4339–42) and the poet stresses the lovers' unreserved loving (4440–43).

The final episode of this double love story establishes Joli's presence in that garden of love. The idyllic nights of love by moonlight end when a dwarf in the hire of Florete's father chances upon the couples and betrays them to the emperor. The dwarf reports seeing Florete and another young woman in the orchard with two knights who " 'En font totes lor volentez' " (4499) ["Do their will with them"]. Although the emperor rushes immediately to the orchard with his soldiers, the lovers, warned by Joli, escape to Floriant's camp where they marry with King Arthur's blessing. When the dwarf sees the lovers, Joli sees the dwarf, and so it follows that he, too, is an observer of that intimate scene, but while his presence is demonstrable, no reader would notice that he was there. Technically a go-between who watches love's feast, Joli does not exist emotionally and effectively. Although a plot summary of this poem suggests that he is very much involved in the affairs of these lovers, so little is made of his role that a reader would be unlikely to have any recollection of him.

The fact that the love scenes in idealized stories include many go-betweens explains little about Pandarus's role because they are so unlike him. They do not make jokes like his or act the way he does; they do not throw lovers into beds or preside over deliberately compromising situations—the woman surprised in bed in the middle of the night; they do not break into the atmosphere of the emerging love scene to turn the reader's attention to the carnality of love and suggest that it is amusing. Most important of all, they do not maneuver the woman into a sexual relationship that she may or may not be ready to accept.

Muscatine also implies that tricks like Pandarus's to trap Criseyde are common in "romance intrigue,"[32] but the tricks in romance are critically different from Pandarus's tricks. They are played to protect the lovers against the outside world of hostile relatives and authority figures, not to seduce the woman. Muscatine cites the plot of *Éracle*, but the Old Woman who hides the lovers in the hole in her floor in *Éracle* is carrying out Athanaïs's orders so the lovers can consummate their love despite the empress's guards. Similarly, Alexandrine dresses William and Melior in animal skins so that they can escape from her father's court; Cypriane and Delfin hide Florimont behind a tailor's helper's outfit to win him entrance into Romadanaple's bedroom; Blanchefleur's old nurse disguises her as a beggar to smuggle her into Rivalin's bedroom. This is trickery on behalf of lovers, not seduction tricks like Pandarus's.

In all the idealized stories discussed in this book, only one go-between plays a trick that resembles Pandarus's trick: Glorizia in Boccaccio's *Filocolo* hides Florio behind Biancifiore's bed curtains so that he will be able to awaken her to make love with him. Boccaccio's development of this episode shows how concerned he was that the woman not seem to be tricked. Before Biancifiore goes to sleep, with Florio overhearing her from his hiding place, she tells Glorizia how much she desires Florio and how much she wishes he were with her; she prays to Venus to bring Florio to her; she talks to herself about loving Florio as she falls asleep; she is dreaming about making love with him when he awakens her; and the couple takes formal marriage vows before consummating their love. Glorizia is reuniting two already passionately committed people separated by an evil admiral who purchased Biancifiore for his harem, and yet this is as close as the idealized stories come to portraying a go-between tricking a woman into love.

Claris lies to Marine by pretending to be Laris and hugs and kisses her to revive her from a deadly faint. But Marine loves too much, not too little, and Claris is lying to her to convince her of a truth: this lover she believes is dead is in fact alive and in love with her. And while Claris's behavior is intimate, it never becomes sensual. As soon as Marine revives, she denounces him, and sexual possession by trickery is never even momentarily at issue. Everything important to Pandarus's tricking of Criseyde is missing in this episode.

Everything relevant is also missing from the going between of the third and last of these romance figures, Lunete, from Chrétien de Troyes' *Yvain*. When Lunete initially convinces Laudine to accept Yvain as her husband three days after Yvain killed her first husband, Lunete does not use any trickery at all. Her one weapon is a deductive argument: if one man kills another, then which is the better warrior? Lunete does trick Laudine into reaccepting Yvain as her husband when he breaks his promise to return to her after a year of tourneying. This time Lunete convinces Laudine that she must recruit the Knight of the Lion to stop the attacks of a knight whose storms are threatening her town. She can only recruit him by promising to help him regain his lady's love, and since both the Knight of the Lion and the attacking knight are Yvain himself, Lunete has tricked Laudine into resuming her marriage and so saving her town without losing face, but the trap Lunete lays for Laudine has nothing to do with Pandarus's traps. The romances do not account for the tricks Pandarus plays on Criseyde any more than they explain his presence in the bedroom during the consummation scene.

Becoming Lovers and the Double Go-Between Tradition

Before the Deiphebus episode, it is possible to believe that, despite Pandarus's officiousness and questionable pressuring, he is working to win Criseyde's agreement to love Troilus. But once Pandarus sets his traps for Criseyde at Deiphebus's and then at his own house, his going between shifts definitively to the techniques of the stories about sexual conquest: elaborate deceptions and lies about who is or is not where. Consent is essential in the idealized stories. Both partners must love each other and agree to consummate their love. Idealized go-betweens do not trick one of the couple into loving because idealized loving is impossible without consent. It takes consent to nullify sex as male power. The crux of the typical story about lust, however, is sex without consent. Someone is tricked or trapped into having sexual relations, just as Pandarus tricks and traps Criseyde.

For a medieval audience, what was going on in *Troilus and Criseyde* would have been obvious at once: a romance go-between was using the methods of the go-betweens for sexual conquest; and the contradictory meanings evoked by the traditional depictions of these two figures would have flooded Pandarus's scenes in Books II and III. Pandarus's going between is greatly sophisticated compared with the going between in the tales of lust, but it is deeply rooted in them. The Old Woman in the *Decameron* story who lectures the young woman on how soon she will lose her good looks, and how important it is for her to enjoy love while she is still young sounds quite a lot like Pandarus. And so do Davus from *De nuntio sagaci*, the Old Woman from

Pamphilus, Houdée from *Pamphile et Galatée,* and Trotaconventos and several other go-betweens from the *Libro de buen amor* as they urge the woman to embrace the joys of life while she is still young and lovely, and assure her that her suitor is an ideal person: noble, rich, clever, and faithful. The most important similarity between these go-betweens and Pandarus, however, and their most important difference from their idealized counterparts, is the stance they take toward the woman. For them, going between means putting something over on someone else, just as it always does for Pandarus. His technique is far more subtle than Houdée's or the Old Woman's or Davus's, all of whom pooh-pooh the young women's fears and assure them that the young men just want to be their friends; and Criseyde is a far more formidable and sophisticated adversary than the young women in these stories; but all these go-betweens, Pandarus included, are equally predatory.

Interpretations of *Troilus and Criseyde* diverge notoriously. C. David Benson describes the poem as sanctioning "no single consistent attitude towards the romance between Troilus and Criseyde." Instead, readers "find in the love-affair everything from passionate sensuality to divine harmony and from comic cynicism to lyrical idealism."[33] Peter Christmas registers less satisfaction with the poem's contradictions: "We are left finally. . .baffled in the natural desire to grasp a singleness of meaning," he writes, and he portrays the characters as each containing "ingredients which deliberately cancel each other out, leaving behind a turbid and uncomfortable tension."[34] Instead of grasping for "a singleness of meaning," Carolyn Dinshaw sees the disparateness of the poem as a virtue and its core. She argues against unified interpretations that depend on a reductive critical "flight into order and stability," and reads the text as depicting the "instability and disorder in human experience" as it resists closure, just as "The narrative itself resists expedient ending and final closure."[35] John Hermann, like Dinshaw comfortable with the poem's contradictions, writes about the "labyrinth of interpretations that *Troilus and Criseyde* has spawned," "the plurality of the text, the joyfully puzzling game it establishes for the interpreter by supplying evidence for conflicting interpretations."[36]

Critical responses to the consummation scene, even more so than to the poem in general, create the impression that the responders are struggling to follow the poem in manifold conflicting directions at the same time. After describing the discordant interpretive indications Chaucer offers the reader for the beginning of the consummation scene, and Criseyde's yielding hidden "behind a kaleidoscopic discourse of events and images that defeats precise decoding," Hanning writes, "at its moment of highest aspiration, *Troilus and Criseyde*'s discourse of desire finds (or rather constructs) an interpretive impasse."[37] Louise Fradenburg puts the problem more bluntly: "The consummation scene is written to produce an ambiguity that *cannot be resolved* through interpretation."[38]

Along side the many readings that find ambiguity, contradiction, and unresolvable incongruity in the consummation scene, others take often categorically opposed stands on how it should be read. Two essays published back-to-back in *Masculinities in Chaucer: Approaches to Maleness in the* Canterbury Tales *and* Troilus and Criseyde, for instance, disagree totally about Troilus's sexual capabilities. Derek Brewer, in "Troilus's 'Gentil' Manhood," contends that "there is simply no evidence nor any reason to suppose that Troilus may fear sexual impotence. His love is naturally sexual."[39] But Maud McInerney, in " 'Is this a mannes herte?': Unmanning Troilus through Ovidian Allusion," claims that Troilus's problem in the consummation scene is that he cannot get an erection: "Falling in love, for Troilus, renders *making* love impossible."[40]

During the scene at Deiphebus's house and the consummation scene, the double go-between tradition lies behind every word, action, and gesture, complicating them with their double contexts, incorporating into the poem the interpretive discord that these critical responses bear witness to. When Carolyn Dinshaw argues for a deconstructive reading of *Troilus and Criseyde* that will include "the disruptive Other," "the disturbing," and "the unstable and threateningly destabilizing,"[41] she is still far from denoting the explosive clash of the literary traditions that lie behind Chaucer's poem. Their effect is the repeated engagement and disengagement of the audience from the most fundamental concepts of the poem, a moving in and out of such profoundly conflicting ways of understanding desire that, again and again, the contradictions overturn the experience of reading a love story. In the romances, passion is spiritual, a redemptive virtue; love ennobles, transforms, and elevates; and the go-betweens are motivated by friendship, devotion, and love. In the stories about lust and sexual conquest, woman is a victim to be seduced or raped, or a rampantly highly sexed seductress who robs or devours men; love is an exploitative game; the sex act is Ovidian farce or bestial rutting; and the go-between is trafficking in women. Through the double go-between tradition, Troilus and Criseyde's two meetings are projected against opposing conceptions of desire.

The elegant and high-ranking dinner guests at Deiphebus's reaffirm the romance context, but the episode itself is shaped like an incident from a story about lust and sexual conquest. The complexity of the trick and the amount of detail it involves—the fictitious lawsuit, the dinner party, Troilus in bed, the double set of doors on Troilus's bedroom, the alleged chaperons, the document for Deiphebus and Helen to read in the garden— match the plot convolutions in fabliaux in which much of the pleasure of the story depends on its difficulty and neatness: Dame Auberee's hidden thimble and needle in the surcoat underneath the bedcovers; or Hercelot's trick that beds down the priest with the prostitute instead of the twelve-year-old. On the other hand, compared to Criseyde's violated consent, the surface resemblance of the Deiphebus episode to a fabliau plot is a minor link to the stories of sexual conquest. The lies about Poliphete and his lawsuit that Pandarus creates to bring Criseyde to Troilus's side leave her feeling weak, threatened, and ideally ready to appreciate the protection a powerful lover offers a single woman. Moreover, threatened and vulnerable, she loses that conviction of her independence that she values so highly when she first considers the merits of loving: " 'I am myn owene womman, wel at ese—/ I thank it God' "(II, 750–51). Pandarus's trick exerts double pressures on Criseyde. It increases her awareness of a desirable aspect of loving and it subtracts a desirable aspect of remaining unattached.

When Criseyde and Troilus first meet, she has only agreed to see him, chaperoned by Helen and Deiphebus, to ask his help to protect her against Poliphete. Once she and Pandarus are alone at Troilus's door with Pandarus summing up how important Troilus is and how near death he is from love, she surely realizes that her uncle has been misrepresenting this meeting. Nevertheless, she never consents to join Troilus in a bedroom to hear him talk about love. She is maneuvered under triple false pretenses— Poliphete is threatening her, Troilus is sick, and Helen and Deiphebus are with Troilus—into a situation that subtracts the need for her decision. Instead of choosing to love, she is swept along by Pandarus's machinations. Criseyde's passivity, like Troilus's immobility, is in part a function of Pandarus's manipulating. Pandarus deceives the audience of high-ranking Trojans about just what sort of crowd is in Troilus's bedroom, but that part of his deception is trivial compared to his manipulating and pressuring of Criseyde. She may be willing or even eager for this meeting, but she is delivered to Troilus's bedside by a go-between, in direct violation of the most important traditions of idealized going between. Often the appeal of a story of sexual conquest like this one—a woman tricked into an intimate setting with a man who wants to become her lover—derives from the reader's identification with the male as he overpowers her. But while Pandarus goes between from the tradition of the Latin comic tales and the fabliaux, Troilus loves from the tradition of the romances. As Criseyde asks him to continue protecting her against Poliphete, the conceptions of men from the two traditions collide. In this double context, romance and story about lust at once, Troilus is struck dumb, blushes, forgets his prepared speeches, and dissolves in agonies of shame over the role reversal generated by his part in deceiving his lady. As the romance lover, he should be begging her to take pity on him; instead, she is asking him for political protection. As the episode proceeds, it ricochets from type to type and mood to mood. Troilus's exquisitely lyrical first words to Criseyde, " 'Mercy, mercy, swete herte!' " (III, 98), are the quintessence of the romantic lover's humble desperation, but then Pandarus intervenes "And poked evere his nece new and newe"(III, 116). No idealized heroine has ever been moved to love by poking. When Pandarus pleads with Criseyde to " 'make of this thing an ende' " and Criseyde replies, she sounds as inelegant as her uncle: " 'I! what?' quod she, 'by God and by my trouthe, / I not nat what ye wilne that I seye' " (III, 120–21). This dialogue, with its repeated "I, whats," is the antithesis of Troilus's songlike idiom, lush with the formulas of love poetry. Criseyde is " 'O goodly, fresshe free,' " " 'my lady right and chief resort,' " and he will find joy under her " 'yerde.' " His reply even has a verbal frame. It begins, " 'What that I mene, O swete herte deere?' " and closes, " 'Lo, this mene I, myn owen swete herte' " (III, 127–47).

Like Troilus, Criseyde can speak the language of romantic love. He is her " 'deere herte and al my knyght,' " and she will receive him fully into her service and turn all his bitterness into sweetness, repaying every woe with bliss (III, 161, 176–79). To play the woman's role in a plot from the stories of lust and sexual conquest, Criseyde has been tricked into this bedroom. To play the woman's role in an idealized plot, she must consent to be there. She does so by action as well as in her formal acceptance of Troilus. Like Guinevere in the meadow with Lancelot, Criseyde takes Troilus in her arms and kisses him.

Troilus's language of love ascends beyond carnality, but as this episode closes, Pandarus reverses perspective to the lust story's relishing of sexual satisfaction. With a half-concealed leer, he offers to have Troilus and Criseyde meet at his house:

"And eseth there youre hertes right ynough;
And lat se which of yow shal bere the belle
To speke of love aright!"—therwith he lough—
"For ther have ye a leiser for to telle." (III, 197–200)

Pandarus's imperviousness to the values of romance switches focus back to the stories where love-talk like Troilus's is a cover-up for lust. In both perspective and mood, again and again, Pandarus's joking frames Troilus and Criseyde's moments together, calling into question the meaning of love and the sources of energy of romance.

Two brief passages describing the feelings and activities of Criseyde and Pandarus in the period following the Poliphete episode illustrate the impact of the two kinds of story on *Troilus and Criseyde*. After explaining that Troilus stood so high in his lady's grace that Criseyde thanked God twenty-thousand times over that she had met him, Chaucer lists the qualities she values in Troilus:

> She fond hym so discret in al,
> So secret, and of swich obëisaunce,
> That wel she felte he was to hire a wal
> Of stiel, and sheld from every displesaunce. (III, 477–80)

A few lines later Chaucer notes the activities of Pandarus:

> And Pandarus, to quike alwey the fir,
> Was evere ylike prest and diligent;
> To ese his frend was set al his desir.
> He shof ay on, he to and fro was sent;
> He lettres bar whan Troilus was absent;
> That nevere man, as in his frendes nede,
> Ne bar hym bet than he, withouten drede. (III, 484–90)

Criseyde's shield and wall of steel evoke Troilus in his role as knight, and discretion, obedience, and protecting her honor are traditional virtues for a romance lover, conventional qualities presented in conventional language. This is elevated, idealized, romantic loving. Pandarus instead is talking about passionate physical feeling, desire imaged as a fire that can be quickened—fueled and blown into flame—the desire that is the stock-in-trade of the go-between in the service of lust and sexual conquest. Feeling is manipulable here, capable of being worked on, rather than idealized above all intervention like Troilus's loving. Love as Pandarus conceives of it is so susceptible to effort that one can be "diligent" about quickening it. Finally, this is love that will "ese" his friend. Love that gives relief, that eases, is not idealistically elevated love. And "shof" is a blatantly inelegant word and concept. In even such a small way, *Troilus and Criseyde* invokes the double tradition of the literature of going between.

All the elements that link the first meeting of Troilus and Criseyde to the stories of lust and sexual conquest reappear magnified, intensified, and greatly problematized in the consummation scene. As before, the crucial issue is violated consent, and this time Criseyde's consent is even more egregiously violated. She is literally trapped. To create this archetypically dangerous situation—a woman awakened in the middle of the night by a man in her bedroom—Pandarus must have Criseyde spend the night at his home. Neither her palace nor the daytime would produce the impact he needs. In the dark, in a strange environment that she does not normally control, Criseyde is as sexually vulnerable as Pandarus can make her. Even the presence of her attendants becomes a weapon against her. If she calls them, she has no uncompromising way to explain the presence of either Troilus or Pandarus. For self-protection, she must keep quiet—let sleeping hounds lie, as Pandarus puts it (III, 764). Criseyde's situation approaches the young wife's in *Auberee* when the young man gets into bed with her. When the wife threatens to scream, he warns her that she will be publicly shamed if anyone discovers her naked with him in the middle of the night.

Pandarus has created a standard scenario for a rape, and his trick is the most ordinary trick of the literature of sexual conquest: get the woman into a room with a bed, bring in the man, and shut the door. This is the trick Dame Auberee plays, as does Davus in *De nuntio sagaci*, the Old Woman in *Pamphilus*, Houdée in *Pamphile et Galatée*, and Trotaconventos in the *Libro de buen amor*. Moreover, these stories loom just behind *Troilus and Criseyde*. Chaucer certainly made use of one of these and probably three of them as sources for this episode. T.J. Garbáty established that *Troilus and Criseyde* uses *Pamphilus* and he also suggested that Chaucer may well have heard the *Libro de buen amor* sung by minstrels when he was in Spain.[42] John V. Fleming and I have argued that *Pamphile et Galatée* is one of *Troilus and Criseyde*'s sources.[43] More than any other moment in *Troilus and Criseyde*, the consummation scene is deeply embedded in the stories in which go-betweens serve lust.

Chaucer sets up the consummation itself with extreme contrasts in language and attitude that pit the traditions of going between for lust and going between for idealized love against each other. As in earlier episodes, Pandarus is not merely an alien speaker using jarring vocabulary and behaving unceremoniously. He acts and speaks from the conception of lovers as lustful bodies and loving as coupling, an eminently accomplishable enterprise to laugh at and peek in on. For Troilus, as always, desire is transfigured into passionate, ecstatic romantic loving. When Pandarus tells Troilus, hidden in the "stewe," that the plot has succeeded and it is time for them to go to Criseyde's bedroom, Troilus, overcome by the near-sacredness of the enterprise, launches into appeals for aid from Venus, Jove, Mars, Apollo, Mercury, Diana, and the three Fates, evoking all the principals in the names of lovers they have desired and lost—" 'O help now at this nede!' " (III, 728). The prosaic, self-confident, altogether earth-bound voice of Pandarus, who does not doubt the probability of success, frames Troilus's anguished petition. As Troilus begins,

"Now, blisful Venus, thow me grace sende!
. . .For nevere yet no nede
Hadde ich er now, ne halvendel the drede" (III, 705–07)

Pandarus interrupts:

> "Ne drede the nevere a deel,
> For it shal be right as thow wolt desire;
> So thryve I, this nyght shal I make it weel,
> Or casten al the gruwel in the fire." (III, 708–11)

Beside Troilus in desperate prayer, Pandarus talks about throwing porridge in the fire. To him, Troilus's spiritualization of love is a simple failure of nerve, and as Troilus appeals to the Fates, Pandarus breaks in with: " 'Thow wrecched mouses herte, / Artow agast so that she wol the bite?' " (III, 736–37).

Throughout the goings-on preparatory to Troilus and Criseyde's loving, Chaucer tugs his audience back and forth between idealized conceptions of desire and desire as the stories of sexual conquest portray it. When Criseyde invites Troilus to sit down, Pandarus interjects with a knowing leer:

> "Now wol ye wel bigynne.
> Now doth hym sitte, goode nece deere,
> Upon youre beddes syde al ther withinne,
> That ech of yow the bet may other heere." (III, 974–77)

Pandarus's legendary triple non-exit lines sustain the tension between the two conceptions of love. He is never shown leaving Criseyde's bedroom. No sooner is the audience confident that the lovers are alone than Pandarus reintroduces the raised eyebrows of carnality: " 'Light is nought good for sike folkes yën!' " (III, 1137). Once the love scene seems to have begun in elevated, romantic earnestness and Troilus has Criseyde in his arms, Pandarus jokes about Troilus's faint, raising the potency issues Pandarus has associated with the faint: " 'If ye be wise, / Swouneth nought now, lest more folk arise!' " (III, 1189–90).

The double go-between traditions collide most spectacularly when Troilus faints. Of all the go-betweens in medieval literature, only Pandarus literally throws a lover into bed. Throwing lovers into beds would suit the ambience of the stories of sexual conquest, but most of the men who hire go-betweens are so brazen and full of lust that the occasion does not arise. Consider, for instance, the priest in *Du Prestre et d'Alison*, or the young man in *Auberee*, or Pyrrhus who disguises himself as his sister in *Alda*, or Raoul who tries to rape Jehanne, and many others. Only the Pamphilus figures have to be warned to "be men" when the situation presents itself, but the go-betweens shut them into rooms with the young women rather than actually throwing them into bed. In Boccaccio's *Filostrato*, Pandaro is never present in the bedroom of love. In the idealized stories, the couple, not the go-between, controls their situation, and both the man and the woman agree to consummate their love before they reach the point of physical union. Moreover, most of the idealized couples in these stories involving go-betweens only consummate their relationships after they marry, which eliminates these issues.

For many contemporary critics, Troilus's faint undercuts whatever is left of his stature as a lover. Diane Steinberg, for instance, writes that "love becomes a debilitating and a feminizing experience" for Troilus. "The fainting Troilus, who must be lifted onto the bed next to his lady, is as passive and inept a lover as he is a fearsome and deadly warrior."[44] Sealy Gilles, writing about love and disease, describes Troilus's response to Criseyde's tears as a "hysterical reaction" and sees a "comic scenario" in "the swooning, perhaps impotent, lover tossed into bed with his bewildered beloved and rubbed and coaxed out of his stupor."[45] Maud McInerney observes that "Troilus's faint is perceived as funny not only by every class of undergraduates which encounters it, but also by Pandarus, who pokes fun at it as he falls asleep. It is funny precisely because it suggests not restraint, which is voluntary, but impotence, which is involuntary, and a favorite source of Chaucerian humour."[46]

Troilus's feminization and infantilization in this episode are essential for Elaine Hansen's argument about male/female relationships in *Chaucer and the Fictions of Gender*. Discussing "masculine anxiety" and the "difficulty that men face in securing masculine identity and dominance," she writes that "the courtly model of aristocratic behavior feminizes the male lover— rendering him subservient, weakened, infantilized, privatized, and emotional."[47] She explains Troilus's unmanliness in the "infamous bedroom scene" as follows: "if the lover is as conventionally submissive, frightened, infantilized, and unmanned by love as he is supposed to be, he will not be able to perform like a man in an actual heterosexual encounter."[48]

The roles of males in several romances initially match the pattern Hansen describes. Like Troilus in Book I, the man gives up all aggression because he idealizes the woman so much that he cannot imagine himself as her lover and therefore cannot begin to court her. In the typical story, however, the power implications of the role-reversal, the male acting as the female's servant, do not come into play because the woman loves and idealizes the man equally and is equally paralyzed by love. This is Alexander's situation with Soredamors, William of Palerne's with his Melior, and Generydes' with Clarionas, which, of course, is why they all need go-betweens. Once their go-betweens bring these couples together, on the other hand, they become lovers or agree to marry, and there is no

suggestion that the men have been emasculated and infantilized by partici-
pating in the emotional capacity of women. In romances, being capable of
extraordinarily intense, idealizing love is a sign of manliness rather than of
effeminacy.

Moreover, the fainting hero is a romance convention, and, far from
suggesting the hero's inability to perform like a man, fainting traditionally
bears witness to his spirituality and the great strength of his love. The fainting
hero appears in many works that make heavy use of conventions, for
instance, *Floriant et Florete*, *Generydes*, and *Claris et Laris*. When Floriant
catches sight of Florete, he faints despite the fact that he is in the middle of
a battle, and he has to be carried off the field to safety (3949–70).
Generydes faints when Clarionas accuses him of infidelity (4702–17). Claris
faints twice out of despair and extreme love suffering, and both times his
comrade-in-arms believes Claris is about to die (3950, 8090). In two far
more adventuresome and less conventional works, Lancelot, in the Prose
Lancelot, falls as if he were about to faint during his first interview with
Guinevere and Galehot has to rush forward to catch him (346), and
Florimont, in *Florimont*, collapses in such a deadly faint that Delfin, his
comrade, believes it will be fatal and revives him by promising to help him
court Romadanaple (8197–221). There is no anxiety in these stories about
the virility of these fainting men, or suggestion that they are not successful
lovers. Quite the reverse, Floriant is Florete's lover night after night in her
father's garden, and Lancelot is such a spectacular lover that he is honored
magically. When he and Guinevere first make love, a mysterious split
shield given to Guinevere by the Lady of the Lake reunites so that the
knight and lady painted on it are joined in an embrace (556). Generydes,
Claris, and Florimont wait until after their marriages to consummate their
relationships, but there is no implication that they wait because the men
lack virility. In the romance convention, it is great lovers who faint.
Fainting may indicate their gender instability in the sense of their openness
to emotions identified as appropriate for females, but in none of these cases
is there any indication that their fainting is supposed to suggest weakness,
infantilization, feminization, or lack of virility. Moreover, all these men are
great warriors. As Lancelot faints, for instance, Guinevere has just discovered
that he is the greatest warrior of their time and that she and King Arthur
owe their kingdom to him. By romance convention, a swoon is an impressive
expression of extreme emotion, as appropriate to men as to women.

Moreover, there is another equally important complication to the reading of Troilus's swoon. He does not faint because he fears making love to
Criseyde; he faints because he has wronged her. Pandarus's arguments to
convince Criseyde to allow Troilus into her bedroom strike directly against
her sense of herself as a loving woman. She is ashamed, and her despair in

the false felicity speech shows how deeply Troilus's alleged lack of faith in her moves her. Later, when Troilus is seated on her bed, she talks for ten stanzas about the kinds and causes of jealousy, concluding by swearing her innocence and crying a little. It is Troilus who is hurt most by Pandarus's no-holds-barred going-between. With all the emotional tension generated between Pandarus and Criseyde, it is easy to overlook the fact that while Pandarus is berating Criseyde, Troilus hears everything they both say. He is hidden from Criseyde by her bed curtains, but he is present while Pandarus is accusing her of loving Horaste and he hears her despair, her repeated attempts to convince Pandarus to wait until morning, and Pandarus's overpowering her with arguments, objections, and threats.

At Deiphebus's house, when Criseyde begged Troilus's help with Poliphete's alleged lawsuit, Troilus was overwhelmed by shame because of his involvement in Pandarus's lies. Here the same situation is greatly magnified. It is unthinkable that gentle, loving, protective, honorable Troilus, worshipping Criseyde as he does, could pressure her to the point of despair, but Pandarus is his agent, that is what Troilus has done by proxy, and he sinks under the awareness of his guilt: " 'God woot that of this game, / Whan al is wist, than am I nought to blame' " (III, 1084–85). But of course he is to blame, and he knows it. As James Wimsatt writes, "In his passive complicity both in the duping of Deiphebus with the story of 'false Poliphete' and in the fabrication about his jealousy of Horaste, his integrity is compromised."[49] Troilus has good reason to faint.

Troilus's faint and its motivation, then, would both be appropriately manly for a romance hero. And yet critic after critic reads this scene as if it implies Troilus's impotence. They do so because Pandarus's actions shift the scene from romance to farce. As Pandarus throws Troilus into Criseyde's bed and strips him to his "bare sherte," the perspective of the stories of sexual conquest floods back to take possession of the scene, leaving Troilus's behavior as a lover to be judged by their pragmatic, realistic view of sex. The poem, which had been edging back toward high romance, turns into fabliau, with its attendant concerns about performance, flaccidness, and lack of bodily fluids. In this context, impotence brought on by fear of sex becomes the meaning of Troilus's faint, as we hear in Pandarus's " 'Is this a mannes herte?' " and Criseyde's " 'Is this a mannes game?' " (III, 1098, 1126). The new perspective applies such pressure that McInerney reads as empty a line as "He [Troilus] seyde, 'O mercy, God, what thing is this?' " (III, 1124) to mean, "Troilus, it appears, has now got an erection, but does not know what to do with it."[50] It is Pandarus's wiles that make Troilus's faint so comically inappropriate, not Troilus's emotion.

Playing the woman's part inherited from the stories of lust and sexual conquest that lie behind *Troilus and Criseyde*, Criseyde is a victim, but at the same time, as the woman in the idealized stories, Criseyde is the loving beloved. The victim is trapped, but the loving beloved gives her consent to love. Troilus, recovered from his faint and embracing Criseyde in bed, speaks to her as the victim: he has caught her, he tells her, and she must yield to him. Criseyde replies as the loving beloved: " 'Ne hadde I er now, my swete herte deere, / Ben yolde, ywis, I were now nought here!' " (III, 1210–11). Here are the two perspectives, side by side. Jill Mann, reading *Troilus and Criseyde* as a romance, sets aside the importance of Pandarus's "coercive manipulation," traces with great subtlety the ins and outs of Troilus and Criseyde's shifting sex roles as they approach the consummation, and attributes Criseyde's willingness to surrender to her appreciation of Troilus's 'obeisaunce' to her. Criseyde recognizes, Mann writes, "that the pressures that have brought her to the consummation scene have been inner as well as outer, and that these inner pressures are now strong enough to bear the whole responsibility of her surrender; coercion is overtaken and swallowed up in the full tide of her volition."[51]

But has Criseyde consented, or has she simply been trapped? Does she answer to the idealized stories or the stories of lust and conquest? The baffling lines in which she accepts Troilus are poised just after Troilus's faint but before the love scene gains firm, though temporary, control over the poem's mood. Her "consent" can therefore be read from either perspective.

Undaunted by the many critics who emphasize Troilus's impotence, Elaine Hansen, Christopher Cannon, and Louise Fradenburg speculate about Criseyde's rape. Criseyde puts her yielding in the past tense, "ben yolde," and Hansen contends, "we can never determine exactly when—or even if—Criseyde 'yielded,' because her consent is a fiction, one that she is forced to invent, believe in, invoke, and revise at crucial points in order to save face and survive."[52] Cannon, writing about the legal implications of Pandarus's and Troilus's entrapment of Criseyde, concludes similarly that "the careful handling of consent in this scene keeps the crime just beyond our judgement; we *may* accept Criseyde's 'yielding' as consensual even as that consent is qualified to the very edge of freedom."[53] Fradenburg, noting the allusions to rape and violence that introduce the consummation scene, argues that "The possibility of Criseyde's rape can be spoken only through a kind of intertextual haunting. . . . We cannot 'decide' whether Criseyde has consented or not, whether she has been raped or not. We can only see that the possibility has been raised and then made undecidable."[54] A possibility that "has been raised and then made undecidable" describes aspect after aspect of the double go-between tradition's impact on *Troilus and Criseyde*. Like so much else, Criseyde moves back and forth, unresolvably, between the two perspectives.

Idealized go-betweens act out of friendship and commitment. The go-betweens for lust and sexual conquest are paid, one way or another.

Pandarus's principal payoffs are the consummation scene and his encounter with Criseyde the morning after the consummation. The consummation scene is afloat with homoerotic and heterosexual desire, the one merging into the other as opportunities unfold. Tison Pugh describes "the queerness of Pandarus's gaze in which he brings a level of sexual satisfaction to himself through the staging of scenes designed for his pleasure,"[55] and that is surely part of what is going on here. But Pandarus's satisfactions exceed significantly the pleasures of voyeurism. Through an elaborate Girardian analysis that plots out desiring subject, mediator, and object of desire as they shift for Pandarus throughout this scene, Richard Zeikowitz describes Pandarus's varying goals and how he fulfills them. One of Pandarus's objectives, for instance, is that Troilus possess Criseyde, and when he does, Pandarus shares her vicariously. In another configuration, he and Criseyde are rivals competing for Troilus, and Pandarus must work through Criseyde as his mediator. In a third, he and Criseyde use each other as mediators as they both labor to bring Troilus out of his faint. The boundary between homoerotic and heterosexual desires is fluid and undefined, and one slips into the other.[56]

Considering the consummation scene from the point of view of hetero-sexual and gay desire at once shows up rarely noted aspects of it. When Pandarus throws Troilus into bed and strips him to his shirt, Zeikowitz observes, "Pandarus appears ready to rape Troilus."[57] And when Pandarus and Criseyde together rub Troilus's wrists and wet his forehead to help him regain consciousness, Zeikowitz continues, "Troilus, who is lying in bed wearing nothing but his 'bare sherte,' is acted upon equally by both"; Pandarus's and Criseyde's two "streams of desire—one homoerotic, the other heterosexual" run parallel to each other. Pandarus also acts vicari-ously through Criseyde in this "homoerotically charged" scene, Zeikowitz points out. As Criseyde kisses Troilus to rouse him from his faint, Pandarus stands beside her, sharing.[58] To appreciate how these moments look and how these characters are interacting, it is important to remember that Chaucer never suggests that Criseyde herself is wearing anything. People usually slept nude in the Middle Ages and she is never said to take anything off before the stanza in which her naked body is so memorably described (III, 1247–50).

The romance tradition elevates and cocoons the long-sought, blissful night of the consummation itself, but just as romance seems finally to have taken over *Troilus and Criseyde*, Pandarus and his payoff regain control. Does Pandarus actually have sex with Criseyde the morning after the consummation scene? Irate Chaucerians—and there are many of them—contend that nothing in the rest of the poem supports such a reading. T.A. Stroud, for instance, after describing Criseyde's attempts to keep

Troilus from entering her bedroom the night before, protests: "Can we believe that the woman who acts this way would feel so little sexual restraint the next morning when Pandarus returns that she would fornicate with him? Are not readers being asked to equate this young widow with one of the virgins in pornographic fiction who instantly become nymphomaniacs?"[59] Similarly outraged, R.P. apRoberts entitled an article on the subject "A Contribution to the Thirteenth Labour: Purging the *Troilus* of Incest."[60] Many other Chaucerians, however, are equally adamant in contending that the repeatedly sexually charged double meanings of this scene yield strong intimations of incest. Fleming, for instance, writes that "The whiff of incest is everywhere in the poem,"[61] and he is joined by James Maybury[62] and Richard Fehrenbacher,[63] among others, who trace the importance of incest throughout the first three books of *Troilus and Criseyde* in preparation for this scene.

Two patterns are present in the language and situation of this brief scene, and they function much as the double go-between tradition functions when it provides the contradictory meanings for Pandarus and his role. Read one pattern and you have Pandarus and Criseyde teasing and joking together; read the other, and you have them committing incest. The second meaning of the scene emerges so entirely from implication and innuendo that it is always possible to refuse to see it, but this second refusable meaning is Pandarus's payoff as a go-between for lust and sexual conquest. His reward—sexual possession of Criseyde—occurs only on the second level of meaning of this language; the first level is left intact to tell the story of Troilus's love for his bright lady Criseyde.

Sarah Stanbury, discussing "And Pandarus hath fully his entente" (III, 82), the concluding line of the scene, describes it as "shifting the visual and imaginative project away from Pandarus onto the reader, who can only imagine what has ensued between Pandarus's aggressive thrusting of his hand beneath Criseyde's covers and the narrator's assertion that Pandarus has satisfied his desire."[64] It is literally up to the readers to decide, which leaves them, as Fehrenbacher writes, "confronted with the realization that as readers they are always complicit in generating a text's meaning."[65] Pandarus's final scene with Criseyde is a text each reader must construct.

As would be expected, the idealized stories provide no serious precedents for this morning-after scene. Only one episode bears any resemblance to it. In the fifteenth-century English version of *William of Palerne* (although not in the Old French original), when Melior's confidante Alexandrine returns at sunset to the garden where Melior and William have saved each other from dying of lovesickness by becoming lovers under William's apple tree, Alexandrine jokes with them. She had promised to find an herb to cure Melior when she was first dying of love, and she greets her with " 'have ʒe geten þe gras þat I ʒou geynliche hiʒt?' " (1030) ["have you gotten the herb

that I promised you in friendship?"] When Melior admits to having found
the healing herb in the garden of love, Alexandrine observes what good
doctors Melior and William are for each other's illness: " 'alle þe surgyens
of Salerne so sone ne couþen / have 3our langoures alegget, I leve for
soþe!' " (1033–34) ["Truly, I do not believe that all the surgeons of Salerne
could have relieved your sickness so quickly."]

Alexandrine's gentle teasing has none of the qualities of Pandarus's
suggestive remarks about the "litel laiser" Criseyde has had to sleep and dream.
Pandarus conjures up the night of love viewed from beneath raised eyebrows
(III, 1557–61); Alexandrine alludes only to shared knowingness: consummated love as the cure she and Melior now both acknowledge. There is no
false note here or contrast between Alexandrine's and the lovers' attitudes
toward love. She understands love better than they do because she is not overwhelmed by it. However, she is never the voice of sexual experience.

The stories about going-between for lust and sexual conquest, several of
which were sources for Chaucer, include a substantial tradition of after-
the-event scenes, a tradition that stretches from the late eleventh through
the mid-fourteenth century. All the versions of the *Pamphilus* story contain
these episodes. Even the *Libro de buen amor*, which lost its rape scene, probably to a moralist,[66] retains the encounter between the go-between and the
raped woman following the rape. These episodes occur immediately after
the event instead of the next morning, and the raped women bewail their
lost virginity or chastity and denounce the go-between who pretended
friendship, but whose real function has been unmasked by the rape.

The oldest of these after-the-event scenes appears in *De nuntio sagaci*,
from the late eleventh century, and has some emotional similarities to the
Troilus and Criseyde episode. It begins with the young woman who has just
been raped accusing Davus, the go-between, of tricking her. Davus first
denies knowing anything at all about what happened, but he then argues
the young woman into accepting her lost virginity, comforts her, and
finally convinces her to kiss the young man and continue with him as her
lover (205–80). The other poems, however, offer no such resolutions
of the rapes. They all conclude with the betrayed women denouncing the
go-betweens for the traps and snares that have destroyed their innocence.

Pandarus's and Criseyde's encounter clearly derives from these scenes.
Like the other women, she denounces him:

> "Nevere the bet for yow,
> Fox that ye ben! God yeve youre herte kare!
> God help me so, ye caused al this fare,
> Trowe I," quod she, "for al youre wordes white.
> O, whoso seeth yow knoweth yow ful lite." (III, 1564–68)

All these women curse the go-between the same way: "What a liar you've turned out to be! You caused all this, you and all your cover-ups. No one knows you who only sees you from the outside!" But no scene in any previous work then opens out the way Chaucer's does to allow and disallow at once the sex act between the woman and the go-between.

Woman: The Most Valuable Gift

On the two occasions that going between is discussed explicitly in *Troilus and Criseyde*, its shamefulness is accepted as self-evident. The devoted confidantes, comrades-in-arms, and governesses who go between in the idealized stories never talk about themselves as go-betweens and there is never any suggestion that they believe they are playing a socially unacceptable role. Their going between is an honorable activity both in their own eyes and in the eyes of the people for whom they go between. The only idealized story that mentions going between is Chrétien de Troyes' *Yvain*, and there Laudine dismisses out of hand the possibility that Lunete could be acting the part of a hired go-between. Laudine reflects upon her lady-in-waiting's loyalty and is certain she did not argue on Yvain's behalf "por loiier ne por desserte / Ne por amor, que a lui et" (1742–43) ["for reward or profit or for any love she felt for him"]. None of the other idealized stories raise the issue of going between even to this very slight degree.

The go-betweens of the stories about lust and sexual conquest, on the other hand, are engaged in an objectively shameful business, and its shamefulness is a given. Some have to be tempted with gifts or money before they will admit to being go-betweens; others camouflage their operations by spending time in church or with nuns; some hide behind other occupations—peddling, in particular—and they caution their customers to help maintain their cover. The notoriousness of going between yields the comedy of the rich passage in the Spanish *Libro de buen amor* that lists forty-one ways to refer to a go-between—sledge hammer, knocker, shoe-horn, etc.—without saying the word.[67] And when John Gower writes solemnly about go-betweens in the *Confessio Amantis*, he describes God taking vengeance on them by cursing them with their own tricks.[68]

The shamefulness of going between is one of Pandarus's points of reassurance as he first tries to interest Criseyde in Troilus in Book II. He could not be intending to encourage more than friendship, Pandarus insists, because he would rather have all three of them hanged than be Troilus's "baude" (II, 351–57), and this is the only time in *Troilus and Criseyde* that Pandarus uses the word "baude." Once the agreement is reached that Criseyde is to be exchanged for Antenor, Pandarus slips right back into his role of go-between. Troilus needs another woman to get over loving

Criseyde, Pandarus advises, citing his usual proverbs and authorities: " 'The
newe love out chaceth ofte the olde' "—(IV, 415), " 'as writ Zanzis, that
was ful wys' " (IV, 414). Troy is full of women, lots of them are prettier
than she is, and Pandarus knows just where to find them:

> "Fairer than swiche twelve
> As evere she was, shal I fynde in som route—
> Yee, on or two, withouten any doute.
> Forthi be glad, myn owen deere brother!
> If she be lost, we shal recover an other." (IV, 402–06)

The old elements of Pandarus's role and his special relationship to Troilus
are present once again: the plural pronouns—"we shal recovere an
other"—and the saving grace of Pandarus's effective activity—"Forthi be
glad." Loving is just pleasurable sex to Pandarus. As he tells Troilus, trying
to convince him that he will forget Criseyde in any case: " 'For syn it is but
casuel plesaunce, / Som cas shal putte it out of remembraunce' " (IV,
419–20). But obvious as the real nature of his role is, Pandarus does not
acknowledge that he is offering to go between.

The crucial conversation about going between in *Troilus and Criseyde*
occurs the evening following their first meeting at Deiphebus's. Chaucer is
rewriting the *Filostrato* passage in which Pandaro calls himself a "mezzano"
and Troilo defends him, but Chaucer's Pandarus is too ashamed to speak
forthrightly as Boccaccio's Pandaro had. Pandarus hides behind painfully
constrained circumlocutions; he is " 'swich a meene / As maken wommen
unto men to comen; / Al sey I nought, thow wost wel what I meene' "
(III, 254–56). And he is both ashamed and afraid of more shame. A single
stanza from the *Filostrato* becomes forty tiresome, proverb-ridden verses
about how important it is that no one find out about the affair and his part
in it (III, 288–329).

Chaucer turns Troilo's reply to Pandaro into Troilus's most shameful
speech in *Troilus and Criseyde*. He is incredulous that Pandarus could imagine
he would consider him a bawd, and his lines ring with conviction, but then
he argues that going-between for friendship is " 'gentilesse,' " " 'compas-
sioun,' " " 'felawship,' " and " 'trist,' " while going-between for money is
procuring (III, 402–03). Troilo had offered his sisters to convince Pandaro of
his good feelings toward him. Troilus instead offers them for a more ambi-
tious purpose, to establish that he does not think " 'this servise' " is shameful.
The more he describes what he is offering, the more definitively it is procuring: "You name her, I'll get her for you"—procuring reduced to its essence.
Chaucer expands Boccaccio's already remarkable list of offered women to
include not only Cassandra, but any of the "frape," which means a very large

group, a crowd, a multitude, or a mob. The more sisters, the more imper-
sonal this transaction becomes. Similarly, Chaucer avoids even the hint of
possible romantic interest that Boccaccio had introduced, "-apri il cor tuo
se te ne piace alcuna-" [" 'Open your heart, if either of them pleases
you' "](III, 18), and instead adds the " 'wel yshape' " detail—he is offering
any of his sisters, no matter how fair or well shaped she is—nudging the
reader to keep in mind just what sort of relationship is being offered. Finally,
while the first meaning of " 'lat me thanne allone' " is "let me arrange it,"
there is also a suggestion of impatience or irritation in the line, of "leave me
alone," "don't bother me about this any more," with an overtone of evening
things off: a sister for a niece, a woman for a woman.

Ida L. Gordon marvels that "this passage does not seem to have troubled
those critics who see Troilus as a pure and noble lover," and she proposes
that "the aura of 'gentilesse' created by the courtly language acts as a veil
between the reader and the narrative."[69] Something surely has veiled the
narrative effectively, and continues to veil it. In the 1960s, Elizabeth Salter
described Troilus's offer as a "jaunty passage" carelessly adapted from
Boccaccio.[70] Henry Ansgar Kelly, intent upon defending Troilus's moral
stature, repeated her argument that Chaucer had allowed inappropriate
Filostrato material to slip into his poem. In addition, Kelly proposed, among
other exculpatory readings, that Troilus's offer of his sisters might be "a rare
attempt to give Troilus a sense of humor."[71] John Fleming dismisses Salter's
explanation with deadly accuracy: "It will not do to explain away Troilus'
remarkable speech as a bit of fossilized Boccaccio, since its more remarkable
features were never in Boccaccio in the first place."[72]

Instead of reading Troilus's offer of his sisters as a mistake or a joke, contemporary feminists see it as a momentary glimpse into his true attitude
toward women. Carolyn Dinshaw, for example, understands these lines as
acknowledgment of "a more fundamental system of trade of women" and
proposes that "in the ease with which Troilus offers his 'servise'—indeed,
his *sister*—we sense that this view of women as gifts, tokens of exchange, is
more basic to the relations between men in Troy than is the view of
women as singular and unique."[73] Either despite or in response to such
readings, two contemporary male critics remain eager to justify Troilus's
offer of his sisters. Derek Brewer, for instance, proposes that "It illustrates
masculine bonding. . . .Even if it is deplorably masculine it is highly masculine, though Troilus's youthful enthusiasm may be thought to have
rather carried him away."[74] John Hill focuses much of an article on creating a context that can explain this conversation between Troilus and
Pandarus. Pandarus's self-description as a go-between, Hill writes, fills "the
private space these two friends share, at a peak moment in the progressing
affair, with a hellish vision of unworthiness." Troilus must dispel that vision

by offering an equal or greater gift, and therefore

> he offers the very best service he can: help with the highest noblewomen in
> the realm, including Helen and his own sister. . . .To exclude his family
> would be equivalent to saying that his own kin are too good for Pandarus.
> Such an implication would indeed confirm part of the lurking nightmare
> indicated earlier—that in some corner of his being Troilus thinks less well of
> Pandarus for the help Pandarus has provided with his close niece.[75]

Hill's imaginative, sensitive reading of Troilus's offer cannot evade the real
"lurking nightmare": Troilus must offer to procure for Pandarus to make
Pandarus feel better about procuring for him. And if there was ever any
serious question about the meaning of this conversation in the *Filostrato*,
there can no longer be any question about it in *Troilus and Criseyde* because
now the go-betweens for lust and sexual conquest cast their heavy, corrupting shadows over this scene of aristocratic friends. Chaucer has already
added the Deiphebus trick to the *Filostrato* and will next add Criseyde's
entrapment. His go-between is firmly positioned at once within the tradition
of loving friends who unite consenting men and women and the tradition
of the go-betweens who set up rapes for a price. Given that double context,
these generous, sympathetic excuses for Troilus are grounded in sand.
Idealistic as Troilus sounds when he sings his Boethian hymns to love,
when Pandarus is his avenue to Criseyde, he is willing to believe whatever
he needs to believe to keep Pandarus in action. Boccaccio introduces the
procuring theme, but Chaucer strengthens it at every turn.

While Pandarus is delivering his arid forty-verse monologue on not
telling anyone anything about the forthcoming love affair, Troilus is
responding to his lecturing in a highly improbable way. The reader is swept
up by poetry that is full of life, warmth, and emotion, and rich with
imagery like the imagery of the opening of *The Canterbury Tales*. At first the
images are below the surface of the lines: "His [Troilus's] olde wo, that
made his herte swelte, / Gan tho for joie wasten and tomelte." (III,
347–48). Woe that wastes away and melts, suggesting snow melting and ice
breaking up in springtime; and then the underlying metaphors burst
through with the new life of spring:

> But right so as thise holtes and thise hayis,
> That han in wynter dede ben and dreye,
> Revesten hem in grene when that May is,
> Whan every lusty liketh best to pleye;
> Right in that selve wise, soth to seye,
> Wax sodeynliche his herte ful of joie,
> That gladder was ther nevere man in Troie. (III, 351–57)

Pandarus's self-conscious tiptoeing around what he is doing and his anguished fear of public shame have conveyed to Troilus that he will be able to possess Criseyde. This is one of *Troilus and Criseyde*'s most intensely idealized passages, but, virtually oxymoronically, it is arrived at via aggressively compromised material. The means to Troilus's ecstatic realization is Pandarus's shame at going between, just as Troilus's means to Criseyde's bed will be Pandarus's shameful actions, and the elevated, aristocratic, courtly love affair of the knight and his lady will ride at once upon the double, incongruous traditions of the idealized go-betweens and the go-betweens for lust and sexual conquest.

The Double Go-Between Tradition

The double go-between tradition functions in *Troilus and Criseyde* as a spectacularly flamboyant instance of the intertextuality through which medieval works so often speak to one another—"the complex interaction among texts, ideologies, and traditions, the play of cross-references, echoes, and cultural symbols."[76] Like audiences of all eras and all literatures, Chaucer's hearers would have encountered *Troilus and Criseyde* against the backdrop of their previous literary experience, and that would have included these two dramatically different kinds of go-betweens identified with opposed conceptions of love and lust and presiding over opposed ways of bringing about relationships.

The double go-between tradition is critical for the much vexed question of the genre of *Troilus and Criseyde*. Simon Gaunt, discussing twelfth-century Old French chivalric romances, argues that form and content cannot be clearly distinguished, that "form in itself signals content" and "genres are inherently ideological constructs; the formal and structural features of a text do not produce aesthetic effects that can be divorced from content and thereby from ideology, but on the contrary they signal participation in a discursive framework that implies a world-view with a heavy ideological investment."[77] *Troilus and Criseyde*, however, cannot be understood as an instance of a single genre, in large measure because of Chaucer's use of the double go-between tradition. The poem is neither exemplum, fabliau, Latin comic tale, novella, or chivalric romance. As it shifts content and context, then, by implication it shifts its "discursive framework," "world-view," and "ideological investment."

Karla Taylor, struggling to establish the genre of *Troilus and Criseyde*, characterizes it as an "anti-romance." In *Troilus and Criseyde*, she writes, "By setting lyric, romantic, and unromantic voices next to one another, Chaucer gives his audience the opportunity to discover the fabrications involved in any version of love," and she acknowledges that these "competing perspectives on love" leave the audience analyzing the experience rather than judging it.[78] The double go-between tradition is the backbone of the process Taylor is describing—that setting of voice against voice that leaves the *Troilus and Criseyde* audience assessing loving rather than empathizing with lovers.

It is tempting to look to Old French romances to clarify the genre of *Troilus and Criseyde*. Gaunt finds in the romances "an interest in individual psychology and identity: thus romances frequently narrate an individual's quest for his 'true' identity through love and chivalric exploits."[79] Barry Windeatt argues that Chaucer was reworking this focus in a new way in *Troilus and Criseyde*. Writing about the nature of romance and Chaucerian romance's place within it, Windeatt proposes that the adventures that typically test Old French knights take another form in Chaucer's poem. He sees Troilus's "intense and transfiguring experience of love" as "a kind of adventure," and likens it to that of the "typical protagonists of romance." The "all-possessing nature of the experience of love" for Troilus, Windeatt argues, constitutes "a kind of inward equivalent of 'aventure'."[80] Later, in his *Oxford Guide* to *Troilus and Criseyde*, Windeatt elaborates his point:

> Chaucer's emphasis on the hero's *in*experience in love makes experience itself an adventure into an unknown, something marvellously out of this world, which is reflected in that language of heaven's bliss, of love as a religion, as worship, in which Chaucer's Troilus thinks of his experience. His aspirations and conceptions are those of the idealistic hero of romance, and this restores to Chaucer's story that characteristic sense in romance that the hero's experiences include a process of learning, and that romance develops an education of the heart.[81]

However, if the romance hero's quest yields " 'true' identity," as Gaunt proposes, and if loving is Troilus's equivalent of that quest, as Windeatt suggests, then Troilus fails his quest. He does not acquire true identity in this "aventure"; indeed, he is so inadequately self-aware at crucial moments that he lets identity slip through his fingers. Eager, attractive, boyishly engaging as he often is, Troilus is deeply personally duplicitous. Except when Pandarus's recognition of his own role as a pander surfaces so aggressively that he cannot silence it without acknowledgment, Pandarus operates within the double conventions of going between with great ease and cynically amused awareness of their many possible implications. Troilus, on the other hand, does not acknowledge either the contradictions between the two traditions or the fact that he is functioning within them both. At the same time that he acts his part in a story about sexual conquest, he insists upon experiencing his relationship with Criseyde exclusively and extravagantly as an idealized love story. Instead of forging a more encompassing and mature identity as a typical hero of romance would, Troilus grounds his selfhood in an unrealistically idealized Criseyde, and when she betrays him, his sense of himself caves in so catastrophically that he is left futilely suicidal (V, 1716–22). In the romances, the hero's inner world—his self-awareness and self-consciousness—emerges through his loving and questing, and his success in love and quest establishes his identity. No such development of identity occurs, however, for Troilus, and it is the double go-between tradition's testing of him that isolates his personal failure most definitively. As Windeatt argues, *Troilus and Criseyde* depicts "the unsustainable nature of human idealisms" by portraying at once the romance experience and "the qualifications and exhaustion of romance," and he identifies "Chaucer's most distinctive development" of romance as its "disenchantment."[82] Pandarus's going between for sexual conquest, with Troilus as his beneficiary, is romance at its most thoroughly disenchanted.

Gayle Margherita describes " 'plot' " as "always less significant than the genre's exploration of its own history and expectations," and she sees medieval romance as "unique in its insistence upon the conceptual complicity of narrative structure and thematics."[83] By Chaucer's time, she argues, the romance genre was "so overdetermined as to be necessarily self-referential and at least somewhat ironic."[84] According to Margherita, then, Chaucerian romance is "overdetermined"; according to Taylor, it is "anti-romance"; and according to Windeatt, it is disenchanted. Writing about Old French romance and "the combining of spiritual and sexual elements, which is characteristic of so many 'courtly love' texts," Sarah Kay proposes:

> In my view, the reason why courtly love is so elusive of definition is precisely that courtly representations of love are built upon internal tensions, while also seeking to mask them. Courtly texts do not so much propound precepts as raise alternatives, permitting contradictions to surface, but within a restricted agenda of shared preoccupations.[85]

The difference between the Old French texts Kay is describing and Chaucer's *Troilus and Criseyde* is that Chaucer breaks out of the "restricted agenda of shared preoccupations" that the courtly texts accept as limits, and once his romance is in illegitimate territory, when the contradictions surface, they cannot be resolved. It is these unresolved and unresolvable contradictions that set *Troilus and Criseyde* apart most definitively from traditional romance; the double go-between tradition, *Troilus and Criseyde*'s intertextual context, generates the prime instances of these unresolved and unresolvable contradictions.

One of the stronger currents of late twentieth-century criticism of *Troilus and Criseyde* describes the poem as alive with disparate impulses, energies, and ways of conceptualizing itself that pull frankly against one another in restless contradiction rather than building together to create a coherent whole. Carolyn Dinshaw, Rosemarie McGerr, and H. Marshall Leicester, Jr. all stress the many forms "resistance to closure"[86] takes in *Troilus and Criseyde*. McGerr writes about the poem's "dialectic of Christianity and courtly love" that proceeds through pagan speakers whose dialogue echoes scripture and through passages in which *caritas* and *amor* are indistinguishable even in context.[87] Leicester describes the first three books of *Troilus and Criseyde* as embodying "a deliberate attempt to conflate past and present, here and there, speaker, audience, and characters, and 'vapour eterne' with love 'in tymes' (III, 11), in a transparency of meaning that can be felt to exist in some unmediated way *beyond* the text, the words." He sees the "failure of this attempt," among other instances, in the impression that the consummation of the love affair "cannot sustain the symbolic weight that has been put upon it." How radically Leicester believes *Troilus and Criseyde* "defers our access to final meaning" is clear when he writes, "What began by pretending to be the presentation of an experience to listeners ends by identifying the activity it embodies as the construction for readers of a text whose meaning has yet to be determined."[88] Carolyn Dinshaw describes *Troilus and Criseyde* as refusing "expedient closure and final meaning."[89] In "Readers in/of *Troilus and Criseyde*," she analyzes the two most influential mid-twentieth-century interpretations of the poem, D.W. Robertson's approach via biblical exegesis and E. Talbot Donaldson's formalist New Critical reading. Despite the fact that these interpretations rest on opposed theoretical conceptions, Dinshaw finds them both, for contrary reasons, insisting upon controlling "disorder and disruption in the text by appealing to secure visions of order and hierarchy."[90] Donaldson's and Robertson's critical moves are identical; the foundations of both readings are "a vigorous limitation of the disturbing, a rigorous structure controlling the potentially uncontrollable."[91] In *Troilus and Criseyde*, Dinshaw argues, Chaucer creates "a text which is larger than the totalizing readings in it or of it: he not only acknowledges instability and disorder in human experience but also exposes merely expedient resolutions of such disruptions. The narrative itself resists expedient ending and final closure."[92]

Varied as their points of view are, all three of these critics, McGerr, Leicester, and Dinshaw, are arguing that the energies and implications of *Troilus and Criseyde* that earlier Chaucerians homogenized, overlooked, or subordinated to larger structures must be maintained in all their contradictory difference. Recognition of the double go-between tradition's impact on *Troilus and Criseyde* brings to the surface of the poem another panoply of disruptions of meaning. That impact triggers the movement in and out of contradictory ways of understanding and relating to desire and sexuality; it generates the repeated engagement and disengagement of the audience from the concepts that seem to be governing the poem; it shifts the audience out of one genre and its ideologically invested world view into another. Pandarus's literary ancestors can be found in both the idealized tradition and the stories of lust and sexual conquest, but that is just the beginning of the point. Pandarus cannot derive from both traditions at once and maintain the poem's "discursive framework," "world view," and "ideological investment," as Simon Gaunt puts it. And so *Troilus and Criseyde* shifts from one governing concept to the other, again and again.

Nevertheless, unsettling as they are, the double points of view built into *Troilus and Criseyde* account for much of its intellectually daunting appeal. Writing about twelfth-century Old French courtly fiction's scrutinizing of "its own 'performance' of gender," Roberta L. Krueger describes how "these fictions move their audiences into a space beyond debate and invite them to participate in an interrogation of cultural conventions, codes, and norms." This interrogation, she argues, is "one of the enduring legacies of courtly fictions" which prompted the "self-reflective scrutiny" of its own culture and ideology.[93] The process Krueger identifies here is perhaps the fundamental function of the double go-between tradition in *Troilus and Criseyde*: the interrogation of cultural conventions, codes, and norms, prompting a culture's "self-reflective scrutiny." Instead of presenting either love, friendship, and romance, on the one hand, or lust, procuring, and sexual satisfaction, on the other, the double contexts Chaucer manipulates interrogate their culture's approaches to dealing with desire, turning them this way and that, over and over, as one tradition yields place to or gains predominance over the other. Chaucer's poem continues to engage audiences so complexly because instead of generating a single point of view on the nature of desire and taking its stand within it, it entices its readers into experiencing contradictory approaches. Surely this demand for play of mind and responsiveness is one of the most important reasons why *Troilus and Criseyde*, undergirded by the warp and weft of the double go-between tradition, is still read with such intensity in the twenty-first century.

NOTES

Introduction: Going Between

Unless otherwise noted, translations are mine and citations are to line numbers of poems.

1. For example, see William Witherle Lawrence, "The Love Story in 'Troilus and Cressida,' " in *Shaksperian Studies by Members of the Department of English and Comparative Literature in Columbia University*, ed. Brander Matthews and Ashley Horace Thorndike (New York: Columbia University Press, 1916), pp. 202–03 [187–211].
2. Thomas J. Garbáty, "The *Pamphilus* Tradition in Ruiz and Chaucer," *Philological Quarterly* 46 (1967): 457–70.
3. John V. Fleming, *Classical Imitation and Interpretation in Chaucer's* Troilus (Lincoln: University of Nebraska Press, 1990), pp. 157–59.
4. Leyla Rouhi, *Mediation and Love: A Study of the Medieval Go-Between in Key Romance and Near-Eastern Texts*, Brill's Studies in Intellectual History 93 (Leiden: Brill, 1999), pp. 120–23.
5. I first argued this position in a working paper: Gretchen Mieszkowski, "Going-Between: Chaucer's Pandarus and Medieval Literary Go-Betweens," Mary Ingraham Bunting Institute of Radcliffe College, 1979.
6. Joseph de Morawski, ed., *Pamphile et Galatée*, Jean Brasdefer (Paris: Champion, 1917), pp. 105–55.
7. William Matthews, "The Wife of Bath and All Her Sect," *Viator* 5 (1974): 413–43.
8. Paul Strohm, *Social Chaucer* (Cambridge, Mass.: Harvard University Press, 1989), p. 112.
9. C.S. Lewis, *The Allegory of Love: A Study in Medieval Tradition* (1936; repr. Oxford: Oxford University Press, 1971), pp. 1–4, 11–14.
10. Gretchen Mieszkowski, "Chaucer's Much Loved Criseyde," *Chaucer Review* 26.2 (1991): 109–32.

Part I: Choreographing Lust: Go-Betweens for Sexual Conquest

1. Elizabeth Robertson, "Medieval Medical Views of Women and Female Spirituality in the *Ancrene Wisse* and Julian of Norwich's *Showings*," in

Feminist Approaches to the Body in Medieval Literature, ed. Linda Lomperis and Sarah Stanbury, New Cultural Studies (Philadelphia: University of Pennsylvania Press, 1993), pp. 143–45, 147 [142–67].

2. Ann E. Matter, "The Undebated Debate: Gender and the Image of God in Medieval Theology," in *Gender in Debate from the Early Middle Ages to the Renaissance*, ed. Thelma S. Fenster and Clare A. Lees, New Middle Ages (New York: Palgrave, 2002), pp. 41, 43–44 [41–55].

3. Katharine M. Rogers, *The Troublesome Helpmate: A History of Misogyny in Literature* (Seattle: University of Washington Press, 1966), p. 66.

4. R. Howard Bloch, *Medieval Misogyny and the Invention of Western Romantic Love* (Chicago: University of Chicago Press, 1991), pp. 9, 46.

5. Joyce E. Salisbury, "Gendered Sexuality," in *Handbook of Medieval Sexuality*, ed. Vern L. Bullough and James A. Brundage (New York: Garland, 1996), p. 86 [81–102].

6. Quoted in Alcuin Blamires, *The Case for Women in Medieval Culture* (Oxford: Clarendon Press, 1997), p. 127.

7. Quoted in Rogers, *Troublesome Helpmate*, p. 74.

8. Rogers, *Troublesome Helpmate*, pp. 74–75.

9. Dorothy M. Robathan, "Ovid in the Middle Ages," in *Ovid*, ed. J.W. Binns (London: Routledge & Kegan Paul, 1973), pp. 191, 193–98 [191–209]. For a list of the eleventh to thirteenth-century appearances of Ovidian works and references, see Peter L. Allen, *The Art of Love: Amatory Fiction from Ovid to the* Romance of the Rose (Philadelphia: University of Pennsylvania Press, 1992), "Appendix," pp. 114–17.

10. Allen, *Art of Love*, p. 47.

11. Allen, *Art of Love*, p. 52.

12. Morawski provides the most extensive overview of this literary figure and her roots. Morawski, ed., *Pamphile*, pp. 105–55. William Matthews adds others in "The Wife of Bath," pp. 413–43, although many of the old women he includes are not go-betweens. Rouhi describes the parallel Persian and Islamic tradition in her chapter on "The Medieval Near-Eastern Go-between," *Mediation*, pp. 135–203.

13. Morawski, ed., *Pamphile*. Date and manuscript, pp. 66–68.

14. *Dame Sirith*, in *Early Middle English Verse and Prose*, ed. J.A.W. Bennett and G.V. Smithers, 2nd edn. (Oxford: Clarendon Press, 1968), pp. 77–95. Robert E. Lewis dates the manuscript containing this poem from the last quarter of the thirteenth century. "The English Fabliau Tradition and Chaucer's 'Miller's Tale'," *Modern Philology* 79 (1982): 245, 247 n. 34 [241–55].

15. *Le Prestre teint*, Fabliau 81, in *Nouveau recueil complet des fabliaux*, eds. Willem Noomen and Nico van den Boogaard, 8 vols. (Assen: Van Gorcum, 1983–93), 7:307–30. Date and authorship, pp. 309–10. Citations to texte critique.

16. *Petri Alfonsi Disciplina clericalis: III. Französische Versbearbeitungen*, ed. Alfons Hilka and Werner Söderhjelm, Acta societatis scientiarum fennicae (Helsingfors: Druckerei der finnischen Literatur-Gesellschaft, 1922) 49, No. 4: version A, pp. 29–35. Dating, p. ix.

17. Giovanni Boccaccio, "Giornata quinta, novella decima," *Il decameron*, ed. Aldo Rossi (Bologna: Cappelli, 1977), pp. 317–22. "Fifth Day, Tenth Story," in *Decameron*, trans. Mark Musa and Peter Bondanella (New York: W.W. Norton, 1982), pp. 369–76.

18. Juan Ruiz, *Libro de buen amor*, ed. Giorgio Chiarini (Milan: Ricciardi, 1964). References to stanza numbers. Trans. Rigo Mignani and Mario A. Di Cesare, *The Book of Good Love* (Albany, NY: State University of New York Press, 1970). Two extant manuscripts of this work are dated, variously, 1330 and 1343; perhaps different editions of the poem; Mignani, pp. 25–26.

19. Matthews, "Wife of Bath," pp. 420–21.

20. Fleming, *Classical Imitation*, p. 161.

21. Philippe Ménard, *Le Rire et le sourire dans le roman courtois en France au moyen âge (1150–1250)*, Publications romanes et françaises 105 (Geneva: Droz, 1969), n. 120, p. 211.

22. Eberhard Hermes, trans. and ed., P.R. Quarrie, trans. into English, *The Disciplina clericalis of Petrus Alfonsi* (Berkeley: University of California Press, 1977), pp. 124–25.

23. John Tolan, *Petrus Alfonsi and His Medieval Readers* (Gainesville: University Press of Florida, 1993), pp. 132–33.

24. Rouhi, *Mediation*, pp. 162–64.

25. Jole Agrimi and Chiara Crisciani, "Savoir médical et anthropologie religieuse: Les représentations et les fonctions de la *vetula* (XIIIe-XVe siècle)," *Annales ESC* 48 (1993): 1298 [1281–1308].

26. Shulamith Shahar, "The Old Body in Medieval Culture," in *Framing Medieval Bodies*, ed. Sarah Kay and Miri Rubin (Manchester: Manchester University Press, 1994), p. 164 [160–186].

27. Quoted in Shahar, "Old body," in *Framing Medieval Bodies*, p. 163.

28. Agrimi, "Savoir médical," pp. 1298, 1302.

29. Agrimi, "Savoir médical," pp. 1303, 1298.

30. Agrimi, "Savoir médical," p. 1298.

31. Agrimi, "Savoir médical," p. 1299.

32. Agrimi, "Savoir médical," p. 1301.

33. Agrimi, "Savoir médical," pp. 1299–1300.

34. Agrimi, "Savoir médical," p. 1302.

35. "Dame Sirith," ll. 243–48.

36. Ruth Mazo Karras, *Common Women: Prostitution and Sexuality in Medieval England* (Oxford: Oxford University Press, 1996), p. 15.

37. Karras, *Common Women*, p. 15.

38. Karras, *Common Women*, p. 62.

39. Karras, *Common Women*, p. 62.

40. Alison Goddard Elliott, ed. and trans., "Intro.," *Seven Medieval Latin Comedies* (New York: Garland, 1984), pp. xxvi–xxvii.

41. Charles Muscatine, *The Old French Fabliaux* (New Haven: Yale University Press, 1986), pp. 14–15; Marjorie Curry Woods, "Rape and the Pedagogical

Rhetoric of Sexual Violence," in *Criticism and Dissent in the Middle Ages*, ed.
Rita Copeland (Cambridge, UK: Cambridge University Press, 1996), p. 58
[56–86].

42. 1080: Gabriella Rossetti, ed., *De nuntio sagaci* in *Commedie latine del XII e
XIII secolo*, 6 vols. (Genova: Istituto di filologia classica e medievale,
1976–98), 2:21–25 (1980) [11–125]. Rossetti reviews the arguments for
dating *De nuntio* and agrees with Peter Dronke's suggestion of 1080.
c. 1100: Stefano Pittaluga, ed., *Pamphilus*, in *Commedie latine*, 3:13–15 (1980)
[11–137]. Pittaluga accepts Dronke's dating. Peter Dronke, "A Note on
Pamphilus," *Journal of the Warburg and Courtauld Institutes* 42 (1979): 225–26.
c. 1155: Edmond Lackenbacher, ed., *Lidia*, in *La "Comédie" latine en France
au XIIe siècle*, ed. Gustave Cohen, Société d'édition "les belles-lettres,"
2 vols. (Paris, 1931) 1:214 [211–46].
[1150–75: Giovanni Orlandi, ed., *Baucis et Traso*, in *Commedie latine*,
3:248–49 (1980) [243–303].
[c. 1170: Marcel Wintzweiller, ed., Guillaume de Blois, *Alda*, in *La
"Comédie" latine*, 1:111–13 [107–51].

43. Woods, "Rape and pedagogical rhetoric," in *Criticism*, pp. 56–58.

44. Ovid, *The Art of Love*, trans. James Michie (New York: Modern Library,
2002) Book I, ll. 673–78.

45. Wintzweiller, ed., Guillaume de Blois, *Alda*, in *La "Comédie" latine*, 1:107–51.

46. Peter Dronke, "Pseudo-Ovid, Facetus, and the Arts of Love,"
Mittellateinisches Jahrbuch 11 (1976): 129–30 [126–31].

47. Alison Goddard Elliott, ed. and trans., "The *Facetus*: or, The Art of Courtly
Living," *Allegorica* 2 (1977): 44–45 [27–57].

48. Rossetti, ed., *De nuntio* in *Commedie latine*.

49. Elliott, "The *Facetus*," 267–68, pp. 44–45. Elliott's trans.

50. Anne Howland Schotter, "Rape in the Medieval Latin Comedies," in
Representing Rape in Medieval and Early Modern Literature, ed. Elizabeth
Robertson and Christine M. Rose, New Middle Ages (New York:
Palgrave, 2001), p. 242 [241–53].

51. Rouhi, *Mediation*, p. 90.

52. Alphonse Dain, ed., "Intro.," *Ovidius puellarum (De nuncio sagaci)*, in *La
"Comédie" latine*, 2:109, 116 [109–65].

53. Rossetti, ed., *De nuntio* in *Commedie latine*, pp. 17–19.

54. Elliott, "Intro.," *Seven Medieval*, p. xxxiii.

55. Pittaluga, ed., *Pamphilus*, in *Commedie latine*, pp. 41–44; Morawski, ed.,
Pamphile, Jean Brasdefer, pp. 13–20.

56. Garbáty, "The *Pamphilus* Tradition."

57. Ernest Langlois, *Origines et sources du* Roman de la rose (Paris: 1891), p. 27.
Morawski, ed., *Pamphile* discusses Langlois's argument pp. 31–34. Alastair
Minnis, however, contends that "direct influence of the genre is possible
but unprovable." *Magister amoris: The* Roman de la Rose *and Vernacular
Hermeneutics* (Oxford: Oxford University Press, 2001), p. 179.

58. Pittaluga, ed., *Pamphilus*, in *Commedie latine*.

59. Morawski, ed., *Pamphile*, ll. 1946–47.

60. Ruiz, *Libro*, citations to stanza numbers.

61. Minnis, *Magister amoris*, pp. 197–98, 183–84.

62. Jill Mann, *Geoffrey Chaucer* (Atlantic Highlands, NJ: Humanities Press International, Inc., 1991), p. 97.

63. Elliott, "Intro.," *Seven Medieval*, p. xxix.

64. Anne Schotter, "Rhetoric versus Rape in the Medieval Latin *Pamphilus*," *Philological Quarterly* 71.3 (1992): 249–51 [243–60].

65. Elliott, "Intro.," *Seven Medieval*, pp. xxx–xxxi; Schotter, "Rhetoric versus Rape," 243; Woods, "Rape and Pedagogical Rhetoric," in *Criticism*, p. 73.

66. Schotter, "Rhetoric versus Rape," 256.

67. Woods, "Rape and Pedagogical Rhetoric," in *Criticism*, pp. 60, 73.

68. Kathryn Gravdal, *Ravishing Maidens: Writing Rape in Medieval French Literature and Law*, New Cultural Studies Series (Philadelphia: University of Pennsylvania Press, 1991), p. 110.

69. Orlandi, ed., *Baucis et Traso*, in *Commedie latine*.

70. Rouhi, *Mediation*, p. 207.

71. Lackenbacher, ed., *Lidia*, in *La "Comédie" latine*, 1.

72. Sheila Fisher and Janet E. Halley, ed., "Intro.," *Seeking the Woman in Late Medieval and Renaissance Writings: Essays in Feminist Contextual Criticism* (Knoxville: University of Tennessee Press, 1989), p. 5.

73. This outlandish copulation scene caught the imaginations of both Chaucer and Boccaccio. Boccaccio based the "Seventh Day, Ninth Story" of the *Decameron* directly on *Lidia*; Chaucer's "Merchant's Tale" in *The Canterbury Tales* ends with the pear-tree trick. Boccaccio turns the duke and Lydia into an old/young marriage, but he picks up Lusca's appeal to Pyrrhus as a fellow subordinate. While friends and relatives have to be loyal to each other, Lusca tells Pirro, no servant owes his master loyalty. Pirro should imagine what would happen if he had a pretty relative that appealed to the duke. If the duke could not seduce her, he would rape her, Lusca points out, and Pirro does not contradict her.

74. Woods, "Rape and Pedagogical Rhetoric," in *Criticism*, p. 76, n. 13.

75. Woods, "Rape and Pedagogical Rhetoric," in *Criticism*, p. 72.

76. Muscatine, *Fabliaux*, p. 4.

77. Muscatine, *Fabliaux*, p. 46.

78. Muscatine, *Fabliaux*, p. 152.

79. Muscatine, *Fabliaux*, pp. 5, 10.

80. R. Howard Bloch, *The Scandal of the Fabliaux* (Chicago: University of Chicago Press, 1986), p. 5.

81. Muscatine, *Fabliaux*, pp. 55, 152–53

82. *Le Prestre teint*, in *Nouveau recueil*, 7:307–30.

83. Muscatine, *Fabliaux*, pp. 14–15.

84. Muscatine, *Fabliaux*, p. 10.

85. Elliott, "Intro.," *Seven Medieval*, p. xxxiii.

86. *Dame Sirith*, in *Early Middle English Verse*, pp. 77–95.

87. Bruce Moore, "The Narrator within the Performance: Problems with Two Medieval 'Plays,'" in *Drama in the Middle Ages: Comparative and Critical Essays: Second Series*, ed. Clifford Davidson and John H. Stroupe, AMS Studies in the Middle Ages 18 (New York: AMS Press, 1990), pp. 152–55 [152–67]. J.A.W. Bennett and G.V. Smithers, editors of *Dame Sirith*, suggest, however, that *Dame Sirith* would suit a minstrel who could change his voice for the different characters. *Early Middle English Verse*, pp. 78–79.

88. *Auberee*, in *Nouveau recueil*, 1:160–312. Citations to texte critique. Dating and authorship (perhaps Jean Renart), pp. 166–67.

89. Muscatine, *Fabliaux*, p. 4.

90. Muscatine, *Fabliaux*, p. 92.

91. Rouhi, Mediation, p. 132.

92. Rouhi, Mediation, pp. 132, 100–101.

93. María del Pilar Mendoza Ramos, "Auberée la alcahueta: Similitudes y diferencias con sus homólogas literarias hispanas," in *Actas del IX Simposio de la Sociedad Española de Literatura General y Comparada*, ed. Túa Blesa, María Teresa Cacho, Carlos García Gual, Mercedes Rolland, Leonardo Romero Tobar, and Margarita Smerdou Altolaguirre (Zaragoza: Universidad de Zaragoza, 1994), 1:263–64 [263–68].

94. *Dame Sirith*, in *Early Middle English Verse*, pp. 77–95.

95. *Dame Sirith*, "Intro.," in *Early Middle English Verse*, p. 79.

96. John Hines, *The Fabliau in English*, describes Margery as "not much more than a dumb blonde" who is ambiguous about her willingness to be seduced. The lines Hines cites, however (135–38), are not ambiguous in context, and the seducing clerk shows no signs of hearing ambiguity in them. Longman Medieval and Renaissance Library (New York: Longman, 1993), pp. 50–51, 53.

97. E. Jane Burns, "Raping Men: What's Motherhood Got To Do With It?" in *Representing Rape*, p. 156 n. 3 [127–60].

98. See note 87.

99. Philippe Ménard, *Les Fabliaux: contes à rire du moyen âge.* (Paris: Presses universitaires de France, 1983), pp. 131, 138.

100. Lesley Johnson, "Women on Top: Antifeminism in the Fabliaux?," *Modern Language Review* 78.2 (1983): 298 [298–307].

101. Muscatine, *Fabliaux*, p. 122.

102. *Constant du Hamel* in *Nouveau recueil*, 1:29–126. Citations to texte critique. Dating and authorship, pp. 33–34.

103. Norris J. Lacy, "Fabliau Women," *Romance Notes* 25.3 (1985): 320 [318–27].

104. 602–603, 820–21, Text A; 586–87, Text B; 748–49, Text J.

105. Guillaume le Normand, *Le Prestre et Alison* in *Nouveau recueil*, 8:182–206. Citations to texte critique. Dating and authorship, pp. 185–87.

106. Lacy, "Fabliau Women," p. 322.

107. Otto Rank, *The Myth of the Birth of the Hero: A Psychological Interpretation of Mythology*, trans. F. Robbins and S.E. Jelliffe (New York: Robert Brunner, 1957).

108. Thomas Malory, *The Works of Sir Thomas Malory*, ed. Eugène Vinaver (1954: repr. London: Oxford University Press, 1962), p. 4.

109. Rosemary Morris compares nine versions of this story, beginning with Geoffrey of Monmouth's early twelfth-century account, and finds that all include Igerne's "uncourtly" deception or rape. "Uther and Igerne: A Study in Uncourtly Love," in *Arthurian Literature IV*, ed. Tony Hunt and Toshiyuki Takamiya (Woodbridge, Suffolk: D.S. Brewer, 1985), p. 70 [70–92].

110. *Lancelot: Roman en prose du XIIIe siècle*, ed. Alexandre Micha, Textes littéraires français, 9 vols. (Paris: Librairie Droz, 1978–83), 2:XLVII, 32–45, XLVIII, 1–27.

111. Malory, *Works*, pp. 584–86. *Lancelot*, ed. Micha, 4:LXXVIII, 53–58, LXXIX, 1–4; 6:CV, 33–38, CVI, 1–2.

112. *Le Roi Flore et la belle Jehanne*, in *Nouvelles en prose du XIIIe siècle*, ed. L. Moland et Ch. d'Hericault (Paris: Bibliothèque elzévirienne, 1856), pp. 85–157. Citations to page numbers.

113. This is very probably the name of a type figure. The go-between in *Le Prestre teint* (see pages 13–14, 39–40 above) is also called Dame Hersent, and so is the wolf's wife in the *Roman de Renart*.

114. See Sheila Delany for an interesting feminist, new historicist reading of this story. *Writing Woman: Women Writers and Women in Literature, Medieval to Modern* (New York: Schocken Books, 1983).

115. Guillaume de Lorris and Jean de Meun, *Le Roman de la rose*, ed. Félix Lecoy, Les Classiques français du moyen âge 92, 95, 98, 3 vols. (Paris: Champion, 1965–70), 3:21157–80.

116. Guillaume, *Le Roman*, 3:21162–64.

117. Ovid, *Metamorphoses*, ed. Frank Justus Miller, Loeb Classical Library (1916; Cambridge, Mass: Harvard University Press, 1958), Book X, ll. 309–467.

118. Sarah Kay, "Sexual Knowledge: The Once and Future Texts of the *Romance of the Rose*," in *Textuality and Sexuality: Reading Theories and Practices*, ed. Judith Still and Michael Worton (Manchester: Manchester University Press, 1993), p. 70 [69–86].

119. Guillaume, *Le Roman*, 2.

120. Marta Powell Harley, "Narcissus, Hermaphroditus, and Attis: Ovidian Lovers at the Fontaine d'Amors in Guillaume de Lorris's *Roman de la rose*," *PMLA* 101.3 (1986): 334 [324–37].

121. Karl D. Uitti, " 'Cele [qui] doit estre Rose clamee' (*Rose*, vv. 40–44): Guillaume's Intentionality," in *Rethinking the Romance of the Rose: Text, Image, Reception*, ed. Kevin Brownlee and Sylvia Huot (Philadelphia: University of Pennsylvania Press, 1992), p. 40 [39–64].

122. Simon Gaunt, "Bel Acueil and the Improper Allegory of the *Romance of the Rose*," *New Medieval Literatures* 2 (1998): 70, 91 [65–93].

123. Sarah Kay, "Women's Body of Knowledge: Epistemology and Misogyny in the *Romance of the Rose*," in *Framing Medieval Bodies*, p. 213 [211–35].

124. E. Jane Burns, *Courtly Love Undressed: Reading Through Clothes in Medieval French Culture* (Philadelphia: University of Pennsylvania Press, 2002) pp. 81–83.

125. E. Jane Burns, Sarah Kay, Roberta L. Krueger, and Helen Solterer, "Feminism and the Discipline of Old French Studies: *Une Bele Disjointure*," in *Medievalism and the Modernist Temper*, ed. R. Howard Bloch and Stephen G. Nichols, Jr. (Baltimore: Johns Hopkins University Press, 1996), p. 243 [225–66].

126. Kay, "Women's body," in *Framing Medieval Bodies*, pp. 217–18.

127. *The Pseudo-Ovidian De Vetula*, ed. Dorothy M. Robathan (Amsterdam: Adolf M. Hakkert, 1968), p. 8. Dating, p. 30.

128. Jean Lefèvre, *La Vieille ou les dernières amours d'Ovide*, ed. Hippolyte Cocheris (Paris: Auguste Hérissey, 1861). Dating of translation, p. xxxiv.

129. Lee Patterson, " 'For the Wyves love of Bathe': Feminine Rhetoric and Poetic Resolution in the *Roman de la Rose* and the *Canterbury Tales*," *Speculum* 58.3 (1983): [656–95].

130. Lee Patterson, *Chaucer and the Subject of History* (Madison: University of Wisconsin Press, 1991), pp. 292–96.

131. Lee Patterson, "Feminine Rhetoric and the Politics of Subjectivity: La Vieille and the Wife of Bath," in *Rethinking the Romance of the Rose: Text, Image, Reception*, ed. Kevin Brownlee and Sylvia Huot (Philadelphia: University of Pennsylvania Press, 1992), pp. 316–58.

132. Patterson, *Chaucer and History*, pp. 295–96.

133. Patterson, *Chaucer and History*, p. 296.

134. Patterson, *Chaucer and History*, p. 295.

135. Patterson, *Chaucer and History*, pp. 295–96.

136. Lefèvre, *La Vieille*, ed. Cocheris, p. xxxiv.

137. Morawski, ed., *Pamphile*, Brasdefer, p. 68.

138. Mignani, trans., *Book of Good Love*, p. 25.

139. Ruiz, *Libro de buen amor*, stanzas 576–891.

140. Vittore Branca, *Boccaccio: The Man and His Works*, trans. Richard Monges (New York: New York University Press, 1976), p. 77.

141. Garbáty, "*Pamphilus* Tradition," pp. 457–61.

142. Kay, "Sexual Knowledge," in *Textuality and Sexuality*, p. 70.

143. Christine Ryan Hilary, notes to "The Wife of Bath's Prologue," in Geoffrey Chaucer, *The Riverside Chaucer*, gen. ed. Larry D. Benson, 3rd edn. (Boston: Houghton Mifflin Co., 1987), p. 864.

144. Chaucer, "General Prologue to the Canterbury Tales," in *Riverside*, ll. 127–36. Guillaume and Jean, *Le Roman*, 1966, vol. 2., ll. 13378–402.

145. Fisher and Halley, *Seeking the Woman*, p. 4.

146. John Gower, *The Confessio Amantis*, *Complete Works of John Gower*, ed. G.C. Macaulay, 4 vols. (Oxford: Clarendon Press, 1899–1902), 2:bk. 1, ll. 840, 847.

147. Gower, *Confessio Amantis*, 3: bk. 5, ll. 2706, 2709.
148. Anne Laskaya, "The Rhetoric of Incest in the Middle English *Emaré*," in *Violence Against Women in Medieval Texts*, ed. Anna Roberts (Gainesville, FL: University Press of Florida, 1998), p. 98 [97–114].
149. Fisher and Halley, *Seeking the Woman*, p. 5.
150. Boccaccio, "Giornata terza, novella nona," *Decameron*, pp. 199–204. "Third Day, Ninth Story," *Decameron*, pp. 226–35.
151. *Le Roman du comte d'Artois*, ed. Jean-Charles Seigneuret (Geneva: Librairie Droz, 1966), pp. 113–35. Dating, p. xxix.
152. Boccaccio, "Eighth Day, Tenth Story," *Decameron*.
153. Boccaccio, "Eighth Day, First Story," *Decameron*.
154. Boccaccio, "Giornata quinta, novella decima," *Decameron*, pp. 317–22. "Fifth Day, Tenth Story," *Decameron*, pp. 369–76.
155. Karras, *Common Women*, p. 61.

Part II: Choreographing Love: Idealized Go-Betweens

1. Lewis, *Allegory*, pp. 1–4, 11–14.
2. Lewis, *Allegory*, pp. 32–43.
3. For a recent discussion of the twentieth-century arguments about medieval literary love, see Neil Cartlidge, *Medieval Marriage: Literary Approaches, 1100–1300* (Woodbridge, UK: D.S. Brewer, 1997), pp. 5–10.
4. E. Talbot Donaldson, "The Myth of Courtly Love," *Ventures: Magazine of the Yale Graduate School* 5 (1965): [16–23].
5. A.R. Press, "The adulterous nature of *fin' amors*: a reexamination of the theory," *Forum for Modern Language Studies* 6 (1970): 328–31 [327–41].
6. Sarah Kay, "Courts, Clerks, and Courtly Love," in *The Cambridge Companion to Medieval Romance*, ed. Roberta L. Krueger (Cambridge, UK: Cambridge University Press, 2000), p. 88 [81–96].
7. Cartlidge, *Medieval Marriage*, p. 10.
8. Cartlidge, *Medieval Marriage*, p. 14.
9. Cartlidge, *Medieval Marriage*, p. 16.
10. Cartlidge, *Medieval Marriage*, p. 12.
11. Eugene Vance, "Chrétien's *Yvain* and the Ideologies of Change and Exchange," *Yale French Studies* 70 (1986): 45 [42–62].
12. Vance, "Chrétien's *Yvain*," p. 45.
13. Vance, "Chrétien's *Yvain*," p. 46.
14. Cartlidge, *Medieval Marriage*, pp. 20–21.
15. Simon Gaunt, "Romance and Other Genres," in *Cambridge Companion*, pp. 48–49 [45–59].
16. Gaunt, "Romance," in *Cambridge Companion*, p. 49.
17. Elspeth Kennedy, ed., "Intro.," *Lancelot do Lac: The Non-Cyclic Old French Prose Romance*, 2 vols. (Oxford: Clarendon Press, 1980), 1: vi.
18. Muscatine, *Fabliaux*, p. 4.

19. Elliott, "Intro.," *Seven Medieval*, p. xxxiii.
20. Sylvia Huot, "The Manuscript Context of Medieval Romance," in *Cambridge Companion*, p. 75 [60–77].
21. Helen Cooper, *The English Romance in Time: Transforming motifs from Geoffrey of Monmouth to the death of Shakespeare* (Oxford: Oxford University Press, 2004), pp. 29–31.
22. Chrétien de Troyes, *Cligés, Les Romans de Chrétien de Troyes*, ed. Alexandre Micha, Les Classiques français du Moyen Age 84, 2 vols. (Paris: Champion, 1957), 2. Dating, p. viii. *Cligés* in *Arthurian Romances: Chrétien de Troyes*, trans. D.D.R. Owen (London: J.M. Dent, 1987), pp. 93–184.
23. *William of Palerne: an alliterative romance*, ed. G. H. V. Bunt (Groningen: Bouma's Boekhuis, 1985). Date *c.* 1335–61, pp.14–15.
24. *Guillaume de Palerne: Roman du XIIIe siècle*, ed. Alexandre Micha, Textes littéraires français (Geneva: Droz, 1990). Date *c.* 1220, p. 23.
25. Erik Kooper, "*Grace*: The Healing Herb in *William of Palerne*," *Leeds Studies in English* 15 (1984): 85–87, 90 [83–93].
26. For a discussion of this homoerotic/heterosexual love triangle, see Gretchen Mieszkowski, "The Prose *Lancelot*'s Galehot, Malory's Lavain, and the Queering of Late Medieval Literature," *Arthuriana* 5 (1995): [21–51].
27. Kennedy, ed., *Lancelot do Lac*, references to vol. 1. Dating, *c.* 1214–30, 2:41–42.
28. Kennedy, ed., "Intro.," *Lancelot do Lac*, 2:1–10.
29. William Calin, *The French Tradition and the Literature of Medieval England*, University of Toronto Romance Series (Toronto: University of Toronto Press, 1994), p. 140.
30. Kennedy argues convincingly that the long, cyclic version was expanded from the short, non-cyclic version rather than the short version abridged from the longer version. Kennedy, ed., "Intro.," *Lancelot do Lac*, 2:39–40.
31. *Lancelot: Roman en prose*, 8: sections LIIa, pp. 86–118.
32. Gravdal, *Ravishing Maidens*, p. 15.
33. Gottfried von Strassburg, *Tristan*, ed. Friedrich Ranke, commentary Rüdiger Krohn, 3 vols. (Stuttgart: Philipp Reclam Jun., 1981), 1: citations, 3:226–30, dating. A.T. Hatto, trans., *Tristan* (1960: repr. New York: Penguin Books, 1982).
34. Aimon de Varennes, *Florimont*, ed. Alfons Hilka, Gesellschaft für romanische literatur 48 (Göttingen, 1932). Date, Anthime Fourrier, *Le Courant réaliste dans le roman courtois en France au moyen-âge*, 2 vols. (Paris: Nizet, 1960) 1:384 n. 142.
35. Thomas, *The Romance of Horn*, ed. Mildred K. Pope, 2 vols.; vol. 2 revised and completed by T.B.W. Reid, Anglo-Norman Texts 9–10, 12–13 (Oxford: Basil Blackwell, 1955, 1964). Date, 2:121–24.
36. Judith Weiss, "The wooing woman in Anglo-Norman romance," in *Romance in Medieval England*, ed. Maldwyn Mills, Jennifer Fellows, and Carol M. Meale (Cambridge, UK: D.S. Brewer, 1991), p. 155 [149–61].
37. Weiss, "Wooing woman," in *Romance in Medieval England*, p. 155.

38. Giovanni Boccaccio, *Il filocolo*, ed. Salvatore Battaglia (Bari: Gius. Laterza & Figli, 1938). Citations to book and section numbers. Dating, Antonio Enzo Quaglio as quoted in "Intro.," Thomas G. Bergin, *Giovanni Boccaccio: Il Filocolo*, trans. Donald Cheney, Garland Library of Medieval Literature 43, Series B (New York: Garland, 1985), p. xi. Karl Young argued this episode was a source for the Book III consummation scene in Chaucer's *Troilus and Criseyde*: "Chaucer's Use of Boccaccio's 'Filocolo,' " *Modern Philology* 4 (1906–07): 169–77. Henry Ansgar Kelly argues, based on this episode, that Troilus and Criseyde enter into a secret marriage: *Love and Marriage in the Age of Chaucer* (Ithaca: Cornell University Press, 1975), pp. 219–25.

39. Boccaccio, *Filocolo*, Bk. 4, 118.

40. René d'Anjou, *Oeuvres complètes du Roi René*, ed. M. le Comte de Quatrebarbes, 4 vols. (Angers, 1846), 3. References to pages. Internally dated, p. 195.

41. Quatrebarbes, ed., *Roi René* 3: ii–iii.

42. *Partonopeu de Blois: A French Romance of the Twelfth Century*, ed. Joseph Gildea, 2 vols. (Villanova, PA: Villanova University Press, 1967, 1968, 1970), 1:text, 2 pt. 1, *Partonopeu de Blois, The Continuation*; vol. 2, pt. 2, Leon Smith, "Introduction," Joseph Gildea, "Commentary."

43. Fourrier, *Le Courant réaliste*, p. 315.

44. "Middle High German, Old Norse, Middle Dutch, medieval Spanish and Catalan, and medieval Italian." "Introduction," *Partonopeus de Blois*: An Electronic Edition, ed. Penny Eley, Penny Simons, Mario Longtin, Catherine Hanley, and Philip Shaw (Sheffield: HriOnline, 2005), www.hrionline.ac.uk/partonopeus, p. 1.

45. *The Middle-English Versions of Partonope of Blois*, ed. A. Trampe Bödtker, EETS, E.S. 109 (London: Oxford University Press, 1912). Citations to Addit. MS. 35,2888, British Museum.

46. Matilda Tomaryn Bruckner, *Shaping Romance: Interpretation, Truth, and Closure in Twelfth-Century French Fictions* (Philadelphia: University of Pennsylvania Press, 1993), p. 124. For recent debates over the gender roles in *Partonopeus*, see Bruckner, *Shaping Romance*, pp. 109–56; Colleen P. Donagher, "Socializing the Sorceress: The Fairy Mistress in *Lanval, Le Bel Inconnu* and *Partonopeu de Blois*," *Essays in Medieval Studies* 4 (1987): [69–90]; Penny Eley and Penny Simons, "*Partonopeus de Blois* and Chrétien de Troyes: A Re-Assessment," *Romania* 117 (1999): 329 [316–41]; Sarah Kay, *Courtly Contradictions: The Emergence of the Literary Object in the Twelfth Century* (Stanford: Stanford University Press, 2001), pp. 275–99; Gretchen Mieszkowski, "Urake and the Gender Roles of *Partonope of Blois*," *Mediaevalia* 25.2 (2004): [181–95]; Penny Simons and Penny Eley, "Male Beauty and Sexual Orientation in *Partonopeus de Blois*," *Romance Studies* 17 (1999): [41–56].

47. Chrétien de Troyes, *Yvain (Le Chevalier au lion)*, ed. Wendelin Foerster; intro., notes, glossary, T.B.W. Reid (Manchester: Manchester University Press, 1942). Trans. Owen, *Yvain* in *Arthurian Romances*, pp. 281–373.

Dating, Karl D. Uitti, "*Le Chevalier au lion (Yvain),*" in *The Romances of Chrétien de Troyes: A Symposium,* ed. Douglas Kelly, Edward C. Armstrong Monographs on Medieval Literature 3 (Lexington, KY: French Forum, 1985), pp. 182–90 [182–231].

48. Roberta Krueger citing Lefay-Toury, *Women Readers and the Ideology of Gender in Old French Verse Romance* (Cambridge, UK: Cambridge University Press, 1993), p. 45.

49. Stephen Knight, *Arthurian Literature and Society* (New York: St. Martin's Press, 1983), p. 99.

50. Ménard, *Le Rire,* pp. 230–31.

51. A.R. Press, "Chrétien de Troyes's Laudine: A *Belle Dame sans mercy?*", *Forum for Modern Language Studies* 19 (1983): 162 [158–71].

52. Robert W. Hanning, *The Individual in Twelfth-century Romance* (New Haven: Yale University Press, 1977), p. 120.

53. Joan M. Ferrante, "Male Fantasy and Female Reality in Courtly Literature," *Women's Studies* 11 (1984): 85 [67–97].

54. Tony Hunt, *Chrétien de Troyes: "Yvain" (Le Chevalier au Lion)* (London: Grant & Cutler, 1986), p. 90.

55. J.M. Sullivan, "The Lady Lunete: Literary Conventions of Counsel and the Criticism of Counsel in Chrétien's *Yvain* and Hartmann's *Iwein,*" *Neophilologus* 85.3 (2001): 336 [335–54].

56. Hanning, *Individual in Twelfth-century,* pp. 119–20.

57. Donald Maddox, *The Arthurian Romances of Chrétien de Troyes: Once and Future Fictions,* Cambridge Studies in Medieval Literature 12 (Cambridge, UK: Cambridge University Press, 1991), p. 60.

58. Uitti, "*Le Chevalier,*" in *Romances of Chrétien,* p. 217.

59. Roberta L. Krueger, "Love, Honor, and the Exchange of Women in *Yvain*: Some Remarks on the Female Reader," *Romance Notes* 25.3 (1985): 304–06 [302–17].

60. Krueger, "Love, Honor," p. 309.

61. Krueger, *Women Readers,* p. 46.

62. Hunt, *Chrétien,* p. 92.

63. Hanning, *Individual in Twelfth-century,* p. 121.

64. *Li Romans de Claris et Laris,* ed. Johann Alton, Bibliothek des Litterarischen vereins in Stuttgart 169 (Tübingen: 1884). Dating, p. 863.

65. Ménard, *Le Rire,* p. 209.

66. Penny Simons and Penny Eley, "The Prologue to *Partonopeus de Blois*: Text, Context and Subtext," *French Studies* 49 (1995): 11–12, 14 [1–16].

67. Laurence Harf-Lancner, *Les Fées au moyen âge: Morgane et Mélusine: la naissance des fées* (Paris: Champion, 1984), p. 317; Kay, *Courtly Contradictions,* p. 327 n. 28.

68. Hue de Rotelande, *Protheseläus: ein altfranzösischer Abenteuerroman,* ed. Franz Kluckow, Gesellschaft für romanische Literatur 45, 2 vols. (Göttingen: Niemeyer, Halle, 1924). Date pre-1190 when patron Hue mentions dies, intro., p. 2.

Judith Weiss discusses the comic elements of *Protheseläus*, in particular
Hue's pleasure in ridiculing "conventional themes, figures and motifs."
"A Reappraisal of Hue de Rotelande's *Protheselaus*," *Medium AEvum* 52.1
(1983): 106 [104–111].

69. Edmond Faral, *Les Jongleurs en France au moyen âge*, 2nd edn. (Paris:
    Champion, 1964), pp. 147–48.
70. Weiss, "A Reappraisal," 107.
71. Gautier d'Arras, *Éracle*, ed. Guy Raynaud de Lage, Les Classiques français
    du moyen âge (Paris: Champion, 1976). Dating, Corinne Pierreville,
    Gautier d'Arras: L'autre Chrétien (Paris: Champion, 2001), pp. 13–15.
    Pierreville argues that *Éracle* was influenced by *Cligés*, pp. 62–63.
72. Penny Eley argues that exploring breaches of faith is a thematic constant in
    Gautier's work. "Patterns of Faith and Doubt: Gautier d'Arras's *Eracle* and
    Ille et Galeron," *French Studies* 43.3 (1989): 257 [257–70].

Part III: Choreographing Lust and Love: Chaucer's Pandarus

1. Larry D. Benson, "Courtly Love and Chivalry in the Later Middle Ages,"
   in *Fifteenth-Century Studies: Recent Essays*, ed. Robert F. Yeager (Hamden,
   CT: Archon Books, 1984), p. 240 [237–57].
2. See Mary Hamel, "The Franklin's Tale and Chrétien de Troyes," *Chaucer
   Review* 17.4 (1983): [316–31].
3. Notes 143 and 144, part 1.
4. Garbáty, "*Pamphilus* Tradition," 457–70; Mieszkowski, "Chaucer's
   Pandarus and Jean Brasdefer's Houdée," *Chaucer Review* 20 (1985): [40–60];
   Fleming, *Classical Imitation*, p. 159.
5. For *Pamphilus*, see p. 25; for the *Roman*, p. 61.
6. Eleanor Prescott Hammond, ed., "The Chance of the Dice," *Englische Studien*
   59 (1925): 9 [1–16], stanza 23. Caroline F.E. Spurgeon dates this poem
   c. 1440. *Five Hundred Years of Chaucer Criticism and Allusion, 1357–1900*,
   3 vols. (Cambridge, UK: Cambridge University Press, 1925), 1:44–45.
7. John Hill, "Aristocratic Friendship in *Troilus and Criseyde*: Pandarus,
   Courtly Love and Ciceronian Brotherhood in Troy," in *New Readings of
   Chaucer's Poetry*, ed. Robert G. Benson and Susan J. Ridyard (Cambridge,
   UK: D.S. Brewer, 2003), pp. 165–82.
8. Geoffrey Chaucer, *Troilus and Criseyde*, ed. Stephen A. Barney, in *Riverside
   Chaucer*. Citations to book and line number.
9. Karl Young, *The Origin and Development of the Story of Troilus and Criseyde*,
   Chaucer Society, 2nd Series 40 (London: Kegan Paul, 1908).
10. William George Dodd, *Courtly Love in Chaucer and Gower*, Harvard Studies
    in English 1 (Boston: Ginn, 1913), p. 147.
11. Albert C. Baugh, ed., *Chaucer's Major Poetry* (New York: Appleton-
    Century-Crofts, 1963), p. 80.

12. Paolo Savj-Lopez, "Il *filostrato* di G. Boccaccio," *Romania* 27 (1898): 468–69 [442–79].

13. Lawrence, "Love Story," in *Shaksperian Studies*, pp. 202–03.

14. Charles Muscatine, *Chaucer and the French Tradition* (1957: repr. Berkeley: University of California Press, 1964), p. 137.

15. Mann, *Geoffrey Chaucer*, p. 104.

16. Fleming, *Classical Imitation*, p. 163.

17. Laura F. Hodges, "Sartorial Signs in *Troilus and Criseyde*," *Chaucer Review* 35.3 (2001): 231 [223–58].

18. Richard W. Fehrenbacher, " 'Al that which chargeth nought to seye': The Theme of Incest in *Troilus and Criseyde*," *Exemplaria* 9.2 (1997): 344 [341–69].

19. Giovanni Boccaccio, *Il filostrato*, ed. Vincenzo Pernicone, trans. Robert P. apRoberts and Anna Bruni Seldis, Garland Library of Medieval Literature 53, Series A (New York: Garland, 1986). References to section and stanza.

20. Richard E. Zeikowitz, *Homoeroticism and Chivalry: Discourses of Male Same-Sex Desire in the 14th Century* (New York: Palgrave Macmillan, 2003), pp. 134–35.

21. Zeikowitz, *Homoeroticism*, p. 140.

22. Steven R. Guthrie, "Chivalry and Privacy in *Troilus and Criseyde* and *La Chastelaine de Vergy*," *Chaucer Review* 34.2 (1999): 150, 154, 167, 172 [150–73].

23. Robert W. Hanning, "Come in Out of the Code: Interpreting the Discourse of Desire in Boccaccio's *Filostrato* and Chaucer's *Troilus and Criseyde*," in *Chaucer's* Troilus and Criseyde *"Subgit to alle Poesye": Essays in Criticism*, ed. R.A. Shoaf (Binghamton, New York: Pegasus Press, 1992), pp. 135, 133 [120–37].

24. Muscatine, *Chaucer*, pp. 140–41.

25. Guthrie, "Chivalry," 155, 168.

26. See pp. 96–99 above.

27. Muscatine, *Chaucer*, p.141.

28. See pp. 87–88 above.

29. Muscatine, *Chaucer*, p. 141.

30. *Generydes*, ed. W.A. Wright, EETS, O.S. 55, 70 (London, 1873, 1878). Dating, derivation from French original: Carol M. Meale, "The Morgan Library copy of *Generides*," in *Romance in Medieval England*, pp. 90–91 [89–104].

31. *Floriant et Florete*, ed. Harry F. Williams (Ann Arbor: University of Michigan Press, 1947). Dating p. 7.

32. Muscatine, *Chaucer*, p. 140.

33. C. David Benson, *Chaucer's* Troilus and Criseyde (London: Unwin Hyman, 1990), p. 120.

34. Peter Christmas, "*Troilus and Criseyde*: The Problems of Love and Necessity," *Chaucer Review* 9.4 (1975): 286 [285–96].

35. Carolyn Dinshaw, "Readers in/of *Troilus and Criseyde*," *Yale Journal of Criticism* 1.2 (1988): 87 [81–105].

36. John P. Hermann, "Gesture and Seduction in *Troilus and Criseyde*," *Studies in the Age of Chaucer* 7 (1985): 107–35, in *Chaucer's* Troilus *"Subgit,"* p. 160 [138–60].
37. Hanning, "Come In," in *Chaucer's* Troilus *"Subgit,"* p. 136.
38. Louise O. Fradenburg, "'Our owen wo to drynke': Loss, Gender and Chivalry in *Troilus and Criseyde*," in *Chaucer's* Troilus *"Subgit,"* p. 100 [88–106].
39. Derek Brewer, "Troilus's 'Gentil' Manhood," in *Masculinities in Chaucer: Approaches to Maleness in the* Canterbury Tales *and* Troilus and Criseyde, ed. Peter G. Beidler (Cambridge, UK: D.S. Brewer, 1998), p. 239 [237–52].
40. Maud Burnett McInerney, "'Is this a mannes herte?': Unmanning Troilus through Ovidian Allusion," in *Masculinities in Chaucer*, p. 223 [221–35].
41. Carolyn Dinshaw, *Chaucer's Sexual Poetics* (Madison: University of Wisconsin Press, 1989), pp. 28, 37–38.
42. Garbáty, "*Pamphilus* Tradition," 457–61, 463–68.
43. Fleming, *Classical Imitation*, p. 159; Mieszkowski, "Chaucer's Pandarus and Houdée," pp. 40–60.
44. Diane Vanner Steinberg, "'We Do Usen Here No Wommen For To Selle': Embodiment of Social Practices in *Troilus and Criseyde*," *Chaucer Review* 29.3 (1995): 264 [259–73].
45. Sealy Gilles, "Love and Disease in Chaucer's *Troilus and Criseyde*," *Studies in the Age of Chaucer* 25 (2003): 191 [157–97].
46. McInerney, "'Is this a mannes herte?,'" in *Masculinities in Chaucer*, p. 225.
47. Elaine Tuttle Hansen, *Chaucer and the Fictions of Gender* (Berkeley: University of California Press, 1992), pp. 12–13, 20.
48. Hansen, *Chaucer and the Fictions*, p. 149.
49. James I. Wimsatt, "Medieval and Modern in Chaucer's *Troilus and Criseyde*," *PMLA* 92.2 (1977): 208 [203–16].
50. McInerney, "'Is this a mannes herte?,'" in *Masculinities in Chaucer*, p. 224.
51. Mann, *Geoffrey Chaucer*, pp. 107–09.
52. Hansen, *Chaucer and the Fictions*, p.170.
53. Christopher Cannon, "Chaucer and Rape: Uncertainty's Certainties," in *Representing Rape*, p. 269 [255–79].
54. Fradenburg, "'Our owen wo,'" in *Chaucer's* Troilus *"Subgit,"* pp. 100–01.
55. Tison Pugh, "Queer Pandarus? Silence and Sexual Ambiguity in Chaucer's *Troilus and Criseyde*," *Philological Quarterly* 80.1 (2001): 18 [17–35].
56. Zeikowitz, *Homoeroticism*, pp. 54–61.
57. Zeikowitz, *Homoeroticism*, p. 59.
58. Zeikowitz, *Homoeroticism*, p. 60.
59. T.A. Stroud, "The Palinode, the Narrator, and Pandarus's Alleged Incest," *Chaucer Review* 27.1 (1992): 23 [16–30].
60. Robert P. apRoberts, "A Contribution to the Thirteenth Labour: Purging the *Troilus* of Incest," in *Essays on English and American Literature and a Sheaf of Poems*, ed. J. Bakker, J.A. Verleun, and J.v.d. Vriesenaerde (Amsterdam: Rodopi, 1987), pp. 11–25.

61. John V. Fleming, "Deiphoebus Betrayed: Virgilian Decorum, Chaucerian Feminism," *Chaucer Review* 21.2 (1986): 188 [182–99].

62. James F. Maybury, "Pandarus and Criseyde: The Motif of Incest in Chaucer's *Troilus*," *Xavier Review* 2 (1982): 82–89.

63. Fehrenbacher, " 'Al that which chargeth,' " pp. 344, 351–57.

64. Sarah Stanbury, "The Voyeur and the Private Life in *Troilus and Criseyde*," *Studies in the Age of Chaucer* 13 (1991): 155 [141–58].

65. Fehrenbacher, " 'Al that which chargeth,' " p. 343.

66. Ruiz, Mignani, ed., *The Book of Good Love*, n. 61.

67. Ruiz, *Libro de buen amor*, stanzas 923–26.

68. Gower, *Confessio Amantis*, 3: bk. 5, ll. 4573–80.

69. Ida L. Gordon, *The Double Sorrow of Troilus: A Study of Ambiguities in* Troilus and Criseyde (Oxford: Clarendon Press, 1970), pp. 115–16.

70. Elizabeth Salter, "*Troilus and Criseyde*: A Reconsideration," in *Patterns of Love and Courtesy: Essays in Memory of C.S. Lewis*, ed. John Lawlor (London: Arnold, 1966) pp. 99–100 [86–106].

71. Kelly, *Love and Marriage*, p. 63.

72. Fleming, *Classical Imitation*, p. 171.

73. Dinshaw, *Chaucer's Sexual Poetics*, pp. 60–61.

74. Brewer, "Troilus's 'Gentil' Manhood," in *Masculinities in Chaucer*, p. 243.

75. Hill, "Aristocratic Friendship," in *New Readings*, p. 176.

76. Laurie A. Finke and Martin B. Shichtman, ed., "intro.," *Medieval Texts & Contemporary Readers* (Ithaca: Cornell University Press, 1987), p. 9 [1–11].

77. Gaunt, "Romance," in *Cambridge Companion*, p. 46 [45–59].

78. Karla Taylor, "*Inferno 5* and *Troilus and Criseyde* Revisited," in *Chaucer's* Troilus "*Subgit*," p. 246 [239–56].

79. Gaunt, "Romance," in *Cambridge Companion*, p. 47.

80. Barry Windeatt, "*Troilus* and the Disenchantment of Romance," in *Studies in Medieval English Romances: Some New Approaches*, ed. Derek Brewer (Cambridge, UK: Boydell and Brewer Inc., 1988), p. 131 [129–47].

81. Barry Windeatt, Troilus and Criseyde: *Oxford Guides to Chaucer* (Oxford: Clarendon Press, 1992), p. 148.

82. Windeatt, "*Troilus* and Disenchantment," in *Studies in Medieval*, pp. 131–32.

83. Gayle Margherita, "Criseyde's Remains: Romance and the Question of Justice," *Exemplaria* 12.2 (2000): 261 [257–92].

84. Margherita, "Criseyde's Remains," 271.

85. Kay, "Courts, Clerks," in *Cambridge Companion*, p. 85.

86. Rosemarie P. McGerr, "Meaning and Ending in a 'Paynted proces': Resistance to Closure in *Troilus and Criseyde*," in *Chaucer's* Troilus "*Subgit*," p. 181 [179–98].

87. McGerr, "Meaning and Ending," in *Chaucer's* Troilus "*Subgit*," pp. 182–84.

88. H. Marshall Leicester, Jr., "Oure Tonges *Différance*: Textuality and Deconstruction in Chaucer," in *Medieval Texts*, pp. 17–18, 23 [15–26].

89. Dinshaw, "Readers In/of," 100.

90. Dinshaw, "Readers in/of," 81.

91. Dinshaw, "Readers in/of," 86.

92. Dinshaw, "Readers in/of," 87.

93. Roberta L. Krueger, "Beyond Debate: Gender in Play in Old French Courtly Fiction," in *Gender in Debate*, p. 91 [79–95].

BIBLIOGRAPHY

Agrimi, Jole and Chiara Crisciani. "Savoir médical et anthropologie religieuse: Les Représentations et les fonctions de la *vetula* (XIIIe-XVe siècle)." *Annales ESC* 48 (1993): 1281–308.

Aimon de Varennes. *Florimont.* Ed. Alfons Hilka. Gesellschaft für romanische Literatur 48. Göttingen, 1932.

Allen, Peter L. *The Art of Love: Amatory Fiction from Ovid to the* Romance of the Rose. Philadelphia: University of Pennsylvania Press, 1992.

apRoberts, Robert P. "A Contribution to the Thirteenth Labour: Purging the *Troilus* of Incest." In *Essays on English and American Literature and a Sheaf of Poems.* Ed. J. Bakker, J.A. Verleun, and J.v.d. Vriesenaerde. Amsterdam: Rodopi,1987. 11–25.

Arthurian Romances: Chrétien de Troyes. Trans. D.D.R. Owen. London: J.M. Dent, 1987.

Auberee. In *Nouveau recueil.* 1:160–312.

Baucis et Traso. Ed. Giovanni Orlandi. In *Commedie latine,* 1980. 3:243–303.

Baugh, Albert C., ed. *Chaucer's Major Poetry.* New York: Appleton-Century-Crofts, 1963.

Beidler, Peter G., ed. *Masculinities in Chaucer: Approaches to Maleness in the* Canterbury Tales *and* Troilus and Criseyde. Cambridge, UK: D.S. Brewer, 1998.

Benson, C. David. *Chaucer's* Troilus and Criseyde. London: Unwin Hyman, 1990.

Benson, Larry D. "Courtly Love and Chivalry in the Later Middle Ages." In *Fifteenth-Century Studies: Recent Essays.* Ed. Robert F. Yeager. Hamden, CT.: Archon Books, 1984. 237–57.

Blamires, Alcuin. *The Case for Women in Medieval Culture.* Oxford: Clarendon Press, 1997.

Bloch, R. Howard. *Medieval Misogyny and the Invention of Western Romantic Love.* Chicago: University of Chicago Press, 1991.

———. *The Scandal of the Fabliaux.* Chicago: University of Chicago Press, 1986.

Boccaccio, Giovanni. *Decameron.* Trans. Mark Musa and Peter Bondanella. New York: W.W. Norton, 1982.

———. *Giovanni Boccaccio: Il Filocolo.* Trans. Donald Cheney. Intro. Thomas G. Bergin. Garland Library of Medieval Literature 43, Series B. New York: Garland, 1985.

———. *Il decameron.* Ed. Aldo Rossi. Bologna: Cappelli, 1977.

Boccaccio, Giovanni. *Il filocolo*. Ed. Salvatore Battaglia. Bari: Gius. Laterza & Figli, 1938.

———. *Il filostrato*. Ed. Vincenzo Pernicone. Trans. Robert P. apRoberts and Anna Bruni Seldis. Garland Library of Medieval Literature 53, Series A. New York: Garland, 1986.

Branca, Vittore. *Boccaccio: The Man and His Works*. Trans. Richard Monges. New York: New York University Press, 1976.

Brewer, Derek. "Troilus's 'Gentil' Manhood." In Beidler. 237–52.

Brownlee, Kevin and Sylvia Huot, ed. *Rethinking the* Romance of the Rose: *Text, Image, Reception*. Philadelphia: University of Pennsylvania Press, 1992.

Bruckner, Matilda Tomaryn. *Shaping Romance: Interpretation, Truth, and Closure in Twelfth-Century French Fictions*. Philadelphia: University of Pennsylvania Press, 1993.

Burns, E. Jane. *Courtly Love Undressed: Reading Through Clothes in Medieval French Culture*. Philadelphia: University of Pennsylvania Press, 2002.

———. "Raping Men: What's Motherhood Got To Do With It?" In Robertson and Rose. 127–60.

Burns, E. Jane, Sarah Kay, Roberta L. Krueger, and Helen Solterer. "Feminism and the Discipline of Old French Studies: *Une Bele Disjointure*." In *Medievalism and the Modernist Temper*. Ed. R. Howard Bloch and Stephen G. Nichols, Jr. Baltimore: Johns Hopkins University Press, 1996. 225–66.

Calin, William. *The French Tradition and the Literature of Medieval England*. University of Toronto romance series. Toronto: University of Toronto Press, 1994.

Cannon, Christopher. "Chaucer and Rape: Uncertainty's Certainties." In Robertson and Rose. 255–79.

Cartlidge, Neil. *Medieval Marriage: Literary Approaches, 1100–1300*. Woodbridge, UK: D.S. Brewer, 1997.

Chaucer, Geoffrey. *The Riverside Chaucer*. Gen. ed. Larry D. Benson. 3rd edn. Boston: Houghton Mifflin Co., 1987.

———. *Troilus and Criseyde*. Ed. Stephen A. Barney. In Chaucer, *Riverside*.

Chrétien de Troyes. *Cligés*. *Les Romans de Chrétien de Troyes*. Ed. Alexandre Micha. Les Classiques français du moyen âge 84. 2 vols. Paris: Champion, 1957. 2.

———. *Yvain (Le Chevalier au lion)*. Ed. Wendelin Foerster. Intro., notes, and glossary T.B.W. Reid. Manchester: Manchester University Press, 1942.

Christmas, Peter. "*Troilus and Criseyde*: The Problems of Love and Necessity." *Chaucer Review* 9.4 (1975): 285–96.

La "Comédie" latine en France au XIIe siècle. Ed. Gustave Cohen. Société d'édition "les belles-lettres." 2 vols. Paris, 1931.

Commedie latine del XII e XIII secolo. 8 vols. Genova: Istituto di filologia classica e medievale, 1976–2000.

Constant du Hamel. In *Nouveau recueil*. 1:29–126.

Cooper, Helen. *The English Romance in Time: Transforming Motifs from Geoffrey of Monmouth to the Death of Shakespeare*. Oxford: Oxford University Press, 2004.

Dame Sirith. In *Early Middle English Verse and Prose*. Ed. J.A.W. Bennett and G.V. Smithers. 2nd edn. Oxford: Clarendon Press, 1968. 77–95.

Delany, Sheila. *Writing Woman: Women Writers and Women in Literature, Medieval to Modern*. New York: Schocken Books, 1983.

De nuntio sagaci. Ed. Gabriella Rossetti. In *Commedie latine*, 1980. 2:11–125.

Dinshaw, Carolyn. *Chaucer's Sexual Poetics*. Madison: University of Wisconsin Press, 1989.

———. "Readers in/of *Troilus and Criseyde*." *Yale Journal of Criticism* 1.2 (1988): 81–105.

Dodd, William George. *Courtly Love in Chaucer and Gower*. Harvard Studies in English 1. Boston: Ginn, 1913.

Donagher, Colleen P. "Socializing the Sorceress: The Fairy Mistress in *Lanval, Le Bel Inconnu* and *Partonopeu de Blois*." *Essays in Medieval Studies* 4 (1987): 69–90.

Donaldson, E. Talbot. "The Myth of Courtly Love." *Ventures: Magazine of the Yale Graduate School* 5 (1965): 16–23.

Dronke, Peter. "A Note on *Pamphilus*." *Journal of the Warburg and Courtauld Institutes* 42 (1979): 225–26.

———. "Pseudo-Ovid, Facetus, and the Arts of Love." *Mittellateinisches Jahrbuch* 11 (1976): 126–31.

Eley, Penny and Penny Simons. "*Partonopeus de Blois* and Chrétien de Troyes: A Re-Assessment." *Romania* 117 (1999): 316–41.

Eley, Penny. "Patterns of Faith and Doubt: Gautier d'Arras's *Eracle* and *Ille et Galeron*." *French Studies* 43.3 (1989): 257–70.

Elliott, Alison Goddard, ed. and trans. *Seven Medieval Latin Comedies*. New York: Garland, 1984.

———, ed. and trans. "The *Facetus*: or, The Art of Courtly Living." *Allegorica* 2 (1977): 27–57.

Faral, Edmond. *Les Jongleurs en France au moyen âge*. 2nd edn. Paris: Champion, 1964.

Fehrenbacher, Richard W. " 'Al that which chargeth nought to seye': The Theme of Incest in *Troilus and Criseyde*." *Exemplaria* 9.2 (1997): 341–69.

Fenster, Thelma S. and Clare A. Lees, eds. *Gender in Debate from the Early Middle Ages to the Renaissance*. New Middle Ages. New York: Palgrave, 2002.

Ferrante, Joan M. "Male Fantasy and Female Reality in Courtly Literature." *Women's Studies* 11 (1984): 67–97.

Finke, Laurie A. and Martin B. Shichtman, eds. *Medieval Texts & Contemporary Readers*. Ithaca: Cornell University Press, 1987.

Fisher, Sheila and Janet E. Halley, eds. *Seeking the Woman in Late Medieval and Renaissance Writings: Essays in Feminist Contextual Criticism*. Knoxville: University of Tennessee Press, 1989.

Fleming, John V. *Classical Imitation and Interpretation in Chaucer's* Troilus. Lincoln: University of Nebraska Press, 1990.

———. "Deiphoebus Betrayed: Virgilian Decorum, Chaucerian Feminism." *Chaucer Review* 21.2 (1986): 182–99.

Florimont, see Aimon de Varennes. *Floriant et Florete* Ed. Harry F. Williams. Ann Arbor: University of Michigan Press, 1947.

Fourrier, Anthime. *Le Courant réaliste dans le roman courtois en France au moyen-âge*. 2 vols. Paris: Nizet, 1960.

Fradenburg, Louise O. " 'Our owen wo to drynke': Loss, Gender and Chivalry in *Troilus and Criseyde*." In Shoaf. 88–106.

Garbáty, Thomas J. "The *Pamphilus* Tradition in Ruiz and Chaucer." *Philological Quarterly* 46 (1967): 457–70.

Gaunt, Simon. "Bel Acueil and the Improper Allegory of the *Romance of the Rose*." *New Medieval Literatures* 2 (1998): 65–93.

———. "Romance and Other Genres." In Krueger, *Cambridge*. 45–59.

Gautier d'Arras. *Éracle*. Ed. Guy Raynaud de Lage. Les Classiques français du moyen âge. Paris: Champion, 1976.

Generydes. Ed. W.A. Wright. EETS, O.S. 55, 70. London, 1873, 1878.

Gilles, Sealy. "Love and Disease in Chaucer's *Troilus and Criseyde*." *Studies in the Age of Chaucer* 25 (2003): 157–97.

Gordon, Ida L. *The Double Sorrow of Troilus: A Study of Ambiguities in* Troilus and Criseyde. Oxford: Clarendon Press, 1970.

Gottfried von Strassburg. *Tristan*. Ed. Friedrich Ranke. Commentary Rüdiger Krohn. 3 vols. Stuttgart: Philipp Reclam Jun., 1981.

Gower, John. *The* Confessio Amantis. *Complete Works of John Gower*. Ed. G.C. Macaulay. 4 vols. Oxford: Clarendon Press, 1899–1902. 2–3.

Gravdal, Kathryn. *Ravishing Maidens: Writing Rape in Medieval French Literature and Law*. New Cultural Studies Series. Philadelphia: University of Pennsylvania Press, 1991.

Guillaume de Blois. *Alda*. Ed. Marcel Wintzweiller. In *La "Comédie" latine*. 1:107–51.

Guillaume de Lorris and Jean de Meun. *Le Roman de la rose*. Ed. Félix Lecoy. Les Classiques français du moyen âge 92, 95, 98. 3 vols. Paris: Champion, 1965–70.

Guillaume de Palerne: Roman du XIIIe siècle. Ed. Alexandre Micha. Textes littéraires français. Geneva: Droz, 1990.

Guillaume le Normand. *Le Prestre et Alison*. In *Nouveau recueil*. 8:182–206.

Guthrie, Steven R. "Chivalry and Privacy in *Troilus and Criseyde* and *La Chastelaine de Vergy*." *Chaucer Review* 34.2 (1999): 150–73.

Hamel, Mary. "The Franklin's Tale and Chrétien de Troyes." *Chaucer Review* 17.4 (1983): 316–31.

Hammond, Eleanor Prescott, ed. "The Chance of the Dice." *Englische Studien* 59 (1925): 1–16.

Hanning, Robert W. "Come in Out of the Code: Interpreting the Discourse of Desire in Boccaccio's *Filostrato* and Chaucer's *Troilus and Criseyde*." In Shoaf. 120–37.

———. *The Individual in Twelfth-century Romance*. New Haven: Yale University Press, 1977.

Hansen, Elaine Tuttle. *Chaucer and the Fictions of Gender*. Berkeley: University of California Press, 1992.

Harf-Lancner, Laurence. *Les Fées au moyen âge: Morgane et Mélusine: la naissance des fées*. Paris: Champion, 1984.

Harley, Marta Powell. "Narcissus, Hermaphroditus, and Attis: Ovidian Lovers at the Fontaine d'Amors in Guillaume de Lorris's *Roman de la rose*." *PMLA* 101.3 (1986): 324–37.

Hermann, John P. "Gesture and Seduction in *Troilus and Criseyde*." *Studies in the Age of Chaucer* 7 (1985): 107–35. Repr. in Shoaf. 138–60.

Hilary, Christine Ryan. Notes to "The Wife of Bath's Prologue." In Chaucer, *Riverside*.

Hill, John. "Aristocratic Friendship in *Troilus and Criseyde*: Pandarus, Courtly Love and Ciceronian Brotherhood in Troy." In *New Readings of Chaucer's Poetry*. Ed. Robert G. Benson and Susan J. Ridyard. Cambridge, UK: D.S. Brewer, 2003. 165–82.

Hines, John. *The Fabliau in English*. Longman Medieval and Renaissance Library. New York: Longman, 1993.

Hodges, Laura F. "Sartorial Signs in *Troilus and Criseyde*." *Chaucer Review* 35.3 (2001): 223–58.

Hue de Rotelande. *Protheseläus: ein altfranzösischer Abenteuerroman*. Ed. Franz Kluckow. Gesellschaft für romanische Literatur 45. 2 vols. Göttingen: Niemeyer, Halle, 1924.

Hunt, Tony. *Chrétien de Troyes: "Yvain" (Le Chevalier au Lion)*. London: Grant & Cutler, 1986.

Huot, Sylvia. "The Manuscript Context of Medieval Romance." In Krueger, *Cambridge*. 60–77.

Johnson, Lesley. "Women on Top: Antifeminism in the Fabliaux?" *Modern Language Review* 78.2 (1983): 298–307.

Karras, Ruth Mazo. *Common Women: Prostitution and Sexuality in Medieval England*. Oxford: Oxford University Press, 1996.

Kay, Sarah. *Courtly Contradictions: The Emergence of the Literary Object in the Twelfth Century*. Stanford: Stanford University Press, 2001.

Kay, Sarah and Miri Rubin, ed. *Framing Medieval Bodies*. Manchester: Manchester University Press, 1994.

———. "Courts, Clerks, and Courtly Love." In Krueger, *Cambridge*. 81–96.

———. "Sexual Knowledge: The Once and Future Texts of the *Romance of the Rose*." In *Textuality and Sexuality: Reading Theories and Practices*. Ed. Judith Still and Michael Worton. Manchester: Manchester University Press, 1993. 69–86.

———. "Women's Body of Knowledge: Epistemology and Misogyny in the *Romance of the Rose*." In Kay and Rubin. 211–35.

Kelly, Henry Ansgar. *Love and Marriage in the Age of Chaucer*. Ithaca: Cornell University Press, 1975.

Knight, Stephen. *Arthurian Literature and Society*. New York: St. Martin's Press, 1983.

Kooper, Erik. "*Grace*: The Healing Herb in *William of Palerne*." *Leeds Studies in English* 15 (1984): 83–93.

Krueger, Roberta. "Beyond Debate: Gender in Play in Old French Courtly Fiction." In Fenster. 79–95.

———, ed. *The Cambridge Companion to Medieval Romance*. Cambridge, UK: Cambridge University Press, 2000.

———. "Love, Honor, and the Exchange of Women in *Yvain*: Some Remarks on the Female Reader." *Romance Notes* 25.3 (1985): 302–17.

———. *Women Readers and the Ideology of Gender in Old French Verse Romance*. Cambridge, UK: Cambridge University Press, 1993.

Lacy, Norris J. "Fabliau Women." *Romance Notes* 25.3 (1985): 318–27.

Lancelot do Lac: The Non-Cyclic Old French Prose Romance. Ed. Elspeth Kennedy. 2 vols. Oxford: Clarendon Press, 1980.

Lancelot: Roman en prose du XIIIe siècle. Ed. Alexandre Micha. Textes littéraires français. 9 vols. Paris: Librairie Droz, 1978–83.

Langlois, Ernest. *Origines et sources du* Roman de la rose. Paris: Thorin, 1891.

Laskaya, Anne. "The Rhetoric of Incest in the Middle English *Emaré.*" In *Violence Against Women in Medieval Texts.* Ed. Anna Roberts. Gainesville, Florida: University Press of Florida, 1998. 97–114.

Lawrence, William Witherle. "The Love Story in 'Troilus and Cressida.' " In *Shaksperian Studies by Members of the Department of English and Comparative Literature in Columbia University.* Ed. Brander Matthews and Ashley Horace Thorndike. New York: Columbia University Press, 1916. 187–211.

Lefèvre, Jean. *La Vieille ou les dernières amours d'Ovide.* Ed. Hippolyte Cocheris. Paris: Auguste Hérissey, 1861.

Leicester, Jr., H. Marshall. "Oure Tonges *Différance*: Textuality and Deconstruction in Chaucer." In Finke. 15–26.

Lewis, C.S. *The Allegory of Love: A Study in Medieval Tradition.* 1936; repr. Oxford: Oxford University Press, 1971.

Lewis, Robert E. "The English Fabliau Tradition and Chaucer's 'Miller's Tale.' " *Modern Philology* 79 (1982): 241–55.

Lidia. Ed. Edmond Lackenbacher. In *La "Comédie" latine.* 1:211–46.

Maddox, Donald. *The Arthurian Romances of Chrétien de Troyes: Once and Future Fictions.* Cambridge Studies in Medieval Literature 12. Cambridge, UK: Cambridge University Press, 1991.

Malory, Thomas. *The Works of Sir Thomas Malory.* Ed. Eugène Vinaver. 1954; repr. London: Oxford University Press, 1962.

Mann, Jill. *Geoffrey Chaucer.* Atlantic Highlands, New Jersey: Humanities Press International, Inc., 1991.

Margherita, Gayle. "Criseyde's Remains: Romance and the Question of Justice." *Exemplaria* 12.2 (2000): 257–92.

Matter, Ann E. "The Undebated Debate: Gender and the Image of God in Medieval Theology." In Fenster. 41–55.

Matthews, William. "The Wife of Bath and All Her Sect." *Viator* 5 (1974): 413–43.

Maybury, James F. "Pandarus and Criseyde: The Motif of Incest in Chaucer's *Troilus.*" *Xavier Review* 2 (1982): 82–89.

McGerr, Rosemarie P. "Meaning and Ending in a 'Paynted proces': Resistance to Closure in *Troilus and Criseyde.*" In Shoaf. 179–98.

McInerney, Maud Burnett. " 'Is this a mannes herte?': Unmanning Troilus through Ovidian Allusion." In Beidler. 221–35.

Meale, Carol M. "The Morgan Library copy of *Generides.*" In Mills. 89–104.

Ménard, Philippe. *Le Rire et le sourire dans le roman courtois en France au moyen âge (1150–1250).* Publications romanes et françaises 105. Geneva: Droz, 1969.

——. *Les Fabliaux: Contes à rire du moyen âge.* Paris: Presses universitaires de France, 1983.

The Middle-English Versions of Partonope of Blois. Ed. A. Trampe Bödtker. EETS, E.S. 109. London: Oxford University Press, 1912.

Mieszkowski, Gretchen. "Chaucer's Much Loved Criseyde." *Chaucer Review* 26.2 (1991): 109–32.

———. "Chaucer's Pandarus and Jean Brasdefer's Houdée." *Chaucer Review* 20 (1985): 40–60.

———. "Going-Between: Chaucer's Pandarus and Medieval Literary Go-Betweens." Cambridge, Mass: Mary Ingraham Bunting Institute of Radcliffe College, 1979.

———. "The Prose *Lancelot*'s Galehot, Malory's Lavain, and the Queering of Late Medieval Literature." *Arthuriana* 5 (1995): 21–51.

———. "Urake and the Gender Roles of *Partonope of Blois.*" *Mediaevalia* 25.2 (2004): 181–95.

Mills, Maldwyn, Jennifer Fellows, and Carol M. Meale, eds. *Romance in Medieval England.* Cambridge, UK: D.S. Brewer, 1991.

Minnis, Alastair. *Magister amoris: The* Roman de la Rose *and Vernacular Hermeneutics.* Oxford: Oxford University Press, 2001.

Moore, Bruce. "The Narrator within the Performance: Problems with Two Medieval 'Plays.'" In *Drama in the Middle Ages: Comparative and Critical Essays: Second Series.* Ed. Clifford Davidson and John H. Stroupe. AMS Studies in the Middle Ages 18. New York: AMS Press, 1990. 152–67.

Morris, Rosemary. "Uther and Igerne: A Study in Uncourtly Love." In *Arthurian Literature IV.* Ed. Tony Hunt and Toshiyuki Takamiya. Woodbridge, Suffolk UK: D.S. Brewer, 1985. 70–92.

Muscatine, Charles. *Chaucer and the French Tradition.* 1957. Berkeley: University of California Press, 1964.

———. *The Old French Fabliaux.* New Haven: Yale University Press, 1986.

Nouveau recueil complet des fabliaux. Ed. Willem Noomen and Nico van den Boogaard. 10 vols. Assen: Van Gorcum, 1983–98.

Ovid. *Metamorphoses.* Ed. Frank Justus Miller. Loeb Classical Library. 1916. Cambridge, Mass: Harvard University Press, 1958.

———. *The Art of Love.* Trans. James Michie. New York: Modern Library, 2002.

Ovidius puellarum (De nuncio sagaci). Ed. Alphonse Dain. In *La "Comédie" latine.* 2:109–65.

Pamphile et Galatée. By Jean Brasdefer. Ed. Joseph de Morawski. Paris: Champion, 1917.

Pamphilus. Ed. Stefano Pittaluga. In *Commedie latine,* 1980. 3:11–137.

Partonopeu de Blois: A French Romance of the Twelfth Century. Ed. Joseph Gildea. 2 vols. 1:text, 2 pt. 1, *Partonopeu de Blois, The Continuation.* 2, pt. 2, Leon Smith, "Introduction." Joseph Gildea, "Commentary." Villanova, PA: Villanova University Press, 1967, 1968, 1970.

Partonopeus de Blois: An Electronic Edition. Ed. Penny Eley, Penny Simons, Mario Longtin, Catherine Hanley, and Philip Shaw. Sheffield: HriOnline, 2005. www.hrionline.ac.uk/partonopeus.

Patterson, Lee. *Chaucer and the Subject of History*. Madison: University of Wisconsin Press, 1991.

———. "Feminine Rhetoric and the Politics of Subjectivity: La Vieille and the Wife of Bath." In Brownlee. 316–58.

———. " 'For the Wyves love of Bathe': Feminine Rhetoric and Poetic Resolution in the *Roman de la Rose* and the *Canterbury Tales*." *Speculum* 58.3 (1983): 656–95.

Petri Alfonsi Disciplina clericalis: III. Französische Versbearbeitungen. Ed. Alfons Hilka and Werner Söderhjelm. Acta societatis scientiarum fennicae. Helsingfors: Druckerei der finnischen Literatur-Gesellschaft, 1922. 49.

Petrus Alfonsi. *The Disciplina clericalis of Petrus Alfonsi*. Trans. and ed. Eberhard Hermes. Trans. into English P.R. Quarrie. Berkeley: University of California Press, 1977.

Pierreville, Corinne. *Gautier d'Arras: L'autre Chrétien*. Paris: Champion, 2001.

Press, A.R. "The Adulterous Nature of *fin' amors*: A Re-Examination of the Theory." *Forum for Modern Language Studies* 6 (1970): 327–41.

———. "Chrétien de Troyes's Laudine: A *Belle Dame sans mercy?*" *Forum for Modern Language Studies* 19 (1983): 158–71.

Le Prestre teint. Fabliau 81. In *Nouveau recueil*. 7:307–30.

The Prose Lancelot, see *Lancelot do Lac Pseudo-Ovidian De Vetula*. Ed. Dorothy M. Robathan. Amsterdam: Adolf M. Hakkert, 1968.

Pugh, Tison. "Queer Pandarus? Silence and Sexual Ambiguity in Chaucer's *Troilus and Criseyde*." *Philological Quarterly* 80.1 (2001): 17–35.

Ramos, María del Pilar Mendoza. "Auberée la alcahueta: Similitudes y diferencias con sus homólogas literarias hispanas." In *Actas del IX Simposio de la Sociedad Española de Literatura General y Comparada*. Ed. Túa Blesa, María Teresa Cacho, Carlos García Gual, Mercedes Rolland, Leonardo Romero Tobar, and Margarita Smerdou Altolaguirre. Zaragoza: Universidad de Zaragoza, 1994. 1:263–68.

Rank, Otto. *The Myth of the Birth of the Hero: A Psychological Interpretation of Mythology*. Trans. F. Robbins and S.E. Jelliffe. New York: Robert Brunner, 1957.

René d'Anjou. *Oeuvres complètes du Roi René*. Ed. M. le Comte de Quatrebarbes. 4 vols. Angers, 1846. 3.

Robathan, Dorothy M. "Ovid in the Middle Ages." In *Ovid*. Ed. J.W. Binns. London: Routledge & Kegan Paul, 1973. 191–209.

Robertson, Elizabeth. "Medieval Medical Views of Women and Female Spirituality in the *Ancrene Wisse* and Julian of Norwich's *Showings*." In *Feminist Approaches to the Body in Medieval Literature*. Ed. Linda Lomperis and Sarah Stanbury. New Cultural Studies. Philadelphia: University of Pennsylvania Press, 1993. 142–67.

Robertson, Elizabeth, and Christine M. Rose, eds. *Representing Rape in Medieval and Early Modern Literature*. The New Middle Ages. New York: Palgrave, 2001.

Rogers, Katharine M. *The Troublesome Helpmate: A History of Misogyny in Literature*. Seattle: University of Washington Press, 1966.

Le Roi Flore et la belle Jehanne. In *Nouvelles en prose du XIIIe siècle*. Ed. L. Moland et Ch. d'Hericault. Paris: Bibliothèque elzévirienne, 1856. 85–157.

Le Roman du comte d'Artois. Ed. Jean-Charles Seigneuret. Geneva: Librairie Droz, 1966. 113–35.

Li Romans de Claris et Laris. Ed. Johann Alton. Bibliothek des Litterarischen vereins in Stuttgart 169. Tübingen, 1884.

Rouhi, Leyla. *Mediation and Love: A Study of the Medieval Go-Between in Key Romance and Near-Eastern Texts*. Brill's Studies in Intellectual History 93. Leiden: Brill, 1999.

Ruiz, Juan. *Libro de buen amor*. Ed. Giorgio Chiarini. Milan: Ricciardi, 1964. *The Book of Good Love*. Trans. Rigo Mignani and Mario A. Di Cesare. Albany, NY: State University of New York Press, 1970.

Salisbury, Joyce E. "Gendered Sexuality." In *Handbook of Medieval Sexuality*. Ed. Vern L. Bullough and James A. Brundage. New York: Garland, 1996. 81–102.

Salter, Elizabeth. "*Troilus and Criseyde*: A Reconsideration." In *Patterns of Love and Courtesy: Essays in Memory of C.S. Lewis*. Ed. John Lawlor. London: Arnold, 1966. 86–106.

Savj-Lopez, Paolo. "Il *filostrato* di G. Boccaccio." *Romania* 27 (1898): 442–79.

Schotter, Anne Howland. "Rape in the Medieval Latin Comedies." In Robertson and Rose. 241–53.

———. "Rhetoric versus Rape in the Medieval Latin *Pamphilus*." *Philological Quarterly* 71.3 (1992): 243–60.

Shahar, Shulamith. "The Old Body in Medieval Culture." In Kay and Rubin. 160–86.

Shoaf, R.A., ed. *Chaucer's* Troilus and Criseyde *"Subgit to alle Poesye": Essays in Criticism*. Binghamton, New York: Pegasus Press, 1992.

Simons, Penny and Penny Eley. "Male Beauty and Sexual Orientation in *Partonopeus de Blois*." *Romance Studies* 17 (1999): 41–56.

———. "The Prologue to *Partonopeus de Blois*: Text, Context and Subtext." *French Studies* 49 (1995): 1–16.

Spurgeon, Caroline F. E. *Five Hundred Years of Chaucer Criticism and Allusion, 1357–1900*. 3 vols. Cambridge, UK: Cambridge University Press, 1925.

Stanbury, Sarah. "The Voyeur and the Private Life in *Troilus and Criseyde*." *Studies in the Age of Chaucer* 13 (1991): 141–58.

Steinberg, Diane Vanner. " 'We Do Usen Here No Wommen For To Selle': Embodiment of Social Practices in *Troilus and Criseyde*." *Chaucer Review* 29.3 (1995): 259–73.

Strohm, Paul. *Social Chaucer*. Cambridge, Mass: Harvard University Press, 1989.

Stroud, T.A. "The Palinode, the Narrator, and Pandarus's Alleged Incest." *Chaucer Review* 27.1 (1992): 16–30.

Sullivan, J.M. "The Lady Lunete: Literary Conventions of Counsel and the Criticism of Counsel in Chrétien's *Yvain* and Hartmann's *Iwein*." *Neophilologus* 85.3 (2001): 335–54.

Taylor, Karla. "*Inferno 5* and *Troilus and Criseyde* Revisited." In Shoaf. 239–56.

Thomas. *The Romance of Horn*. Ed. Mildred K. Pope. 2 vols. Vol. 2 revised and completed by T.B.W. Reid. Anglo-Norman Texts 9–10, 12–13. Oxford: Basil Blackwell, 1955, 1964.

Tolan, John. *Petrus Alfonsi and his Medieval Readers*. Gainesville: University Press of Florida, 1993.

Tristan. Trans. A.T. Hatto. 1960. New York: Penguin Books, 1982.

Uitti, Karl D. " 'Cele [qui] doit estre Rose clamee' (*Rose*, vv. 40–44): Guillaume's Intentionality." In Brownlee. 39–64.

———. "*Le Chevalier au lion (Yvain)*." In *The Romances of Chrétien de Troyes: A Symposium.* Ed. Douglas Kelly. Edward C. Armstrong Monographs on Medieval Literature 3. Lexington, KY: French Forum, 1985. 182–231.

Vance, Eugene. "Chrétien's *Yvain* and the Ideologies of Change and Exchange." *Yale French Studies* 70 (1986): 42–62.

Weiss, Judith. "A Reappraisal of Hue de Rotelande's *Protheselaus.*" *Medium AEvum* 52.1 (1983): 104–11.

———. "The Wooing Woman in Anglo-Norman Romance." In Mills. 149–61.

William of Palerne: An Alliterative Romance. Ed. G.H.V. Bunt. Groningen: Bouma's Boekhuis, 1985.

Wimsatt, James I. "Medieval and Modern in Chaucer's *Troilus and Criseyde.*" *PMLA* 92.2 (1977): 203–16.

Windeatt, Barry. Troilus and Criseyde: *Oxford Guides to Chaucer.* Oxford: Clarendon Press, 1992.

———. "*Troilus* and the Disenchantment of Romance." In *Studies in Medieval English Romances: Some New Approaches.* Ed. Derek Brewer. Cambridge, UK: Boydell and Brewer Inc., 1988. 129–47.

Woods, Marjorie Curry. "Rape and the pedagogical rhetoric of sexual violence." In *Criticism and Dissent in the Middle Ages.* Ed. Rita Copeland. Cambridge, UK: Cambridge University Press, 1996. 56–86.

Young, Karl. "Chaucer's Use of Boccaccio's 'Filocolo.' " *Modern Philology* 4 (1906–07): 169–77.

———. *The Origin and Development of the Story of Troilus and Criseyde.* Chaucer Society, 2nd Series 40. London: Kegan Paul, 1908.

Zeikowitz, Richard E. *Homoeroticism and Chivalry: Discourses of Male Same-Sex Desire in the 14th Century.* The New Middle Ages. New York: Palgrave Macmillan, 2003.

INDEX

Printed in the United States
90194LV00003B/6/A